Insights into Assessing Academic Listening: The Case of IELTS

Also in this series:

IELTS Washback in Context: Preparation for academic writing in higher education
Anthony Green

Examining Writing: Research and practice in assessing second language writing
Stuart D Shaw and Cyril J Weir

Aligning Tests with the CEFR: Reflections on using the Council of Europe's draft Manual
Edited by Waldemar Martyniuk

Examining Reading: Research and practice in assessing second language reading
Hanan Khalifa and Cyril J Weir

Examining Speaking: Research and practice in assessing second language speaking
Edited by Lynda Taylor

IELTS Collected Papers 2: Research in reading and listening assessment
Edited by Lynda Taylor and Cyril J Weir

Examining Listening: Research and practice in assessing second language listening
Edited by Ardeshir Geranpayeh and Lynda Taylor

Measured Constructs: A history of Cambridge English language examinations 1913–2012
Cyril J Weir, Ivana Vidaković, Evelina D Galaczi

Cambridge English Exams – The First Hundred Years: A history of English language assessment from the University of Cambridge 1913–2013
Roger Hawkey and Michael Milanovic

Testing Reading Through Summary: Investigating summary completion tasks for assessing reading comprehension ability
Lynda Taylor

Multilingual Frameworks: The construction and use of multilingual proficiency frameworks
Neil Jones

Validating Second Language Reading Examinations: Establishing the validity of the GEPT through alignment with the Common European Framework of Reference
Rachel Yi-fen Wu

Assessing Language Teachers' Professional Skills and Knowledge
Edited by Rosemary Wilson and Monica Poulter

Second Language Assessment and Mixed Methods Research
Edited by Aleidine J Moeller, John W Creswell and Nick Saville

Learning Oriented Assessment: A systemic approach
Neil Jones and Nick Saville

Advancing the Field of Language Assessment: Papers from TIRF doctoral dissertation grantees
Edited by MaryAnn Christison and Nick Saville

Examining Young Learners: Research and practice in assessing the English of school-age learners
Szilvia Papp and Shelagh Rixon

Second Language Assessment and Action Research
Edited by Anne Burns and Hanan Khalifa

Applying the Socio-cognitive Framework to the BioMedical Admissions Test: Insights from Language Assessment
Edited by Kevin Y F Cheung, Sarah McElwee and Joanne Emery

Lessons and Legacy: A Tribute to Professor Cyril J Weir (1950–2018)
Edited by Lynda Taylor and Nick Saville

Research and Practice in Assessing Academic Reading: The Case of IELTS
Cyril J Weir and Sathena Chan

Language Test Validation in a Digital Age
Edited by Guoxing Yu and Jing Xu

On Topic Validity in Speaking Tests
Nahal Khabbazbashi

Insights into Assessing Academic Listening: The Case of IELTS

John Field
CRELLA, University of Bedfordshire

Shaftesbury Road, Cambridge CB2 8EA, United Kingdom

One Liberty Plaza, 20th Floor, New York, NY 10006, USA

477 Williamstown Road, Port Melbourne, VIC 3207, Australia

314–321, 3rd Floor, Plot 3, Splendor Forum, Jasola District Centre, New Delhi – 110025, India

103 Penang Road, #05–06/07, Visioncrest Commercial, Singapore 238467

Cambridge University Press & Assessment is a department of the University of Cambridge.

We share the University's mission to contribute to society through the pursuit of education, learning and research at the highest international levels of excellence.

www.cambridge.org
Information on this title: www.cambridge.org/9781009102209

© Cambridge University Press & Assessment 2023

This publication is in copyright. Subject to statutory exception and to the provisions of relevant collective licensing agreements, no reproduction of any part may take place without the written permission of Cambridge University Press & Assessment.

First published 2023

20 19 18 17 16 15 14 13 12 11 10 9 8 7 6 5 4 3

Printed in Great Britain by CPI Group (UK) Ltd, Croydon CR0 4YY

A catalogue record for this publication is available from the British Library

ISBN   978-1-009-10220-9

Cambridge University Press & Assessment has no responsibility for the persistence or accuracy of URLs for external or third-party internet websites referred to in this publication and does not guarantee that any content on such websites is, or will remain, accurate or appropriate.

Contents

Acknowledgements	vi
List of abbreviations	viii
Preface	x
Barry O'Sullivan and Nick Saville	
Introduction: Some general considerations	1
Goals and content of the volume	1
Academic listening as a phenomenon	2
Background: The IELTS Listening test	6
The methodological approach underpinning this volume	8
Section 1	
Insights from empirical research	
1 Consequential validity	13
2 Criterion-related validity (1)	22
3 Criterion-related validity (2)	30
4 Test taker characteristics: experiential and behavioural	36
Section 2	
Cognitive and contextual issues in assessing academic listening	
5 A cognitive profile of academic listening	61
6 Test content as text	73
7 Test content as speech	90
8 Checking understanding	102
9 Test formats	110
10 Test items	116
Section 3	
General applications and conclusions	
11 Integrated skills: The way ahead?	125
12 Summary of main recommendations and final remarks	129
13 Issues addressed in this volume	138
Epilogue	140
Barry O'Sullivan and Nick Saville	
References and further reading	148
Author index	164
Subject index	169

Acknowledgements

A volume of this kind inevitably incurs large debts of gratitude for the advice, knowledge and experience of others. In particular, I would like to thank Professor Lynda Taylor, who made a major contribution to the final version of the book – not only drawing upon her background and experience in the field of language testing but also providing informed comment on details at text level. Special thanks are also due to Professor Luke Harding for his thoughtful review of the original manuscript and useful suggestions on the content to be covered. Another early reviewer, Professor Barry O'Sullivan, provided helpful and constructive feedback on various aspects of the manuscript.

On the production side, I would like to acknowledge the assistance of Dr Nick Saville (Director of Research and Thought Leadership at Cambridge University Press and Assessment) who closely monitored the development of the project. Particular thanks are due to John Savage (Publications Administrator at Cambridge English) for overseeing the development of the manuscript throughout and for his sensitive and meticulous copy editing.

The book had its origin in a British Council funded project undertaken by the CRELLA Research Institute, of which I was a member. I was and remain very grateful to the Council and to CRELLA for this opportunity to review the research history of the IELTS Listening test and its impact upon users, and to situate it in relation to our current understanding of the cognitive processes underlying the skill. A second illuminating angle was to use the IELTS test as the point of departure for comparing a range of other tests of second language academic listening skills.

Last but by no means least when acknowledging sources: this book is not the first to approach the testing of academic language skills in the way it does. I was fortunate to inherit a thoughtfully designed framework for the project in a previous volume in the SiLT series, Weir and Chan's *Research and Practice in Assessing Academic Reading: the Case of IELTS* (2019). The present account follows this precedent quite closely: reviewing empirical research and modelling the listening construct before going on to consider the test content in terms of the validity types used in Weir's own model for analysing language skills. Special emphasis in this instance is placed upon cognitive validity. As in Weir and Chan, a final chapter of the book considers possible future developments and how they might affect the teaching and testing of listening for academic purposes.

Acknowledgements

Special thanks go to Barry O'Sullivan (representing the British Council) and to Nick Saville (representing Cambridge English) for contributing a chapter to the book which adds a fresh angle to the validation exercise. And finally, I would like to thank Paul Siedlecki and Hector Garcia for their unstinting support during what has been a difficult stage of my life.

List of abbreviations

AHP	Allied Health Professional
BASE	British Academic Spoken English
CAE	Certificate in Advanced English
CBT	Computer-Based Testing
CEFR	Common European Framework of Reference for Languages
CET	College English Test
CPE	Certificate of Proficiency in English
CRELLA	Centre for Research in English Language Learning and Assessment
D	Doctor
EAP	English for Academic Purposes
EEA	European Economic Area
ELTS	English Language Testing Service
EMI	English Medium Instruction
EPTB	English Proficiency Test Battery
ESL	English as a Second Language
ETS	Educational Testing Service
FP	Final Panel Member
GMC	General Medical Council
GPA	Grade Point Average
IELTS	International English Language Testing System
IMG	International Medical Graduate
IWGs	Item Writer Guidelines
L1	First Language
L2	Second Language
MCQ	Multiple-Choice Question
MM	Multiple Matching
N	Nurse
NCSBN	National Council of State Boards of Nursing
OET	Occupational English Test
OTT	Overseas Trained Teacher
P	Patient
PLAB	Professional and Linguistic Assessments Board
PTE	Pearson Test of English
PTE Academic	Pearson Test of English Academic

List of abbreviations

QAA	Quality Assurance Agency
RO	Responsible Officer/Medical Director
SD	Standard Deviation
SELT	Secure English Language Test
SiLT	Studies in Language Testing
TOEFL	Test of English as a Foreign Language
TOEFL iBT	Internet-based Test of English as a Foreign Language
WPM	Words Per Minute

Preface
Barry O'Sullivan, British Council, UK
Nick Saville, Cambridge University Press & Assessment, UK

SILT 53 is a companion volume to SILT 51, which focused on research and practice in assessing academic reading (Weir and Chan 2019). That volume was aimed at academics and practitioners working in the field of language testing, especially those with an interest in language assessment for academic purposes. The present volume has the same audience and assessment context in mind, but focuses on the testing of academic listening ability which has been a longstanding interest of John Field.

Both volumes build upon a series of research projects undertaken by the Centre for Research in English Language Learning and Assessment (CRELLA) at the University of Bedfordshire (2017–18) focusing on IELTS, and supported by the British Council and Cambridge English Language Assessment (as it was at the time). These projects were designed to take a broad look at the research into the four IELTS papers over the years, with a view to identifying areas that might be addressed in any future revision of the test. Of course, in doing this, the research teams were encouraged to reflect on the broader literature around each skill area.

Field was a member of the CRELLA team and led the review of the research into listening comprehension. In so doing, he drew on his extensive experience and research background in psycholinguistics and cognitive psychology. He also drew on the sociocognitive framework (O'Sullivan and Weir 2011, Weir 2005) that had been employed in other SILT volumes and to which he himself had contributed in shaping the thinking on the validation of listening tests.

In contrast to the study skills approach adopted by Weir and Chan in their volume on academic reading, Field makes the case for a cognitively based approach to academic listening. He argues that the demands placed upon the learner/test taker when listening for academic purposes should be conceived of in terms of processes that have to be acquired in relation to *patterns of thought* and *patterns of language*. He goes on to suggest that this stance is supported by empirically validated models of what listening entails, but which to date have not been successfully operationalised in the assessment of academic listening. He draws attention to features and conventions of current listening tests and argues that the target construct based on the cognitive approach tends to be under-represented and does not fully reflect the real-world conditions in which listening ability is needed. The challenge for test designers is to overcome the conceptual and practical considerations that have prevented such developments, with emerging digital technologies offering promising opportunities for future developments.

Background to the volume

John Field has a well-deserved reputation as a leading voice in *theory-based validity* in language assessment from a cognitive perspective. Coming from a background in psychology and cognitive processing, he was a relative newcomer to language assessment theory when he first began working with Cyril Weir and the Testing and Evaluation Unit at the University of Reading in the early 2000s. Even today he would perhaps deny being a fully-fledged language tester. However, his thinking and research contributions in the field of assessment have had a significant impact – he has recently become a Fellow of the Academy of Social Sciences for his work on L2 listening. The current volume is the latest addition to his long list of publications.

In his chapter on cognitive validity in *Lessons and Legacy: A Tribute to Professor Cyril J Weir (1950–2018)* (SILT 50, 2020), Field comments that Weir, in advancing theory-based validity in language testing, 'did not initially make a connection with a growing body of research, particularly in the USA, that concerned itself with cognitive validity (a term introduced by Glaser in 1991)'. However, once his attention was drawn to this aspect of validity, he enthusiastically incorporated it into the emerging model that was first published as the sociocognitive framework in 2005.

For Weir, it became important for the cognitive dimension to be established *a priori* as part of the construct definition and the test design process. In putting the emphasis on this approach to cognitive validity, he supplements the traditional, statistically based approaches, e.g. using factor analysis, multiple regression and structural equation modelling.

Over many years, Field worked alongside Weir and other colleagues in evolving this aspect of the sociocognitive approach and in using it to inform test design and in carrying out ongoing validation studies. An important aspect of these studies has been 'the building of bridges' between psycholinguistic theory and assessment principles that guide the testing of language skills in practice (Field 2019). Cognitive models account for both the social behaviours that L2 learners are seeking to acquire and also provide a framework for investigating the mental processes a test taps into – some of which may have been 'overlooked or misrepresented' in the past. Field extends this line of argument in the current volume.

Organisation of the volume

The volume is structured in five parts: a general introduction followed by three specific sections, concluding with an epilogue.

In the first section, *Insights from empirical research*, Field comprehensively reviews research findings in relation to the Listening component of the IELTS Academic module, which is principally used for admissions purposes into tertiary-level institutions throughout the world. Field follows a similar approach to Weir and Chan (2019) in summarising the insights from theoretical and empirical research into the cognitive and contextual parameters of the sociocognitive framework (Weir 1983, Weir, Hawkey, Green and Devi 2012). He extrapolates from these insights and empirical findings to propose a comprehensive approach for investigating the cognitive and contextual aspects of listening and for modelling the construct to be deployed. The findings exemplify the types of issue that have arisen over past 25 years in relation to testing in this area. The headings in this section, under which the different aspects of academic listening have been grouped, provide a useful framework of reference for future thinking and research.

The second section, *Cognitive and contextual issues in assessing academic listening*, looks at the construct of listening with a specific focus on the cognitive operations entailed when listening in an academic context. Field notes that, hitherto, established practices and practical constraints have limited the operationalisation in large-scale assessment systems of the cognitively-led approach to construct definition that he proposes (Field 2008, 2013).

In the third section, *General applications and conclusions*, Field anticipates ways in which digital technologies may enhance the assessment of listening for academic purposes and might shape the decisions made by test providers in revising their tests.

The volume concludes with an epilogue, whose aim is to extend this line of thinking about the construct of listening and to suggest ways in which the rapidly changing technological landscape in the digital age might offer new opportunities to transform the way that listening is assessed in future.

Also available in SILT series

Research and Practice in Assessing Academic Reading: The Case of IELTS
ISBN: 978 1 108 73361 8

IELTS Collected Papers 2: Research in Reading and Listening Assessment
ISBN: 978 1 107 60264 9

Examining Listening: Research and Practice in Assessing Second Language Listening
ISBN: 978 1 107 60263 2

Introduction: Some general considerations

Goals and content of the volume

The purpose of this volume is to re-examine current thinking and practice in the assessment of academic listening; and to present some evidence and examples in support of a more rigorous approach to designing, developing and validating current and future listening tests used for academic purposes.

The volume is largely designed for specialists in the testing of language. But its contents have relevance to many other stakeholders – including senior academics and professionals setting standards for entry or performance within institutes of learning. In addition, it is hoped that it will influence the decisions and the creativity of item writers striving to produce test components that are both demanding and fair. Similarly, the contents have implications for language teachers, which hopefully will lead them away from the type of test-wise strategy that often features largely in instruction and towards approaches that embrace the actual processes that underlie the listening experience – processes that will serve the candidate well if and when they succeed in obtaining a place on the course of their choice.

Two general approaches will be adopted in this volume. The first (in Section 1) is to review recent research findings relating to the academic listening paper of one particular test (namely IELTS). The findings in question are wide-ranging, and serve to exemplify the types of issue that have arisen in recent years in relation to testing in this area. These issues continue to merit careful consideration not only by all test providers but also by their stakeholders worldwide. The discussion will draw some concrete conclusions as to how we might ensure that tests of academic listening perform better in respect of various types of validity; and will suggest how present and future versions of tests might benefit from the insights obtained. The general headings in Section 1 under which the different aspects of academic listening have been grouped will serve, it is hoped, to provide a useful framework of reference for future thinking and research.

The second angle will be to approach the construct of academic listening from a perspective that is underpinned by research evidence of the cognitive operations entailed by listening in general, and listening in an academic context in particular. An empirically supported cognitive model of the skill will be outlined in Section 2; and its constraints will then be matched against some of the features of various present-day listening tests, including IELTS. Characteristics of the current IELTS Listening test will help to provide concrete examples of where and how a test may or may not fit the basic criteria. The expectation is that this example of a cognitively led and systematic approach to validation will provide a sustainable model of how any test of listening used for academic purposes might be more relevantly reviewed and validated in future. The exercise also serves indirectly to draw attention to certain features and conventions of current listening tests which may compromise their ability to represent the target construct in a way that reflects real-world conditions.

Section 3 of the volume draws upon the evidence that has been examined to put forward proposals for a general set of precepts worth observing and traps worth avoiding – considerations which, it is hoped, will provide useful guidelines for test providers, current and to come. This final section anticipates the way in which current and future developments in technology may shape some of the decisions made and formats used by test providers, and potentially modify our perceptions as to how this particular skill can best be tested.

The volume complements an earlier volume in the SiLT series by Weir and Chan (2019) on the testing of reading skills for academic purposes. Both volumes originate in and build upon validation research projects generously supported by the British Council and Cambridge English Language Assessment in 2017–18, as well as other research undertaken by the Centre for Research in English Language Learning and Assessment (CRELLA) at the University of Bedfordshire, UK.

Academic listening as a phenomenon

Parallels with reading: Five approaches

In their companion volume to the present one, Weir and Chan (2019) consider various ways in which the content of a test of academic reading might be determined. They identify five possible angles that potentially shape test content and focus:

- *Discipline-specific*: featuring the terminology and lines of argument that characterise a particular subject area
- *Genre-based*: covering a range of different types of reading and reading sources that might feature in an academic context
- *Discourse-based*: representing the various language patterns that a student might encounter when reading an academic text
- *Socially-situated*: representing the different types of reading that occur in an academic culture

- *Study-skills based*: reflecting the type of orientation provided by the general study skills literature (in effect, a mixture of the above) and closely reflecting the linguistic demands that academic study appears to impose

Listening in an academic context clearly has parallels with reading. This is not simply because it is a receptive skill and one on which students rely for the acquisition of subject-specific information that supports learning. It is also because listening requires the novice student to acquire a new repertoire of specialist terminology, events, patterns of discourse and social interactions, but here in the form of speech. Unsurprisingly, some very similar issues will be raised in the overview that follows, and some very similar problems identified.

However, rather than opting for the study-skills approach which Weir and Chan foregrounded, the general direction of argument in this introduction – and indeed in the volume as a whole – will be towards a cognitively based approach, in which the demands upon the learner are conceived largely in terms of the processes that have to be acquired in relation to both patterns of thought and patterns of language. A background to those processes will be found in empirically supported models of what listening (and particularly academic listening) entails.

Academic listening events

The type of listening event taken to be central in academic listening contexts is the lecture or presentation. However, the academic experience also entails attending seminars and following sets of instructions. Commentators even sometimes extend it to include the ability to participate in conversations within the wider academic community.

These may seem rather obvious categories, but it is worth noting that the signal to which an academic listener is exposed differs markedly across the various contexts mentioned. In lecture mode, a speaker's delivery is likely to be measured in pace and carefully structured, with intonation contours serving to highlight important content. There may be occasional summations or repetitions to check understanding. The low prominence of many critical linkers (*but, so, as if*) may prevent the listener from forming all-important connections between propositions, in a way that a reading text does not.

By contrast, in seminar mode, the discourse is likely to be more conversational and interrogative in style, and to include pauses for responses at regular intervals. Pragmatic language may be employed, in line with a tradition of academic hedging (*I was going to suggest that ...*) or criticism (*I'm not sure I agree*). As for instructions, they are typically one-way: precise in terms of lexis and syntax and slowly paced, with occasional comprehension checks. See Laver (1994:66–69) on differences of style and free variation within the productions of a single speaker.

The designer of a test of academic listening has to decide on the extent to which each of these types of interaction should feature. There is a strong preference for lecture-based material, but tests might well include scripts of seminar exchanges or even social encounters in order to feature dialogue material alongside monologue.

Critical thinking

Central to the listener's experience in academic contexts is the need to develop patterns of critical thought. In their overview of academic reading, Weir and Chan (2019) cite a number of characteristics mentioned in a report by the Intersegmental Committee of the Academic Senates of the California Community Colleges, the California State University and the University of California (2002), which apply in the case of listeners as much as they do to readers. They include (2002:16–17):

- summarise information (one might add: distinguishing the relevant from the irrelevant)
- synthesise information and incorporate it into a writing assignment
- relate prior knowledge and experience to new information
- determine major and subordinate ideas
- identify the evidence which supports or contradicts a thesis
- anticipate the direction of the argument
- retain information while searching for answers to self-generated questions.

The last is particularly important in listening given the transitory nature of the signal, which cannot be cross-checked in the way a written text can.

Discourse construction

We can assume that, for a candidate ready to undertake a course of academic study in a second language, the fundamental perceptual skills are relatively well established. Recognition processes at lexical and syntactic level will have become largely automatic – thus freeing up working memory to enable the listener to focus on higher-level information such as patterns of meaning.

At this stage, what is critical to successful academic listening is the ability to a) identify discrete points of information in what a speaker says and then b) build them into a discourse structure. Here, the widely quoted Structure Building Framework (Gernsbacher 1990) provides an accessible account of how readers (and by extension listeners) build a coherent representation of a text or a talk (or even a conversation). A reader/listener begins with a piece of information extracted from the signal. If new incoming information then coheres with what is there, the listener connects it. If it does not, the listener moves on to create a new informational substructure. In this way, an overall discourse pattern emerges, based on closely interconnected sets of propositions. Less-skilled comprehenders are said to shift too often because they fail to make the appropriate connections. They consequently report meaning representations at a very local level and end up with a fragmented line of argument. Skilled listeners, by contrast, are able not simply to report the main points but also to represent the connections between them.

Topics

In a real-world academic lecture, the student is a privileged listener in that they can usually be expected to have some familiarity with the topic area under discussion. In these circumstances, access to background information and specialist terminology may well help them to fill gaps of understanding that may arise. This represents a quandary for designers of tests of academic listening. If (in the interests of authenticity) they focus closely on a particular subject area in the way a lecturer might, they risk disadvantaging those who are studying a different subject area and are unfamiliar with the lexis and patterns of argument that characterise that field. Thus, fully authentic listening texts are rarely used. The consequence is that the raw material for high-stakes academic listening exams typically comes from scripted texts or semi-scripted ones (i.e. lectures that are edited and then re-recorded in a studio). The test designer draws upon neutral issues of debate or sources of information that the test taker is unlikely to have encountered rather than those with which they are familiar.

Test methods and real-world behaviour

Given the transitory nature of speech, the natural response in an academic context is to take notes in order to conserve what has been heard. However, for obvious reasons of standardised scoring, this is an option rarely if ever employed when checking comprehension in high-stakes tests. Instead, the test method usually entails matching text in another modality (a written item) against the information the signal has provided. In the case of (e.g.) a multiple-choice distractor, the text in question is designed to *mislead* the listener – thus (ironically) providing the very opposite of the support that, in real-world circumstances, a student would derive from a lecturer's PowerPoint slide.

Background: The IELTS Listening test

There follows a brief history of the listening section of the IELTS exam, which will provide some points of reference for the discussion in the review chapters of this volume. The aim is to ensure that the reader is familiar with the goals and layout of the IELTS Listening test. But the account also serves to exemplify a few of the issues that any designer of a listening test used for academic purposes may need to consider when planning a new test or revising an existing one – and the types of solution (satisfactory or flawed) that might result.

The present-day IELTS test has an important place in the history of tests of academic listening in that it evolved from one of the very earliest international tests of English for Academic Purposes (EAP). The first standardised test for international students intending to study at universities in the UK was the *English Proficiency Test Battery* (EPTB), developed by the British Council and the University of Birmingham and first available in 1965. The EPTB focused chiefly on reading but one of its three sections tested academic listening. There was no assessment of writing and speaking – either because of a perceived need to focus upon the main sources of information in an EAP context or because of a wish to avoid the subjective scoring that the productive skills require.

The *English Language Testing Service* (ELTS), developed by the British Council and Cambridge Assessment, replaced the EPTB in 1980 and adopted a radically different approach to the testing of Academic English. It attempted to reflect the extent to which the major disciplines demand of the student different types of cognition and different forms of language (self-evidently, studying physics requires a very different type of reading from studying literature). ELTS consisted of six modules, five of which were very broadly domain-specific (life sciences, social studies, physical sciences, technology, and medicine) while the sixth focused on 'general academic' skills. Clearly, this format imposed considerable demands upon item writers, who had to produce specialised content for small numbers of candidates, and upon test designers who had to evaluate the relative difficulty of the modules.

In 1989, ELTS was replaced by IELTS (Alderson and Clapham 1992). The new test was developed by the ELTS partners in conjunction with the International Development Program of Australian Universities and Colleges. Influenced by current principles associated with Communicative Language Teaching, it adopted the convention of testing the four language skills in four distinct modules. Two important issues helped to shape this and subsequent versions. The first was the need to recognise and distinguish between the various purposes that test takers might have in taking the test. Alongside an Academic version aimed at EAP candidates, a General Training version was introduced for those seeking to take the test for vocational training or immigration purposes.

Anomalously, however, the separate versions were provided only for the Reading and Writing tests and not for Listening and Speaking, where a single test, embracing both academic and general material, was offered for each skill. This situation remains true in today's version of the test. The rationales offered (*Guide for Teachers*, IELTS 2018a:3) are that a) 'The distinction between "academic" and "general" literacy has traditionally been seen as most marked in relation to Reading and Writing skills', and b) that 'The more socially-oriented language skills of Listening and Speaking are equally important in an academic study or professional context.' Both of these assertions are open to challenge. The second in particular may underestimate the important differences in the *types* of listening and speaking that take place in general, academic and professional contexts – and indeed within different professional contexts.

A second issue was the vexed question of precisely what should be targeted by a test that provides a criterion for university admission across a range of disciplines. As noted, ELTS had attempted to represent the extent to which the language, discourse patterns and cognitive processes in which L2 users engage are specific to the academic field they are studying. In the first (1989) version of IELTS, this perspective was to some extent retained, with the Academic Reading and Writing tests continuing to offer field-specific papers across three broad subject areas. However, as part of a subsequent revision (1995), the attempt to reflect this level of domain specificity was dropped; and there is now only one generic academic paper for each of the four skills.

The issue of domain specificity is addressed by Murray (2016:Chaps. 3–4), who argues persuasively that tests of academic skills (he mentions IELTS, Test of English as a Foreign Language (TOEFL) and Pearson Test of English (PTE)) need to be viewed as tests of *pre-enrolment*, indicating an individual's potential for embarking upon a course of academic study rather than guaranteeing their ability to do so. This view is endorsed by very precise wording on the IELTS website (retrieved 2018), which specifies the content of the test as follows: 'It assesses whether you are ready to begin studying or training in an environment where English language is used, and reflects some of the features of language used in academic study'. The issue of the extent to which the IELTS Listening test reflects some of the features of language used in academic study will be addressed in rather more detail when considering the contextual validity of the IELTS Listening module. For the moment, the point to be made is that it would appear to be a practical impossibility for any test of academic language to represent and differentiate between the characteristics and demands of a wide range of different domains of study. This is a challenge facing not only the IELTS test developers but also the providers of other international language proficiency tests commonly used for academic purposes, such as TOEFL and Pearson Test of English Academic (PTE Academic).

The panel below summarises the characteristics of the Listening section in the current version of the IELTS test. Note the range of recorded content, which reflects the fact that there is no separate 'General Training' version. The test therefore aims to cover both academic and social contexts. In practice, this means: a) a conversational situation in an everyday social context; b) a monologue, also in a social context; c) a conversation in an 'educational or training' context (e.g. two students planning a research project); and d) a monologue on an academic subject (e.g. a lecture). The implications of this division between social and academic targets will be discussed in due course. For a more detailed history of the development of IELTS, see Davies (2008) and Taylor and Weir (2012).

Characteristics of the IELTS Listening paper
(Source: IELTS 2017)

Number of questions: 40

Number of recordings: 4

Duration: 30 minutes (plus 10 minutes to write up answers)
Mean recording length across versions: 6 mins 47 sec (41 secs per question)*

Content:
    Recording 1: Dialogue: everyday social discourse
    Recording 2: Monologue: everyday social discourse
    Recording 3: Exchange (up to four speakers): set in an academic context
    Recording 4: Monologue: usually presentational style

Question types:
Multiple choice – multiple matching – labelling a graphic – form filling – summary completion – short-answer questions

* Based on a sample of withdrawn tests in *Cambridge IELTS 7* (2009)

The methodological approach underpinning this volume

The terms of reference which shape much of the discussion in this volume draw upon a version of the socio-cognitive framework, a set of criteria for exploring test validation issues that was originally proposed by Cyril Weir in his seminal volume *Language Testing and Validation: An Evidence-based Approach* (Weir 2005).

Chalhoub-Deville and O'Sullivan (2020) describe in their volume entitled *Validity: Theoretical Development and Integrated Arguments* how a socio-cognitive approach steadily took shape through discussions among UK language testers in the early 2000s. This led to the creation of a series of skills-focused frameworks that enabled language test developers and researchers to scrutinise and evaluate key aspects of an assessment as part of the process of constructing a sound validation argument to support claims about test usefulness. One of the innovative features of Weir's approach was the attempt to refine and integrate thinking on how language-related cognition might be better represented within this process, particularly for the receptive skills of reading and listening.

These frameworks subsequently formed the basis of test development and validation projects across the globe. Several volumes in the SiLT series illustrate how the socio-cognitive approach was applied to analyse the Cambridge suite of English language proficiency examinations; for example, a volume edited by Geranpayeh and Taylor (2013) examines the Cambridge listening tests at a range of Common European Framework of Reference for Languages (CEFR, Council of Europe 2001) proficiency levels. Similar volumes focused on the skills of writing, reading and speaking (Shaw and Weir 2007, Khalifa and Weir 2009, Taylor (Ed) 2011, respectively) while other theorists and practitioners demonstrated the relevance of a socio-cognitive approach across a range of test development contexts worldwide (O'Sullivan (Ed) 2011).

Broadly speaking, the socio-cognitive approach, as originally conceptualised by Weir (2005), identifies (amongst others) the following considerations for reviewing tests of language:

- *Consequential validity*: How well do stakeholders understand the purposes of the test and what it measures? What impact does the test have on stakeholder perceptions of the skill? What washback is there on general instruction and on test preparation?
- *Criterion-related validity*: How accurately do a test's scores represent and discriminate between different levels of proficiency, and how well can a test be matched against some external set of criteria which measure the same ability?
- *Test taker characteristics*: Do test tasks take full account of test taker expectations, goals and online behaviour?
- *Context validity*: How does the test material relate to real-world materials and to the real-world circumstances faced by an academic listener?

- *Cognitive validity*: Do the cognitive processes that the test elicits resemble those that would be employed in real-world contexts? Do they take full account of the proficiency level and age of the candidate?
- *Scoring validity*: How are the test scores arrived at (in terms of scoring criteria and marking approaches) and how reliable are the test results for decision-making purposes?

Taken together, these six dimensions provide a theory-derived interrogative framework for reviewing an existing test or developing a new one, which can be adapted and tailored to suit the ability trait or skill of interest. The discussion throughout this volume also draws upon a skill-specific framework for analysing listening tests that was employed by the author in earlier cognitive validity exercises (Field 2013, 2019). This takes due account of both the processes adopted by the test taker and the extent to which test conventions and content can be said to be reflective of normal engagement with spoken input in the target context. It includes consideration of: test taker characteristics – recording as text – recording as speech – conventions of delivery – task formats – items. Though the analysis and commentary will relate primarily to the IELTS Listening test, it should be borne in mind that similar concerns might well be expressed about other widely available tests used to measure academic performance (e.g. Internet-based Test of English as a Foreign Language (TOEFL iBT), PTE Academic), even though they may view the construct of academic listening from a different angle or approach it differently. One of the key issues to be addressed later in the discussion will be the question of how far the IELTS Listening test can be regarded as truly 'academic' in nature, or whether it is more appropriate to see it as containing some features of language that reflect contemporary academic demands alongside features reflecting more generalised listening skills. It should be borne in mind that similar comments may apply in the case of other tests that are widely used to measure academic listening performance – including tests such as TOEFL iBT and PTE Academic, which reflect very different views of the construct of academic listening and how it is operationalised.

Section 1
Insights from empirical research

This section reviews research and other relevant literature on how the IELTS Listening paper operates in terms of:

- *Consequential validity*: stakeholders' understanding of the test's goals and what it measures; the test's washback upon general instruction and test preparation (Chapter 1)
- *Criterion-related validity*: the accuracy of the test's scores in representing and discriminating between different levels of proficiency (Chapter 2); whether listening scores such as those of IELTS can be aligned with criteria specified in the Common European Framework of Reference for Languages (CEFR, Council of Europe 2001) (Chapter 3)
- *Test taker characteristics: Experiential and behavioural*: how accurately the test's tasks target the listening needs of test takers in terms of their experiential, psychological and physical/physiological characteristics (Chapter 4)

Readers will find discussion of the areas of *cognitive validity* and *context validity*, and insights from the related empirical research, covered in Chapters 5 and 6 within Section 2. *Scoring validity* does not have its own chapter in this volume as the IELTS Listening test adopts a largely objective format involving mainly selected-response items and some short, constructed response items. Furthermore, when compared with the number of studies investigating rating and scoring validity issues for the IELTS Writing and Speaking tests, there is relatively little research to draw on to inform the discussion for IELTS Reading and Listening. Nevertheless, the discussion of test formats in Chapter 9 will cover the scoring validity of those formats currently employed and there is also some discussion on the internal consistency of current IELTS Listening test items.

The research literature consulted by the author for this and subsequent sections in the volume included: *IELTS Research Reports*, which have been funded and published by the IELTS partners since 1995; research studies and articles on IELTS published in peer-reviewed journals such as *Language Testing, Language Assessment Quarterly, Applied Linguistics, Journal of English for Academic Purposes*; relevant volumes in the SiLT series published jointly by Cambridge Assessment English and Cambridge University Press; and other academic language testing and assessment volumes in the field. To these more research-orientated sources, we can add published volumes of IELTS practice tests or past papers for teachers and students. All of these items are in the public domain. In addition, as part of the research projects commissioned from CRELLA by the British Council and Cambridge English Language Assessment in 2017–2018, the author was given confidential access to a limited amount of proprietary documentation, such as the IELTS *Item Writer Guidelines* and a selection of retired Listening test material. A comprehensive list of all the references consulted can be found at the end of this volume.

1 Consequential validity

Understanding test consequences

The socio-cognitive approach originally advocated by Cyril Weir in his 2005 volume included a component referred to as 'consequential validity', a convenient umbrella term to encompass matters of test washback and impact, as well as the avoidance of test bias. This built partly upon earlier theoretical work taking into consideration the impact and consequences associated with the use of any test (Messick 1989). Messick stressed the need to ascertain whether the social consequences of test interpretation support the intended testing purpose(s) and are consistent with other social values, such as fairness and justice. In the first of the SiLT volumes to apply the socio-cognitive framework to the Cambridge English tests, Shaw and Weir (2007:7) highlighted concerns for 'the washback of the test on the learning and teaching that precedes it as well as with its impact on institutions and society more broadly'.

Further work has been done over recent years to develop a fuller understanding of consequential validity and the impact of tests within the wider educational and social context. Saville (2009) developed a model for a public examination provider to investigate the impact of their language tests within educational contexts, and Chalhoub-Deville and O'Sullivan (2020:155) promote the concept of impact by design, which places consequences at the top of the evidence chain in support of test validation claims. This broadens out the focus beyond simple matters of washback, impact and test bias. Chalhoub-Deville and O'Sullivan envision validity scholarship as including consequences at the level of the individual, the group and wider interests, whether educational, organisational or societal. Closely associated with this focus on consequences is, they argue, an awareness of the different needs of a wide range of stakeholders.

Stakeholder perceptions

The introduction to this volume touched briefly on the administrative difficulties of providing discipline-specific material in any international high-stakes test. Murray, in his comprehensive survey of English standards in higher education (2016:Chap. 4), characterises such tests as a measure of *pre-enrolment* potential. This entails that some responsibility for the development of the academic literacy of students has to be taken by the accepting university – not least in training incoming students in the logic and the terminology of their area of specialisation. Arkoudis, Baik and Richardson (2012:36) assert that '[A]ll staff involved in setting and administering English language requirements should be made aware of the meaning, limitations and relationship of test scores on different standardised tests, including their limited predictability for future academic performance'. To these individuals, Murray would add university administrators, marketing teams, admission tutors and those responsible for course content within departments.

This raises the intriguing question of how much these personnel understand of the scope and goals of the tests that they choose to accept for admission purposes. On the basis of his extensive experience, Murray (2016:110–111) suggests three factors that chiefly influence their understanding of test results: claims made by the organisation that produced the tests; the skills components of the tests and associated tasks; and performance descriptors which (perhaps in the form of 'can do' statements) characterise the performance that can be expected of successful candidates. The last must surely be very influential in establishing an initial impression of the candidate's receptive skills of reading and listening, given the difficulties of obtaining hard evidence of performance once study begins. Murray also warns against the danger of instructors taking a holistic view of entrants' competence, one which assumes that a student has necessarily mastered all of the functions listed in a set of 'can do' descriptors for a particular band score. One solution that he proposes (2016:Chap. 5) is to ensure that there is a consistent policy across institutions of *post-enrolment* language assessment, which enables tutors to track deficiencies, either specific to the area of study being pursued or not apparent at the time of acceptance.

His other major recommendation is that greater efforts should be made to ensure that stakeholders have a better understanding of what gatekeeping tests claim to do and what their scores indicate. He notes that the equivalence tables comparing scores across different tests are unreliable at best (Davies et al 1999, Taylor 2004) and reports a finding of Murray and Arkoudis (2013) that the interpretation of IELTS scores tends to be more generous than for PTE Academic or TOEFL iBT – thus presumably inflating what is expected of candidates.

There have been a number of general studies (mostly funded by the IELTS partners) which have investigated whether and how well stakeholders understand the scores that a test produces. Research by Coleman, Starfield and Hagan (2003) covered staff and students from China, Australia and the UK. They reported students to be more easily satisfied about their own levels of proficiency than were staff; and commented that staff needed to be better informed about the goals of tests used for admission and the significance of the scores achieved. This view is echoed by Ingram and Bayliss (2007:10), who explicitly link a proper understanding of the function and relevance of scores with the need to determine admission criteria:

> Without a clear understanding of the linguistic behaviour implied by IELTS scores, the setting of appropriate entry levels to different university courses is a speculative exercise. ... At present, IELTS proficiency descriptors provide little information about what a student should or should not be able to "do" with language, making it difficult for university admissions staff and faculties to determine whether they are linguistically equipped to fulfil the task requirements of particular study disciplines.

In a similar vein, O'Loughlin (2012) advocates increasing the assessment literacy of both candidates and university staff. But he makes it clear that what is needed is not a profile-raising exercise that requests a stakeholder's feedback on the handbooks and other information sources; but a sustained project that aims to build bridges between the providers' informed understanding of what the test aims to measure and the interpretations that users bring to bear. An interesting proposal is for online tutorials that explain the principles of EAP testing to stakeholders in an accessible way.

A study by Hyatt and Brooks (2009) interviewed UK stakeholders about their impressions of the IELTS test. There was a consensus that the test was 'a useful indicator of academic English proficiency.' A positive finding was that about 75% of those interviewed showed that they were aware of the need for additional post-entry training; but, less positively, around 65% expressed a wish for tests to serve a more diagnostic purpose.

As with the predictive studies, there have been insufficient attempts by researchers to separate out the four skills represented in the test, either in terms of how they are understood or in terms of stakeholders' perceptions of their differing relevance to particular courses, academic domains or local patterns of instruction. This is especially a matter of concern in the case of listening, which takes place under pressures of time and where students struggling to follow lines of argument in a lecture or even to decode parts of what is said (Field 2011) are much less likely to be detected than those with problems in the other skill areas. An exception was an early stakeholder study by McDowell and Merrylees (1998) which compared target entry scores across institutions. They were highest for Writing (with 62% of institutions requiring a score of 6) and lowest for Listening, with 7% of institutions accepting a score of 4.5 or above. This suggests a rather worrying received view that academic listening can be acquired incidentally after enrolment. It flies in the face of the findings of Ingram and Bayliss (2007, see above) which suggest that, if anything, successful listening to instructional material may merit a relatively higher set of marks than other skills.

Washback effects upon teaching and learning

A further area which has received research attention relates to *washback*, conceived in terms of the effects of tests on teaching and learning (Alderson and Wall 1993, Wall 1997). Interest originally focused on the first of these – in particular, the attitudes of instructors to IELTS as a measure of academic proficiency and how their requirements have shaped EAP course content. More recently, attention has shifted to the attitudes of the learner/test taker and to the types of learning that occur through test practice.

A study by Read and Hayes (2003) of IELTS in New Zealand combined these angles. The researchers reported positive washback in relation to instructors. Among aspects of the test positively received were the inclusion of subjectively marked tests of Speaking and Writing, the use of longer texts with relevant discourse features and the use of a variety of test formats. The last two have implications for Listening as well as Reading. There was a view that the design of the tasks adequately replicated the demands of academic performance. By way of comparison, Read and Hayes (2003) mention a degree of negative washback on the then-current version of the TOEFL test because of its focus on grammar and vocabulary, its reliance on short texts and a single multiple-choice question (MCQ) format and its lack of a free-speaking component. The test was not perceived by Read and Hayes as adequately tapping into the relevant academic language skills.

One has, of course, to separate evaluation of the content of any test from the very different issue of how the test influences EAP instruction. Read and Hayes (2003) also obtained interesting insights into the impact of IELTS on classroom practice by asking learners in what ways they felt their test preparation had assisted them. Some 58.3% of those questioned felt that a major benefit had been an improvement in their English proficiency. But 51.8% identified improved *knowledge of the test* as an important outcome while 58.3% felt that they had gained some useful *test-taking strategies*. This compares with only 38.3% who felt that they had improved their academic study skills. The figures seem to confirm what is often reported anecdotally: namely, a heavy reliance in exam preparation courses upon test practice, with importance attached to developing test-wise strategies of the kind that Field (2012a) demonstrated to be particularly common when taking the IELTS Listening paper.

This raises the long-standing issue of the effects of relying heavily upon this type of instruction. While test designers cannot be held responsible for the use made of their test content by instructors, it is surely reasonable to expect the latter to give careful thought to considerations such as:

- Does extensive test practice constitute time well spent during a general EAP course? Might it distract instructors from equipping learners with the long-term skills that they will need when they eventually arrive in an academic context?
- Is extensive test practice provided not just to ensure familiarity with test method, layout etc. but also to satisfy the assumption that more practice necessarily leads to better test-handling skills and therefore higher scores? If that is the case, might it encourage certain rather inflexible types of training regime, which take more account of test demands than of the relative proficiency and individual needs of the learners?
- Does much of test practice focus on the type of test-wise strategy that exploits a weakness of test design? It might thus be seen as relevant to the task in hand (i.e. finding the correct answer at all costs) but not to employing the target skill in a real-world context. Might it even conduce to frustrating the test's ultimate goal of establishing a test taker's true level of skill proficiency?

In relation to the first, Green (2006) found a degree of congruence between the types of task employed in practice sessions for the IELTS Writing module and the real-world demands of academic writing. However, it appears likely that this relationship is skill-specific. Listening is a much less controllable skill than writing because of its time-constrained nature and a much more approximate one because of the high variability of its basic unit of analysis (the word) when it occurs in connected speech. It is therefore much more subject to strategic behaviour that strives to compensate for uncertainty than are the other three skills. One can understand why the instincts of many instructors lead them to feature both extensive test practice and explicit strategy training when preparing for a Listening module.

In fact, Read and Hayes (2003:182) report that much of the listening instruction in the two classes they observed took the form of test practice, with one group in particular focusing on test-related skills such as answering certain item types. Specific training in listening did not seem to feature as a high priority in either group: in one, it represented 3.6% of class time over the period of observation and in the other 6.5%. In a subsequent study, Hayes and Read (2004) compared a course focusing on exam preparation with one that included wider goals relating to language development and study skills, and found the latter more effective in improving learner performance.

Several studies have attempted to examine the impact of instruction upon scores. Elder and O'Loughlin (2003) report that listening was the skill that benefited most from four intensive 10–12-week courses that were studied. A comparison between pre- and post-test scores across 112 learners showed a mean increase of 0.781 (SD .972) in the band scores for Listening as compared with 0.545 (.948) for Writing, 0.5 (.930) for Speaking and 0.402 (.729) for Reading. Interestingly, the variable that was found to contribute most to this increase in scores was the choice of institution, suggesting a degree of variation in the effectiveness of the teaching methodology employed. In a similar study involving 63 participants, O'Loughlin and Arkoudis (2009) reported the greatest mean improvement in Listening (.500, SD .767) and Reading (.522, SD .772). The score increases for these two skills and for Writing correlated quite closely across participants, with particular benefits seen at lower levels; but scores for Speaking did not fit into the general pattern.

Another longitudinal study exploring the impact of practice upon success (Winke and Lim 2014) specifically focused on the Listening module and the types of approach that might be adopted by instructors. Participants were divided into three groups. For two of them, the training provided was based on test practice sessions: one group focusing on strategy use (including test-wise strategies), the other on the vocabulary of the practice tests that were used. A third group was given conversation-based instruction unconnected to the style or content of any given module.

Contrary to the other findings just reported, no clear effects of training were found upon participants' progress as measured by a post-test. This is perhaps unsurprising as the treatment consisted solely of two 2-hour training sessions a week apart, and therefore cannot be said to replicate the circumstances of the kind of extensive programme studied by Elder and O'Loughlin (2003). On this slim evidence, Winke and Lim conclude (2014:1) that the best function of test preparation 'is perhaps familiarization with test format and the test's item types, especially items that are relatively new or unknown to the test takers'. They even seem at one point (2014:20) to endorse Jafari and Hashim's (2012) acceptance of the value of training learners in test-wise strategies such as employing key words; and fail to address the issue that many techniques of this kind are artefactual, with few direct parallels in real-world listening behaviour. More positively, however, they also make a point of mentioning a major aspect of real-world academic listening that current tests often fail to tackle: namely, identifying which pieces of information constitute main points.

Nguyen (2007) took a rather different approach: contrasting the outcomes of training upon Listening scores in IELTS and in TOEFL iBT. A total of 95 Vietnamese participants were given instruction in handling one of the tests and then asked to take both. Contrary to Winke and Lim's, this study found a strong effect of instruction upon learners' ability to perform well in the IELTS Listening module; but a negligible one so far as the TOEFL iBT paper was concerned. Nguyen attributes this to the demands of the IELTS module, with its wider range and complexity of test formats (as compared with the sole use of MCQs in TOEFL) and its coverage of two discourse types (general as well as academic). However, Nguyen's final conclusion that this illustrates the greater construct validity of TOEFL iBT is ill-founded. It may

Consequential validity

indeed be easier to train learners for a single-format test – but that does not mean that the format in question is necessarily a valid one for representing the target skill (multiple-choice testing of listening is notoriously dependent upon reading competence). The researcher also admits two uncontrolled variables in the study: greater training time given to the IELTS group and the lack of a neutral pre-test to establish the real-world proficiency levels of the participants.

Finally, a general washback study by Allen (2016) examined the effects of IELTS instruction upon test takers within a single learning context – namely the Japanese tertiary system. The population studied scored quite high at the outset in Listening as well as Reading but lower in Writing and much lower in Speaking. The high Listening score may seem a little unusual for the context, and it also seems difficult to explain why this level of listening proficiency had apparently impacted so little on speech production. However, O'Sullivan suggests this may be explained by the fact that Listening has for many years been included in the National Centre Test, meaning that Japanese secondary school learners tend to focus on it (and on reading) with no emphasis on the productive skills (personal communication, February 2022).

Allen's interest lay particularly in the progress resulting from instruction in speaking. He reports that a post-test showed improvements in performance as follows: Speaking > Reading, Writing > Listening. The increase in listening proficiency from 6.6 to 6.7 did not reach significance. This might suggest that (contrary to the Elder and O'Loughlin 2003 results) listening is the skill that benefits least from pre-exam preparation. An alternative, and perhaps more convincing, interpretation is that the result may be evidence of a ceiling effect. It is possible that the pre-treatment IELTS scores over-represented the true capabilities of the learners – in which case, it would be understandable if the subsequent scores showed few signs of progress. See the comments above about the Ingram and Bayliss (2007) findings; and the verbal reports obtained by Golder, Reeder and Fleming (2009), suggesting that many students view the IELTS Listening section as relatively easy. We shall return to the issue of Listening scores in due course.

This review of the washback literature has reported on findings which are largely based upon individual impressions or upon pre-test and post-test scores. It is indeed useful (and good PR) to obtain feedback from experienced practitioners on the extent to which a test is perceived to have relevance to the skills which they are trying to develop in learners. It is also possible to draw some limited conclusions that may be of benefit to them: particularly where there is uncertain evidence whether a heavy focus on test practice necessarily leads to improved performance.

However, whether the source of washback information is the instructor, the learner or a change of band score, it is dangerous to draw conclusions from it that concern the validity of the test. The best one can perhaps argue is that a kind of indirect validation of the test takes place when its components are used as the basis for instruction and that instruction then leads on to a demonstrable improvement in the skills that learners require for their future academic experience. The problem here is that the approach adopted by researchers seeking evidence of progress has usually been a circular one – with pre-treatment scores matched against post-treatment ones rather than against subsequent real-world behaviour. If any test as presently constituted has flaws, then they will not be reliably discovered by comparing results at one stage of training with results at another. Indeed, any increase in scores (particularly in listening) may simply reflect the acquisition of test-wise strategies irrelevant to real-world performance. This is a concern that applies to any listening test (whether major or minor); it is not just a potential issue for IELTS.

Summary and general conclusions

Stakeholders' perceptions

a. The function of tests of academic listening skills should be represented more explicitly as a measure of *pre-enrolment potential* – entailing that some responsibility for the development of the academic literacy of students has to be taken by the receiving university.

b. There is a need to ensure that administrators are better informed about the nature and scope of academic language tests and the significance of their scores. This is critical if informed choices are to be made about admissions criteria, whether in terms of overall score bands or in terms of specific skills. A possible solution (O'Loughlin 2012) would be a set of online tutorials directed at any institution proposing to use a test for its entry procedure. There is some evidence that the role of listening in particular is insufficiently recognised by gatekeepers.

Washback (instructors and candidates)

a. There may be a need to improve the assessment literacy of instructors preparing learners for academic language tests to ensure they are clearer in particular about the goals of a typical listening test and about the behavioural characteristics which underlie the band descriptors.

b. The majority of the evidence suggests that instruction in listening has a positive impact upon test performance. However, it would appear that, in some contexts, the importance of listening skills may be underestimated. A major unresolved issue amongst instructors remains the precise balance to be struck between sessions that involve test practice,

Consequential validity

those that involve skills development and those that focus on other EAP skills.

c. In listening in particular, a case can be made for training learners in compensatory strategies to deal with gaps in comprehension. If such strategies are recommended to instructors as part of test preparation, they should be clearly distinguished from test-wise techniques which exploit loopholes in test method and item information – though inevitably these are likely to feature in the courses offered.

d. There is a need for future washback research which elicits verbal reports from candidates that record their immediate post-test impressions – information which, in the case of listening, cannot be inferred from hard evidence as it sometimes can in writing and speaking.

As suggested in the Introduction to this volume, it is hoped that some of the insights shared above will assist senior academics and professionals tasked with setting standards for entry or performance within institutes of learning. In addition, the observations have practical implications for language teachers and learners, encouraging them away from the type of test-wise strategy that often features in instruction and towards approaches that embrace the actual processes that underlie the listening experience – processes that will serve the candidate well if and when they succeed in obtaining a place on the course of their choice.

2 Criterion-related validity (1)

General findings

What appears to be the most frequently addressed research question in relation to tests of academic language skills concerns the extent to which a test can be said to predict the performance of test takers following their arrival in an academic context. There is a history to this in the case of IELTS. One of the considerations leading to the 1989 revision and the original development of the test was the discovery by Criper and Davies (1988) of a weak correlation between overall ELTS scores and later performance as a student.

For reference in the discussion that follows, Table 1 shows the current scoring scale used in IELTS.

Table 1 The IELTS band score system

Level	
9	Expert user
8	Very good user
7	Good user
6	Competent user
5	Modest user
4	Limited user
3	Extremely limited user
2	Intermittent user
1	Non user
0	Did not attempt the test

A score (to the nearest .5) is attributed to a test taker's performance for each of the four skills (listening, reading, writing and speaking). An overall mean score for the whole test is then calculated, to the nearest .5 above. Acceptance for academic courses at tertiary level is usually determined by an overall score of 6.0, 6.5 or above.

A number of studies have sought correlations between overall IELTS scores and later academic progress. Some have compared the predictive power of different skills modules; of those, very few have focused solely on the Listening test. The measure of academic progress most widely adopted in this type of enquiry has been the candidate's Grade Point Average (GPA), either in the first or second semester of study.

Of the general studies, several (Elder 1993, Feast 2002, Ferguson and White 1994, Kerstjens and Nery 2000, Woodrow 2006) have found a weak positive association between overall scores and in-course performance. Reviewing these and other studies, O'Loughlin (2008) concludes that IELTS offers a 'weak to moderate predictive power of academic success'; but points out that the type of competence tested by the band scores may be simply one amongst a larger set of learner characteristics which contribute to progress. See similar comments by Chalhoub-Deville and Turner (2000), Dooey and Oliver (2002) and Tonkyn (1995).

Hill, Storch and Lynch (1999:65) report a stronger correlation than others ($r = .540$), though they acknowledge possible inconsistencies in their data set. Another strong association was found by Bellingham (1993). Interestingly, what marks out her study is that it includes students with a wide range of scores, from 4.0 upwards. Many other projects have only had access to students already enrolled in university places – in effect, those with a more limited range of scores of 6.0 and above. The Bellingham study thus provides a useful indication that the test has proved reliable in predicting later performance by candidates who did not pass it, as well as by those who did.

Against these positive claims, a number of other researchers (Fiocco 1992, Cotton and Conrow 1998, Dooey and Oliver 2002) have reported the lack of a clear correlation. Dooey (1999) failed to find sufficient evidence that students who fell below the entry criterion of IELTS 6.0 were likely to fail in their later studies and conversely reported that most of those who ultimately failed had entered with high scores.

A point worth noting about much research in this area is its reliance on overall band scores. A few of the studies show a disturbing tendency to equate these general scores quite narrowly with 'language proficiency' (see e.g. Dooey and Oliver 2002, Ferguson and White 1994). They thus implicitly fail to recognise that any modular skills-based test of this kind aims to test not simply language *knowledge* but also *expertise* in using language skills relevantly in response to the challenges of study (Field 2011, 2013). In addition, the focus on overall scores sometimes fails to make due allowance for the fact that the bands are a composite of performance in four different skills, any one of which might have contributed independently to later success.

That said, a number of studies have made a point of focusing on the role of individual skills. There has been particular interest in reading. Amongst those quoted earlier, Hill et al (1999), Kerstjens and Nery (2000) and Dooey and Oliver (2002) go on to report a significant correlation between reading performance and later academic achievement as indicated by grade averages. Cotton and Conrow (1998) did not find any such correlation; but managed to identify a positive link between a) reading and writing scores and b) staff assessments of performance.

Listening scores

Importantly, none of the studies just cited found a positive link in the case of listening; indeed, Cotton and Conrow report a negative correlation between the listening score and later performance. The finding is supported by qualitative evidence from stakeholders. Murray (2016:103) refers to a British Quality Assurance Agency (QAA) report[1] on the Listening paper which quotes both student and staff focus groups as expressing the view (p.13) that the scores obtained 'do not necessarily correlate well with a student's ability to understand conversational English ... or their ability to understand subject specific vocabulary'. An earlier study by Denham and Oner (1992) similarly found a mismatch between students' test scores and later experience of their L2 listening capability.

Two researchers have indeed reported positive correlations; but it may be significant that both studies involved postgraduates with previous experience of academic study. Elder (1993) recorded a correlation of .40 between listening scores and later grade averages, based upon a relatively small sample. A larger-scale study by Woodrow (2006) found a similar correlation of .35 based on students' first semester grade average, but (curiously contrary to other studies cited so far) no correlations in respect of Reading and Writing. Woodrow interpreted the finding in terms of the specific type of teaching and assessment entailed in the study domain investigated (education and social work). This points to another variable that has been all too often neglected in this area of study: namely the extent to which measures of post-test performance are shaped by the balance of skills that a given subject area requires.

How can one explain the fact that (leaving aside Woodrow 2006) Reading scores appear to be consistently predictive of grade average scores; but Lstening scores do not? Picard (2007) would argue that the type of reading text that features in the test engages the specific skills needed for academic study in a way that the content of the other modules does not. She could perhaps have reversed the argument in relation to the content of the Listening test. It may well be that, given the mixture of general and academic material, the recorded material bears quite limited relevance to what is encountered in a real-world study context and does not sufficiently represent the demands associated with the comprehension of complex facts and ideas. This view appears to be endorsed by verbal reports in a Canadian study (Golder et al 2009) which viewed the Listening module as relatively easy. Student perceptions seem consistent with IELTS test performance data officially

---

[1] A British agency tasked with safeguarding the standards and improving the quality of higher education.

reported by the test providers for 2019, the last normal test administration year before the Covid pandemic. The band score data reported for that year shows IELTS Academic test takers receiving their highest modular score on the Listening test, with slightly lower scores on the Reading, Speaking and Writing tests respectively. (A similar pattern applied for test takers taking IELTS General Training, with the Listening module also attracting the highest score of the four skills.)

Of course, in considering any test of the listening skill, one could instead argue for a rather different explanation: one based upon the different roles of listening and reading in academic practice. How meaningful is it for researchers to seek evidence of listening behaviour by reference to later Grade Point Averages, when the course assignments that are set are likely to be in written form and largely informed by reading? Students are also able to compensate for any failures of comprehension during oral instruction by backing up their understanding through reading. In short, the types of measure used in universities to represent successful academic performance *in situ* are strongly biased towards written forms of language.

Research limitations

Summing up, it would seem that, when evaluating the findings on the predictive validity of this type of test (regardless of the test provider), account needs to be taken of a number of factors:

- In-course performance is sometimes measured holistically, with no consideration given to the different contributions made by the four skills to the final band score and/or to the grades obtained.
- Different measures of progress have been used, representing different stages of development: e.g. grade average (after 1st or 2nd semester or both?), final grade, teacher assessment. The use of grade averages has to face the possibility that the data obtained might simply represent an early developmental stage rather than the participant's final capability as an academic initiate.
- Different student populations have been studied (an entire proficiency range versus those with a narrower range of scores that fit admission criteria).
- The nature and importance of auditory input varies across disciplines.
- The importance accorded to auditory input varies across educational cultures.

To these, one might add that the rate of listening skill development varies widely between individuals once they are in an English-speaking setting – partly as a reflection of their social instincts and wish to integrate. It is also clear that language (whether in receptive or productive modes) is just one of a range of variables – or mediating factors – contributing to academic success.

Any predictive validity studies that rely on evidence of achievement can thus only be broadly indicative. A number of researchers in this area (Allwright and Banerjee 1997, Bellingham 1993, Cotton and Conrow 1998) acknowledge that external socio-cultural factors may play a part in academic success. Murray (2016:105) sums it up well: 'results [from predictive validity studies] have been mixed and the territory remains contentious ..., not least because of the many intervening variables, both linguistic and non-linguistic, that have the potential to influence academic performance and success and which therefore make it difficult to draw unambiguous causal links between language proficiency as measured by such tests and subsequent academic performance'. Amongst the factors cited by Murray (2016:106) are: the individual's understanding of university culture, level of motivation, previous experience of study, self-confidence and willingness to interact, critical thinking skills and capacity to manage their studies. In addition, as already noted, there will inevitably be considerable variation in the linguistic and cognitive demands of different disciplines.

Important studies

Ingram and Bayliss (2007)

The most meticulous of the predictive validity studies (Ingram and Bayliss 2007) avoids the convention of relying upon Grade Point Averages. Instead, it draws upon the reported experiences of a group of 28 students as they cope with their first six months of study. In short, it draws upon actual performance rather than measures of achievement. The group was carefully selected to ensure that it represented a range of IELTS overall band scores from 5.5 upwards, with sub-scores on individual skills beginning at 5.0. It was drawn from students across a range of disciplines and levels of study (from undergraduate to MA and PhD). What also makes this paper much more informative than some others is that it separates out the four skills when examining the relationship between entry test score and subsequent academic performance.

The Ingram and Bayliss study employed four sources of evidence: self- and other-rating, interview, observation and lecture notes. Self-assessments were obtained from students during the early stages of their course; in addition, the researchers observed them and allocated grades based on their performance. The general finding here was that the researchers' scores for in-course performance corresponded quite closely to the IELTS band scores, with 25 out of 28 at the same or a higher level. However, the self-assessments varied quite widely, with 36% of students rating themselves higher and 39% lower and a divergence of −1.5 to +1.5.

There followed some semi-structured interviews where students were asked about their ongoing experience of academic study, with a focus on their use of the four skills across 14 different types of academic activity. Two main Listening conditions were covered: listening to lectures and listening in discussions. The figures in Table 2 have been extrapolated from the graphics in Figure 5 of Ingram and Bayliss (2007:26); the percentages are therefore approximate.

Table 2 Student self-assessment of levels of understanding (Ingram and Bayliss 2007:26)

Understood	Lecture		Discussion	
	Approx %	Mean IELTS	Approx %	Mean IELTS
Most/all	22%	7.1	40%	7.14
A lot	53%	6.8	55%	6.53
Some	22%	6.5	5%	6.25
Not much	3%	6.0	0%	

The researchers' initial analysis of the percentage results suggested that the figures did indeed indicate a correlation between students' listening scores and their ability to understand academic discourse. However, closer analysis using a data-plot of the results indicated no such relationship. The figures above provide some indication why. It is noticeable that around a quarter of the participants felt they could not follow lecture material comfortably and that those who reported to this effect received mean test scores of 6.0 and 6.5.

A further question to participants concerned how well they could understand instructors' questions. 68% asserted that they could usually understand what was being asked; but 32% said that they could only do so sometimes. Ingram and Bayliss report (2007:26) that a number of students mentioned that they felt they needed time to reflect on lecturer questions before responding. Two widely reported barriers to comprehension (2007:27) were speed of speech and the use of colloquial expressions. High test scores proved to correlate well with an increased ability to deal with these perceptual factors.

A third source of information employed by these researchers was observation. Lecturers were asked to observe how attentive the target students were as listeners, how much they appeared to understand and how frequently they asked for clarification. The reports suggested that 70% of the group comprehended course content mostly or always. However, only 52% of the target group were bold enough to ask regularly for clarification.

The researchers themselves observed that many of the students took minimal notes in lectures and classes. When examined, the notes proved in many cases to be well organised but were mainly confined to headings and abbreviations, thereby providing little support for later recall. It was not possible to determine if the lack of content was the result of poor listening, the rapid speech rate of the lecturer, lack of focus or simply limited note-taking skills. However, the insight into learner behaviour has implications for pre-sessional study skills training.

Breeze and Miller (2012)

The only major criterion-related study that focuses exclusively on the Listening module is Breeze and Miller (2012). The study controlled for variation between disciplines by covering three domains with different academic practices: Humanities, Law and Medicine. It used final grades rather than grade averages as the measure of achievement; and it investigated a very specific teaching context and culture (a European university where there was no immersion effect of the kind that occurs in a first-language setting).

The correlations between IELTS scores and final grades were calculated across the three domains:

Table 3 IELTS score correlated with final grade (Breeze and Miller 2012)

Area	Correlation: IELTS score/final grade
Humanities (N = 13)	$\rho = 0.408$, n.s
Law (N = 74)	$\rho = 0.283$, $p < 0.01$
Medicine (N = 202)	$\rho = 0.257$, $p < 0.05$

While the figures reach significance with the larger populations, they are nevertheless relatively low; the researchers themselves (2012:507) describe this as evidence of 'a small to moderate correlation'. They also report that students with IELTS Listening scores of Band 6 and above on entry were *not* consistently more likely to pass the university's final exam. Indeed, in Law, the failure rate was slightly higher among those with scores of Band 6 and above than among students with Band 5. This supports a similar finding by Dooey (1999) that an entry criterion of 6.0 did not consistently serve to identify candidates more capable of engaging in academic study.

Summary and general conclusions

a. Research has not shown any clear or consistent correlation between IELTS Listening scores and later measures of listening performance.

In this respect, the Listening test appears to perform differently from the Reading one, where such correlations have been found. The data also suggests disparities between listening scores and the performance of candidates once they begin their studies. One explanation may be that a listening test cannot represent as precisely as a reading one the types of material to which academic study exposes students and the actual processes in which they are required to engage.

b. If research interest and institutional needs continue to attach importance to linking Listening scores to future course performance, then more careful thought may need to be given to the measures that are chosen to represent learner progress. Relying, as many researchers have, on Grade Point Average scores is largely irrelevant in the case of listening because the forms of in-course assessment on which those and other scores are based tend to be chiefly dependent upon performance in writing and evidence of background reading. When considering future research proposals, the Boards responsible for major international tests might do well to encourage use of the kind of multiple-method approach adopted by Ingram and Bayliss (2007), which seeks (*inter alia*) reports of candidate listening behaviour under actual lecture and seminar conditions. Even here, however, due allowance must be made for socio-cultural and other factors which result in students developing divergently as listeners following arrival in the host country. It is also necessary to add the proviso (see Breeze and Miller 2012) that the four skills targeted by academic tests may vary in importance and be employed differently across different disciplines and learning cultures.

3 Criterion-related validity (2)

Alignment with the CEFR

This second chapter on criterion-related validity briefly considers a specific area as conceptualised in the original socio-cognitive framework (Weir 2005): namely, the extent to which it is possible to align listening scores such as those of IELTS with the standards described in the CEFR. Since the mid-1990s, the CEFR has come to represent an established external standard or interpretative framework of reference, articulated through sets of criteria and descriptors, which has proved useful (if sometimes contentious) in the field of language education across Europe and beyond.

A major study by Lim, Geranpayeh, Khalifa and Buckendhal (2013) represents a systematic attempt to align the nine minimally defined IELTS performance levels (ranging from 1 'non-user' to 9 'expert user') with the more specific descriptors of the CEFR scales. The researchers acknowledge a number of difficulties in undertaking this enterprise: among them the fact that the multi-level framework of IELTS represents a set of cut-scores, whereas CEFR descriptors are designed to provide indications of what a learner is capable of achieving within a given level. To this, they add the fact that CEFR descriptors are themselves widely recognised as being under-specified in order to allow them to be used in multiple contexts (see Alderson et al 2006, Green 2018, Jones and Saville 2009, Milanovic 2009, Milanovic and Weir 2010, Weir 2005). This is a particularly telling point with regard to listening, which, for reasons hard to explain, is very thinly profiled at the higher CEFR levels for 'audience listening'. Taylor and Geranpayeh (2011:94) comment: 'What is noticeable about the C-level can-do descriptors (whether for listening or for other skills) is their relative brevity and level of generality'; and this still remains the case despite the extensive 2020 revision of the criteria. It also remains the case that the CEFR criteria continue to focus on the language content and signal quality of what is loosely termed 'comprehension', with relatively little representation of the processes underlying that end-product.

There are two important features of the Lim et al study which distinguish it from earlier attempts to link IELTS and other tests to the CEFR (e.g. ETS 2010, Pearson 2010, Tannenbaum and Wylie 2008). The first is the methodology used. Lim et al employed a standard-setting procedure, where panellists (N = 19) chosen for their familiarity with the IELTS material classified selected Reading and Listening items on a Yes/No basis according to how capable a test taker at a given CEFR level might be of answering them. (The researchers do not make it clear, but it is to be hoped that the Listening exercise included exposure to the recordings used as well as to the script.) They then went on to triangulate the results by means of a separate External Validation study in which test takers (N = 126) took a representative Certificate in Advanced English (CAE, now known as C1 Advanced) test alongside an IELTS test. This was on the rationale that CAE is specifically targeted at C1 level, though its candidates tend to range from B2 to C2.

On the basis of these two substantial sets of evidence, Lim et al concluded that there is a degree of alignment between the IELTS cut-scores and the CEFR as follows:

B1/B2: IELTS 5.5
B2/C1: IELTS 6–7
C1/C2: IELTS 7.5–8

This provides the basis for the figures that are represented in the current IELTS *Guide for Teachers* (IELTS 2018a:24).

However, as the Guide candidly admits (2018a:25), overall band scores present a simplified picture, since they do not represent possible divergences between the four skills. A second valuable feature of the Lim et al study is that it went on to examine the mean scores for each skill separately and attempted to align them to the levels of the CEFR. Here, the results for Listening are especially striking. They are shown in Table 4 below, with the equivalent figures for Reading given in square brackets for the purposes of comparison.

Table 4 IELTS Listening cut-scores aligned with CEFR levels (Lim et al 2013:41)

	B1/B2	B2/C1	C1/C2
Standard setting	6.0 [6.0]	8.5 [7.5]	9.0 [9.0]
External validation (rounded)	6.0 [6.0]	7.0 [7.0]	9.0 [9.0]

The standard-setting exercise seems to have identified anomalies at B2/C1 level that the validation exercise did not. The figures here suggest that it is only when a test taker achieves the high score of 8.5 on the present Listening test (very close to the maximum) that they can be deemed to fall into the C1 category. The authors explain this as a possible by-product of the standard-setting method. But they also mention (2013:42) the 'relative paucity of items at C1 level' and comment: 'Because the Listening test is used for both IELTS Academic and General Training, it is pitched at a slightly lower level than Reading, which would explain why the divergence is more pronounced for Listening'. Thus, they in effect acknowledge an alternative explanation: namely, that the test, with its present combination of general and academic topics, may be too easy for it to discriminate well between listeners from Level B2 upwards. Related to this, it is worth noting that the *Item Writer Guidelines* (IWGs) for Listening (IELTS 2016:10) specifically advise those designing test materials that 'Sections 1 and 2 of the test focus primarily on intermediate level listening skills (CEFR B1, B2) and Sections 3 and 4 on upper-intermediate/advanced listening skills (CEFR C1)'.

Listening also stands out as the exception in Lim et al's figures for correlations between IELTS and CAE. Overall, the researchers report a significant correlation of 0.87, despite the fact that CAE narrowly targets a single higher proficiency level, whereas IELTS embraces a range of such levels. However, when figures for individual skills are cited, it becomes apparent that Listening (0.49) is well below Reading (0.65) and even Writing (0.59) and Speaking (0.58). There can be little doubt that this partly reflects the marked difference in content between the Listening section in IELTS and that in CAE. The more general, less context-specific material in Sections 1 and 2 of the IELTS paper would seem to mark it out as less demanding than CAE. Conversely, the discursive content of the lecture-based Section 4 might make it *more* demanding, given that a sampling of CAE recordings (Field 2012b) suggested that the majority were narrative or expository.

Lim et al conclude their study by expressing some scepticism about the value of attempting to align a test such as IELTS against the CEFR. This would appear to underline what many have argued in relation to attempts to cross-compare tests – or indeed to align them with generalised external criteria such as those in the CEFR. It has been suggested that different tests subserve different goals and different populations, so that comparisons are sometimes meaningless (see e.g. Green 2018, Milanovic and Weir 2010, Taylor 2004).

Lim et al comment that the CEFR does not reflect 'a defined context of use that gives the judgements substantive meaning' (2013:36). In a similar way, one might argue that IELTS's own descriptors remain somewhat under-specified in terms of the specific contexts for which the test is aimed. This may reflect the enduring tension between, on the one hand, the need for a general test which is highly accessible and capable of meeting a variety of needs and, on the other, the desire for a test to be targeted more narrowly in terms of context and purpose. One solution to the cross-comparison issue is for test providers themselves to lay out more clearly what they perceive the needs and goals of their own test takers to be at various levels, whether these criteria are loosely aligned to the CEFR framework or not. This loops back pertinently to the point made in Chapter 1 about the need to keep stakeholders better informed if they are not to misjudge the scope, purpose and outcomes of a test used for academic or professional purposes.

In fairness, one has to take due account of the fact that it is easier to devise performance descriptors for externally observable skills (writing and speaking) for which an answer script or recording can provide hard evidence. By contrast, the principal processes entailed by reading and listening are internalised and far more difficult to match to band score outcomes or calibrated descriptors. Interestingly, Alderson (1991, 1997) reported how difficult it was to develop meaningful descriptors for the Reading and Listening modules as far back as the early days of ELTS, which was the predecessor to IELTS. (See further discussion of this in Taylor and Weir 2012.)

Perhaps reflecting the historic blending of general and academic needs, the IELTS Listening descriptors are short on specific reference to the academic context for which the test is principally designed. They remain for now at the level of general descriptors and are not designed to reflect the precise types of need that test takers will face when entering academe and that the test is designed to assess (Taylor (2004) comments on the relevance of focusing on concrete academic needs). By way of illustration, Table 5 below lists IELTS's current performance descriptors of the nine score bands, abbreviated to

Table 5 Score descriptors for IELTS Bands 0–9 (Source: IELTS 2018a:6)

Level	General descriptor	Comprehension (oral/written)
9 Expert user	Has fully operational command of the language.	*… with complete understanding.*
8 Very good user	Has fully operational command of the language.	*Misunderstandings may occur in unfamiliar situations.*
7 Good user	Has operational command of the language.	*Generally … understands detailed reasoning.*
6 Competent user	Has generally effective command of the language.	*Can … understand fairly complex language particularly in familiar situations.*
5 Modest user	Has partial command of the language … Should be able to handle basic communication in own field.	*Coping with overall meaning in most situations.*
4 Limited user	Basic competence is limited to familiar situations.	*Has frequent problems in understanding …*
3 Extremely limited user	Frequent breakdowns in communication occur.	*Understands only general meaning in very familiar situations.*
2 Intermittent user	No real communication is possible except for the most basic information.	*Has great difficulty understanding spoken and written English.*
1 Non user	Essentially has no ability to use the language beyond possibly a few isolated words.	

cover only receptive skills. As the IELTS test evolves in the future, with both educators and other stakeholders in mind, a case can perhaps be made for aligning the targets more closely to real-world task demands – even if this entails providing two sets of descriptors e.g. one academic and one professional.

Summary and general conclusions

a. Regardless of which test is under discussion, there is general agreement about the difficulty of mapping test scores against an external scale such as the CEFR; as a result, some commentators have questioned the viability of the exercise. An obvious difference is that a test like IELTS relies on band scores while the CEFR describes the performance characteristics of particular proficiency levels. Another is that CEFR levels and descriptors are designed for general purposes whereas many tests used for academic skills purposes, including such as IELTS, TOEFL and PTE Academic, typically have more narrowly specified goals and populations in mind. The conclusion must be that caution in quoting CEFR equivalences for tests is advisable when providing information to stakeholders, particularly university administrators, who may otherwise apply such criteria very narrowly when setting admission targets.

b. Of the four IELTS modules, the Listening test has proved the hardest to match against CEFR standards. This no doubt reflects the fact that the associated IWGs cite 'intermediate' level material as appropriate at CEFR B1 and B2 levels during 50% of the test and restrict the use of C1-level materials to the second part. Unsurprisingly, participants in Lim et al (2013:42) specifically commented that items did not operate sufficiently at the target C1 level. Designers of all tests of this kind would do well to address the issue of the overall difficulty of Listening modules, which, here and elsewhere, show up as markedly lower than that of other skills (including reading). Future developers might perhaps consider how to include a larger number of more demanding test items (targeting the upper proficiency levels) in order to bring the item/task spread across the Listening test more closely into line with the other skills, including reading. See also the comments that follow later in this volume on item targeting.

c. Listening is under-specified at the higher levels of the CEFR – particularly those levels (C1 and C2) that are associated with successful academic performance. In future, it would be useful for test designers to provide their own performance descriptors for Band Levels 2 to 9: descriptors which are not only more detailed but bear relevance to the populations and purposes that the test aims to assess. This would be of value to stakeholders (including instructors, candidates and university administrators charged with setting admission standards). It would also (with a wider readership in mind) represent much more clearly and accessibly the targets set by the test.

4 Test taker characteristics: Experiential and behavioural

Weir's (2005) socio-cognitive framework identifies three distinct categories of test taker characteristic: *experiential, psychological* and *physical/ physiological*, drawing upon earlier work by O'Sullivan (2000). The early part of this chapter considers the first of these characteristics in terms of the background contexts from which candidates come and the types of experience for which they wish to demonstrate their language competence particularly, but not solely, with regard to listening. This section further develops the discussion regarding domain specialisation that was touched upon at the end of Chapter 1. There will be extensive consideration of the multiple uses that a test such as IELTS is currently put to (in academic, professional and immigration contexts) – an important issue given the high-profile, high-stakes use of the test and the level of concern such usage sometimes raises. Later in the chapter, there follows a brief review of findings relating to two particular sets of personality traits (to clearly distinguish from the later cognitive discussion). The chapter ends with a brief closing section considering candidates' physical/physiological attributes and how these may impact on them when being assessed for their listening ability.

Background

As already noted, the IELTS test distinguishes in principle between materials designed for assessing academic readiness and those designed for assessing general skills. In practice, the distinction is only made in relation to tests of Reading and Writing, where there are two different versions for these two skills – IELTS Academic and IELTS General Training. For the oral skills, there is only a single version. The Listening module seeks to combine general material with academic, each of them allocated two sections out of four.

This feature has even greater significance today, when the populations tested by IELTS (and indeed some other tests of academic language performance) cover not one but three distinct areas of experience. The IELTS website (2022) now characterises it as 'the high-stakes English test for study, migration or work'. The same Listening test is thus used to assess readiness to undertake university study, fitness for immigration and the ability to perform in certain professional contexts. The last of these is itself a generalisation, since the contexts in question can be as diverse as early education teaching and nursing and include qualifying for registration within a profession. As will become clear below, the multifaceted use of IELTS today for additional purposes and populations beyond those associated with international higher education is a matter for debate, prompting concerns to be expressed over the years among some language testers and assessment specialists (e.g. Ahern 2009, Hall 2010, McNamara 2000, McNamara and Roever 2006). Understandable questions have been raised concerning IELTS's 'fitness for purpose', i.e. how well suited it is (or is not) for a wider range of constituencies and decision-making contexts beyond the academic.

It is not the author's intention in this volume to either critique or defend the current multifaceted use of IELTS, but rather to examine more closely how the current IELTS Listening test functions as a high-level test of L2 listening skills that is useful for academic-level study and performance. Discussion so far has focused primarily in this direction, both in the Introduction and in the chapters on consequential and criterion-related validity. In this chapter, however, we must fully acknowledge the complexity and challenges associated with the extended uses of IELTS and the potential threat to the validity of inferences drawn from test scores, a situation which has been highlighted most recently by Read (2022). The aim here will be to frame the discussion around the differing characteristics of the 'non-academic' test taker populations that are now taking IELTS (i.e. overseas trained teachers, medical practitioners) to highlight how these characteristics need to be understood and taken into consideration by both test providers and test users if a stronger validation argument is to be developed for the use or non-use of the test in certain contexts. Though the research to validate IELTS for specific populations remains fairly limited, a number of studies will be explored to see what insights they can provide concerning matters of test focus, content, format and score use.

Further discussion of the rationale underpinning the multiple uses of IELTS across differing populations, including those beyond international higher education, can be found in the Foreword to this volume by Nick Saville and Barry O'Sullivan.

Experiential characteristics

Experiential characteristics include aspects such as previous education/training, test preparation/preparedness, communication experience, target-language country residence, and knowledge of the world. O'Sullivan and Green (2011:39–40) describe them as influences external to the test taker which can impact directly on test taker performance and interact with other test taker characteristics such as psychological or physical/physiological factors. Against the background of IELTS being used for professional and immigration as well as academic purposes, it can be helpful to consider performance from an experiential perspective, so to these influences we might consider adding features of workplace and other life experience.

The solution adopted to meet the three very different requirements of university study, professional registration and immigration typically entails adjusting target scores to fit the different circumstances. It is left to the respective sets of stakeholders (university departments, potential employers, professional registrars and border agencies) to define the level of proficiency within the IELTS score bands that is necessary to meet their own perceived needs, though this may often be done with advice from IELTS or (increasingly) from commissioned academics. The range of different conditions that have to be catered for may go some way towards explaining the somewhat indeterminate descriptors exemplified in Table 5 above and indeed the interest (Chapter 3) in attempting to align IELTS scores to the CEFR.

Three questions arise in relation to the multiple purposes to which IELTS and similarly used tests are currently put:

- How distinctive is the L2 content which a candidate has to handle in each of these different domains and to what extent can the content of a given test be said to represent it?
- How distinctive are the language-related functions associated with each of these domains and to what extent can the content of a given test be said to represent them?
- Is it possible that, in certain domains, one or two of the four skills play a more important role than others?

Later in this volume, we will consider these issues in relation to real-world academic contexts and conditions (Chapters 5, 6 and 7). The present focus is on studies that have investigated the needs of the 'non-academic' candidate, especially those working in the education and healthcare professions.

Much of the research in this area has focused attention on the target scores that have been specified by different professional bodies. It thus operates on the basic assumption that the test being examined adequately represents language skills that are central to functioning successfully in a given workplace or place of residence. Accounts of the scores awarded tend to sidestep the issue of test content; but they do serve to shed light on how the test is currently used and understood by stakeholders. It is important to note that the basic assumption regarding 'content fitness' is being increasingly challenged and the body of research investigating context-specific communication skills is steadily growing.

A number of the studies have taken the enquiry one step further by asking stakeholders (both potential employers and potential employees) what their perceived requirements are and how the content and scores of the IELTS test relate to them. Professions targeted have included different types of office-based work (Knoch, May, Macqueen, Pill and Storch 2016, Moore, Morton, Hall and Wallis 2015), where the main interest lies in the use of the written skills. There has also been interest in teachers trained overseas (Gribble, Blackmore, Morrissey and Capic 2016, Murray, Cross and Cruikshank 2014, Sawyer and Singh 2012). But the population attracting the most attention has been applicants to healthcare services (see e.g. Berry, O'Sullivan and Rugea 2013, Gribble et al 2016, Read and Wette 2009, Sedgwick, Garner and Vicente-Macia 2016). The oral skills self-evidently make an important contribution in these last two areas. In particular, the examples cited by researchers provide testimony to how often and importantly listening features when the needs of medical practitioners are under discussion.

Overseas trained teachers

A study by Murray et al (2014) investigated perceptions of the IELTS test by school principals in Australia and New Zealand. The principals were asked about their experience of working with teachers from abroad ('Overseas Trained Teachers' or OTTs) who had been accepted for employment. They were also asked to provide their own impressions of the types of spoken and written discourse that are vital if candidates are to perform effectively in a school context. Responses were gathered from one-to-one interviews with 18 principals from schools at a range of different levels. They were also collected from focus groups, where judgements were passed on both spoken and written samples of L2 English. At this time, the IELTS band scores widely used for acceptance as an OTT were 7 for Reading and Writing and 8 for Listening and Speaking – indicating recognition at ministry level of the important part played in the classroom by oral communication.

Murray et al reported several major findings on the basis of the data they collected:

- The school principals had a very limited understanding of the language proficiency entry requirements and little knowledge of the content of IELTS and of what its scores represent.
- They had unrealistic ideas as to how candidates who attained the requisite band score would perform, especially when interacting with pupils, colleagues and parents (i.e. in areas involving oral communication).
- A large number of problematic areas of communication were identified at discourse and pragmatic levels, alongside some culturally determined assumptions.

So far as listening was concerned, several principals mentioned failures of communication with colleagues – sometimes due to a lack of domain-specific jargon. Teachers with poor oral skills (both receptive and productive) were observed to lack confidence in the classroom; and the compensatory strategies they used tended to be based on avoidance.

A study by Sawyer and Singh (2012) approached the issue of IELTS in relation to would-be educators at an earlier career stage. They investigated whether the current admission scores for those wishing to attend graduate teacher training courses were considered appropriate by the trainers, the teacher registration authorities and the students themselves. A range of language skills specific to teaching competence were identified. An important finding was that students attending such courses expected to be given ample opportunity during their professional training to develop their pre-existing language and communication skills (including listening and speaking). They considered obtaining a good entry-test score to be an important part of qualifying as a teacher and not simply a means of getting accepted on a local training scheme.

A wide-ranging qualitative study by Gribble and colleagues (2016) explored perceptions of the IELTS test amongst two major groups of non-academic candidates wishing to enter employment in Australia and those seeking to employ them. Interviews with potential employers of early-years teachers elicited a generally agreed need for a higher score of 8.0 for Speaking and Listening (as against 7.0 for Reading and Writing). Gribble et al emphasise (2016:20) the importance of oral communication skills in this particular context: 'Early childhood teachers must have the capacity to speak with children, families, staff and other professionals and be able to calibrate their language accordingly'. They also mention that most employers felt the need to make use of interviews to complement IELTS scores; and (like Murray et al 2014) they remark on a general lack of knowledge among these stakeholders as to what IELTS and similar tests really measure.

Medical practitioners

Gribble et al extended their study to include medical recruitment. Two of the employers interviewed supported an entry grade of IELTS 8 for doctors (2016:30). However, potential candidates (international medical graduates) reported the test to be too difficult and insufficiently related to their professional needs. On a similar note, a leading educator in Medicine is quoted (2016:31) as commenting that simple IELTS grades have little practical value because the criteria associated with different band scores are not specific enough; he urged the need for more detailed reporting of candidates' capabilities.

The same researchers then went on to investigate impressions of the specific language skills required in medical practice – with particular emphasis on the importance of the oral skills. Several employers commented on the importance of listening, particularly when L2 entrants were from cultural backgrounds where it is customary for doctors to speak and patients simply to pay attention. The ability to elicit and process information from a patient was seen as especially critical in psychiatry and care of the elderly, given that L1 speakers themselves may not be fully coherent. There were similar responses in relation to nursing, where one nurse manager described much discourse by L2 nurses as broadly task-focused instead of patient-focused. Despite the useful insights obtained from some participants, the researchers concluded (2016:51) that many employers possess insufficient sensitivity to the specific language requirements of the profession that they represent.

The notion that an IELTS score of 8 is a minimal entry criterion for doctors is not clearly sustained in the data obtained by Merrifield (2016). The study reports entry scores for medical professionals across four different countries (the UK, Canada, Australia and New Zealand). Unfortunately, there is some lack of consistency between the agencies cited, which limits direct comparisons; but the figures seem to suggest that, at the time of the study (2014), a typical overall cut-score for physicians was 7.0 to 7.5. The qualitative data obtained from the bodies concerned was relatively uninformative. However, an interesting feature of the statistics obtained is that they illustrate how relevant each of the four skills was deemed to be across a set of medical contexts. This is especially illuminating in the case of listening. Table 6 below provides a selection from the Merrifield data of what were found to be minimal entry criteria in relation to the skill.

Table 6 Minimum band scores for Listening across three countries (no overall score specified for NZ)

Country	Body	Listening score	Overall score
UK	General Medical Council	7.0	7.5
	General Dental Council	6.5	7.0
	General Pharmaceutical Council	7.0	7.0
	College of Veterinary Surgeons	7.0	7.0
Canada	Physicians	7.0	7.0
	Nurses (three authorities)	7.5	7.0
	Pharmacy	6.0	6.5–7.0
New Zealand	Medical Council	7.5	[R/W 7.0]
	Midwives	7.0	7.5
	Veterinary Surgeons	7.0	7.0

There are some curious anomalies here. Whereas listening is treated as a leading skill for doctors in New Zealand (7.5 as compared to 7.0 for reading and writing), it was not at the time of reporting accorded the same importance in the UK for doctors or for dentists, where the required score was actually lower than the four-skill mean. Oddly, the minimum listening score for UK pharmacists and vets (where one would assume considerably less reliance on oral skills) was the same as that for medical practitioners and higher than the score required for dentists. In Canada, listening appears to be recognised as more important in nursing than among physicians; a case can perhaps be made for this. It also seems to make sense that a reduced role was accorded to listening by pharmacists. What these figures show is not simply different interpretations of listening scores from one country to another; but certain instances where there would appear to be a limited understanding by decision-making professional bodies of the part that listening plays in activities within their specialist areas.

Merrifield (2016) claims that awareness of what the IELTS test aims to measure has improved in recent years, and appears to endorse the present situation where different branches of the medical profession determine their own grades. The study certainly recognises the need for a greater level of assessment literacy to enable such decisions to be made more reliably; but rather ducks the question of precisely what steps can be taken to assist practitioner bodies in identifying those functions of language that are most critical to successful practice in their own areas.

A very substantial research project with similar goals was conducted by Berry et al (2013) on behalf of the UK General Medical Council (GMC). It to some extent replicated an earlier study by Banerjee (2004); but was carried out on a much wider scale. Whereas the Banerjee study consulted 17 participants on three panels, this one consulted 62 participants on 11 separate panels, ranging across seven geographical locations. The panels embraced five sets of stakeholders: medical directors, doctors, nurses, allied health professionals, and (curiously omitted in many research designs) patients. It examined the roles of all four skills, whereas Banerjee's study considered only the productive ones, writing and speaking. In addition, it considered two distinct categories of applicant: International Medical Graduates (IMGs) from outside the European Union and students from the European Economic Area (EEA) who at the time were accepted for employment under Freedom of Movement regulations but not consistently tested for language level. Finally, and very importantly, where the 2004 study 'accepted at face value the integrity of IELTS as an assessment instrument for practical purposes', this one approached the issue in a more open-minded way and was concerned to make recommendations to increase the test's validity.

During each of the panel discussions, the participants were requested to:

- discuss the issue of the relative language levels of IMG and EEA applicants;
- brainstorm the characteristics that they thought a minimally competent candidate should possess, and summarise them in the form of 'can do' statements;

Test taker characteristics: Experiential and behavioural

- (amongst other tasks) complete two IELTS Listening tests and specify how many questions from each a minimally qualified candidate might be expected to answer;
- match the task requirements of the tests to the 'can do' statements;
- determine an overall minimally acceptable band level for applicants.

What is ingenious about this approach is that it, in effect, trained panellists to focus on language skills and behavioural evidence within their own professional fields. It thus increased assessment literacy while at the same time eliciting information about aspects of performance that are central to patient safety. It also resulted in a set of concrete 'can do' criteria, against which future test development can be matched. A final meeting of panel representatives reviewed the 'can do' statements and reached agreement as to which IELTS level was appropriate for each of the skills and overall.

One of the more striking findings was in relation to listening, which all six panels rated of high importance, unanimously recommending a band score of 8.5 (as compared with a recommended 7.5 for the other three skills and overall). This is a positive result when compared with Merrifield's data; and appears to be a resounding endorsement of the value of the skill in this particular work environment. As one final panel participant put it (2013:69): '… listening is the key and I do agree with that. Most of [our] communication is about listening and taking in the information and particularly in the patient setting'. Inadequate listening skills were perceived to weaken the authority of a doctor: 'I think also about confidence in your doctor, but a lot of patients wouldn't have the confidence to say "did you understand what I'm saying?" … because the power situation is so different'.

However, it needs to be borne in mind that these judgements were arrived at by reference to two current versions of the test itself rather than to external descriptors. An alternative (or complementary) explanation might be that a high target score was necessary because the test was perceived as too easy. Comments by panellists (2013:33–35) and members of the final panel (2013:68–69) seem to support this interpretation: e.g. 'And that's why we put it so high; we didn't think it would discriminate to any real degree unless you had it at the highest level'.

Of the four different test modules examined, the greatest concerns expressed were about the Listening one. This perhaps reflects the 'blended' nature of the current IELTS Listening test with its dual focus on both general and academically related (i.e. non-professional) content.

The comments of the professionals in the Berry et al (2013) report will be quoted in some detail below because they do not simply relate to the relevance of the test in medical contexts but also provide valuable user insights into certain aspects of the test which will be discussed in later sections of this volume.

Among the comments which questioned the test's relevance for medical applicants were the following[1]. They apply not simply to IELTS but to any test used for testing competence to operate in a medical context.

1) *I don't think these tests are relevant to listening skills that a doctor would need.* (D, p.60)
2) *You could do very well on this test, but how you function in an environment hasn't been tested at all.* (N, p.60)
3) *So carry out a phone conversation, cutting out interruptions, and at the same time processing the thoughts into something more real, so you're not just listening and then get five minutes to recap on the information ... You are listening and the whole time you are making decisions ...* (N, p.35)

It was also suggested that the test did not correspond to the communicative needs of medical professionals as defined by the panels themselves:

4) *I think the reading test is probably a better test than the listening test because I don't think the listening test really picks up on many of the 'can do's.* (FP8, p.68)

A rather idealistic comment expressed the notion that even a single wrong answer in a test is unacceptable:

5) *... if a doctor is going to be able to function in a genuine medical setting, they would need to get all of the questions right.* (D, p.34)

Other comments relate to the quality of the test materials. The test was viewed as easy:

6) *This is too easy, basically. The listening seemed a level below the reading.* (P, p.36)
7) *Everybody seems to think that the reading was much more difficult than the listening, that it's just on a different level altogether.* (Moderator summary)

This view may derive partly from a perceived lack of authenticity in the recorded material:

8) *It's a good test of listening ability but it's too clean, it's not listening in the real world and some of it is too artificial and structured.* (AHP, p.61)
9) *It wasn't like natural conversation where it was flowing quickly and you had to pick things up fast.* (AHP, p.8)

---

[1] Codings indicate the identity of the commentators: D: doctor, P: patient, AHP: Allied health professional, N: nurse, FP: Final panel member, RO: Responsible officer/Medical director.

10) *It was really measured and quite slow and structured and bland accents.* (FP7, p.68)

There are also reservations about the formats and what the items targeted:

11) *The questions run chronologically, which makes it very, very easy.* (N, p.34)
12) *… it runs chronologically so if we are going to assess someone's ability to listen to people in real life, I don't think it's a particularly useful tool to assess people against what we are expecting them to do.* (N, p.34)
13) *It was just sitting down listening to what was said and writing down what was said in a box. It didn't show any need to comprehend or understand what has been said and interpret that, which as a doctor is what you have to do.* (FP8, p.68)

Several commentators reported perceptively on a tendency of the test to focus on discrete low-level facts rather than engaging higher-level interpretation:

14) *I think the one thing it misses out on is understanding whether a person has got the whole gist of a situation.* (D, p.60)
15) *All this test seems to be doing is writing down what you heard.* (D, p.60)

An interesting strand that emerged related to the role of the telephone in medical contexts:

16) *The telephone is difficult, it's harder than face to face, isn't it?* (Telephone conversation with an agitated relative) (RO, p.34)
17) *They need a test like the call handlers' 999 ambulance services. Don't they have a test with agitated, stressed people? They have to get [be] able as part of their test to get accurately location, symptoms with an awful lot of background noise …* (RO, p.61)

There were also suggestions that integrated-skills testing might be a means of modelling real-world activities more closely:

18) *I think the listening was good because it involved a bit of writing so you had to listen and then write down the points.* (AHP, p.38)
19) *Nine times out of ten with GPs you are listening and listening and writing down …* (P, p.38)
20) *They should do something with what they have heard that is completely different like listening to something then writing a referral.* (D, p.38)

In this regard, an interesting comment by a final panellist seemed to align listening needs more closely to the content of a test of speaking:

21) *And I think listening to somebody effectively, it's not just hearing it, it's listening to it and then responding to it as well and that in itself is quite*

> *a complex skill, to be able to reflect to someone that you have actually heard them correctly and that you are clear on what they are telling you.* (FP7, p.69)

The researchers presented a number of conclusions to the UK GMC. They recommended that IELTS be retained as an appropriate entry test of the English language competence of overseas-trained doctors. However, this proposal was qualified by reference to responses from some of the final panellists, who recognised IELTS as a reliable screening test but suggested the need for supplementing it with further tests more specific to the needs of their profession. Typical comments were: 'We said that IELTS as a test of medical communication isn't really [suitable] but as a general test it's fine.' 'Something like IELTS as a screening test is good but it's the first step in a process. It shouldn't be the only step'.

Particular concerns were expressed by the final panel and by a majority of the earlier ones about the suitability of the listening component of the test. Berry and fellow researchers interpret these concerns in terms of domain-specificity, pointing out reasonably that the Listening module was simply not designed to address the particular types of listening in which medical practitioners engage. They mention the existence of the Medical Council's own Professional and Linguistic Assessments Board (PLAB) test, brought into play once the requisite IELTS score has been achieved, which aims to assess a candidate's ability to communicate in specific medical and clinical contexts. They also note a high level of agreement among stakeholders that a possible supplementary test for doctors might be based on integrated skills.

However, this line of argument is rather tangential to the issue of whether the Listening test provides a valid measure of listening competence per se. It does not fully respond to the panellists' perceptions (illustrated above) that the samples reviewed were disproportionately easy, as compared with the Reading test. Nor does it address the comments of some of them that the samples did not tap into a sufficiently wide range of listening processes for the test to be fully representative of the skill in *any* context. These issues will be explored more fully in Section 2 of this volume, when we examine in detail cognitive and contextual issues in assessing listening, including listening for academic purposes.

The stakeholders who were consulted experienced difficulty in determining an overall band score to recommend as an acceptable target; but it is reported that they agreed one of 8, with the score for Listening set at 8.5 and that for Speaking at 8. The panellists also agreed that, despite a directive which at the time exempted EU graduates from providing evidence of language ability when registering with the GMC, a means should be found of ensuring that they did so.

There are currently two widely adopted solutions to the lack of medical content in the IELTS test. One is to use test content that features the types of language which medical professionals employ and that partially replicates the types of real-world encounter that occur. To date, the only major example of this type of test is the Occupational English Test (OET), originally developed in Australia and now administered by Cambridge Boxhill Language Assessment. The other solution is to treat IELTS as a screening test, and to require successful candidates to move on to a professionally oriented test such as the British PLAB. Read and Hirsh (2005:36) note an increasing trend for institutions to design their own diagnostic tests, sometimes modelled on IELTS. Smith and Haslett (2007:29) record that part of the motivation for institutions in New Zealand taking this step was to support certain fields where 'life skills or specific subject knowledge were ... regarded as equally important to academic or English language skills'.

A study by Read and Wette (2009) investigated the experience of healthcare professionals (doctors, pharmacists and nurses) attending an English language training course in New Zealand that was designed to prepare them for either IELTS or the OET. This enabled comparisons to be drawn in terms of candidates' perceptions of the two tests. Before the course, the participants tended to favour OET because of its healthcare-specific content. However, during the period of study, many of them came to conclude that neither OET nor IELTS really assessed their ability to perform effectively in clinical contexts. If anything, there was a preference for IELTS, on the grounds that the registration fees were lower and that more extensive preparatory courses and practice materials were available.

The listening support received by the students in the Read and Wette study consisted of weekly self-study sessions that made use of recorded radio discussions and lectures, both on medical topics. There was little take-up of self-access opportunities to practise listening with these and similar materials; this may indicate a lack of awareness of the importance of the skill in professional contexts or a preference for exam-type practice tasks. When asked to weigh the advantages and disadvantages of the OET Listening module as compared with the IELTS one, the participants mentioned that the medical content of the OET listening texts assisted them. However, they also reported that overall the OET Listening test was considerably more difficult than the IELTS one, partly due to its use of medical terminology and discourse.

Nursing

Some commentators have treated nursing as a special case within medical practice. A study by Sedgwick et al (2016) focused specifically on the nature of nursing encounters and the forms of language involved. It took place against a background of clinical errors which were attributed to the poor communication skills of nurses from overseas (Smith, Allan, Larsen and Mackintosh 2005) – this, despite the fact that applicants to join the UK National Health Service were expected at the time to achieve an overall score of IELTS 7.0.

The project was on a much smaller scale than Berry et al. It employed a tracking study based on weekly interviews with four overseas nurses over a period of a month. The nurses reported on the shift which had just ended, with a particular focus on the communicative needs they had had to meet. In the last interview, they were asked to consider the relevance to their professional practice of three sample IELTS modules (covering Listening, Reading and Writing); this included commenting on recorded extracts from the Listening test. A second part of the study made use of two focus groups: one of seven nurses who were L1 speakers and had trained in the UK, one of four nurses who were L2 speakers of English and had trained overseas. The groups were asked to describe a concrete example of a challenging communicative event, to talk over what nurses have to communicate and why, and to describe the exchanges they had with doctors.

Once again, the main focus of the verbal reports was on oral communication. The researchers concluded from the tracked nurses' accounts that the language employed in nursing is extremely varied, both in the range of situations that need to be covered and in the communicative functions that have to be performed. Various types of spoken encounter were identified, involving patients, colleagues and other medical staff – with listening implicitly playing a part in all of them. Those with patients include social encounters to put individuals at their ease as well as professional ones where medical information has to be elicited or transmitted and questions have to be answered. Listening is mentioned specifically in relation to the critical 'handover' meeting, when an incoming nurse or group of nurses needs not only to master the notes provided by outgoing ones but also to listen to oral explanations and clarifications of those notes. It was deemed vital for nurses to assess their own levels of understanding throughout this process and to ask for clarification whenever necessary. Indeed, there were comments that, if the spoken transmission was not understood, the written notes might not be adequate. Nurses also mentioned particular difficulties arising from the need to engage in social conversations and to adapt to British accents, usage and speech styles.

Some views on the IELTS Listening paper are reported. The nurses commented that the single play of the recording did not represent their situation, where they can seek repetition or explanation; but they agreed that their need to focus carefully on detail was reflected in the test. The everyday topics in Sections 1 and 2 of the paper were felt to have features in common with the informal conversations that take place with patients. Some of the response formats requiring numbers or few words were not unlike the writing of brief notes by nurses.

The researchers themselves trace some features of relevant social conversation in the Listening paper, and conclude that it assesses 'listening for detail, listening for general understanding of information, and listening for specific information'. This seems perhaps a little vague: surely any test would require the first and third and the second is less represented in IELTS than one might expect. They go on to conclude that 'IELTS tests much of the listening that nurses engage in but it does not include the participative listening that is an essential part of their workplace communication' (2016:34). Here, they specifically mention the need to seek clarification or confirmation of important information.

Immigration

We now turn briefly to a very different use made of IELTS and some other academic tests of language: to determine whether a potential immigrant is competent enough in English to integrate into the host community.

Merrifield (2012) investigated immigration policy in relation to IELTS scores, comparing the admission criteria in Australia, New Zealand, Canada and the UK. Table 7 below shows a degree of consistency in the higher-level IELTS scores specified by the different authorities for certain types of applicant at that time.

Table 7 Immigration criteria (Merrifield 2012) as of time of data collection (2009)

Country	IELTS test	Minimum IELTS band
Australia	General	Overall: 6.0 (0 points towards acceptance), 7.0 (10 points), 8.0 (20 points)
New Zealand	General/Academic	Overall: 6.5
Canada	General	Minimum: Listening 4.5, Speaking/Writing 4.0, Reading 3.5 Up to 6.5–7.5 for more highly skilled
UK	General/Academic	Skilled with job offer: Overall 4.0 (CEFR A1) Highly skilled: Overall 6.5 (CEFR C1)

The reliance by three of the four countries on overall band scores seemed to suggest that importance was accorded to the general ability to process information rather than to the minimal oral communicative proficiency that an immigrant might require in order to function in the host country. Canada showed itself more enlightened in that it alone distinguished between the four skills (again, the higher band specified for listening should not go unnoticed). A curious feature is the fact that, in two of the four countries, scores on either the General or the Academic version of IELTS were accepted for general immigration purposes.

Over the past decade, the IELTS test has continued to play a major role in the immigration policy of these four nations. At the time of writing, IELTS is accepted, alongside a number of other proficiency tests, as proof of English language ability for migration in Australia, Canada, New Zealand and the UK. In the UK, for example, IELTS is recognised as one of a handful of Secure English Language Tests (SELTs), i.e. tests which have been formally approved as meeting UK Home Office requirements for secure English language testing arrangements. It is important to note that each country sets its own IELTS score requirements and these may vary (e.g. from Band 4 to Band 7) depending upon the type of visa being applied for within each nation.

In the detail of Merrifield's report, there are one or two rather odd matches between the grade specified and the functions to be performed, and between IELTS and the CEFR. For example, it would seem that, at the time, the UK Border Agency cited CEFR Level A1 for skilled migrants with a job offer but in practice equated this with IELTS 4.0. This suggests some worrying gaps in assessment literacy, even at this level of decision making. The high level of reliance upon IELTS in immigration contexts would seem to confer a degree of responsibility upon test designers to ensure that the performance associated with the grades specified is fully understood by the agencies involved and is as closely aligned as possible to the likely communicative needs of immigrants, as distinct from those of other potential candidates.

Discussion and general conclusions

As the world has changed, with the growth of opportunities for international education and professional employment, as well as increasing migration across borders and continents, so IELTS has been put to new uses over the past quarter century. The IELTS partners (like other EAP test providers) have responded to invitations from professional licensing bodies and have actively promoted their tests to new constituencies. One such example is the consideration and subsequent adoption of IELTS by the US National Council of State Boards of Nursing (NCSBN) as part of the licensure testing programme for internationally trained nurses in the USA (O'Neill, Buckendahl, Plake and Taylor 2007). Another is the UK government's decision to establish a list of officially approved and recognised English language proficiency tests (known as Secure English Language Tests or SELTs) resulting in IELTS being included as part of its Visa and Immigration policy. Test providers are frequently invited to submit tests for scrutiny and consideration with respect to their potential suitability for study, work or

Test taker characteristics: Experiential and behavioural

migration needs. The IELTS website (2022) specifically refers to IELTS as a high-stakes English test 'for study, migration or work'.

The argument that the IELTS test has been put to uses that it was not designed for can only be challenged if it can be represented as an equally valid test for all of: study, migration and work. At the very least, it might be a wise step to provide a greater level of support to the diverse range of stakeholders who opt to use the test for their own purposes: making clear the extent to which it does or does not tap into processes that are central to performance in domains where the test is widely used. In fairness, the IELTS partners have worked hard over recent years to increase awareness and understanding of the test's purpose and content, and of the meaning of the test scores it produces, among a wide range of stakeholder user groups, in order to aid good policy and decision-making. This has sometimes been complemented by work commissioned by the stakeholders themselves to scrutinise their existing policy and practice regarding test usage, sometimes leading to change. One example of such a project commissioned by the UK GMC can be seen in Taylor and Chan (2015).

Any bridge-building initiative between test providers and user groups might also entail a review of the present multi-purpose descriptors. Those who have to interpret IELTS scores cannot be assumed to possess a high level of sensitivity to language and how it is employed in their domains; and may demonstrate a limited understanding of the test and what it measures (Murray 2016:Chap. 4, Murray et al 2014:6, O'Loughlin 2012, Taylor 2009a). Stakeholders badly need more precise details of the level of performance that corresponds to the nine IELTS score bands – and to have any meaningful impact, these specifications should surely be domain-specific. It is not only the gatekeepers in immigration, teaching and medicine who would benefit. So too would the sector for which the IELTS test was originally intended, given the evidence reported earlier that even those responsible for university admissions are sometimes under-informed about what the IELTS band scores represent in terms of actual behaviour in an academic context, despite concerted efforts by the IELTS partners to support appropriate score interpretation and use among admissions personnel. Here, there may be some reluctance due to pressures within higher education institutions to generate increased revenue by recruiting overseas students.

Some of the research studies mentioned here have focused their attention on the target scores chosen by the various agencies which have opted to use the test. Others have taken the enquiry further by asking for the views of stakeholders (gatekeepers, professional bodies and candidates) on the test. These comments, which have been quoted at some length in relation to the Berry et al (2013) study, consistently reflect quite serious reservations about the Listening module, as at present constituted. In particular, the module is sometimes represented as too easy and much easier than the

Reading one – hence the high band score of 8.5 that is demanded in some contexts. One reason for this is no doubt the composition of the test, where two sections cover general and broadly conversational topics and two are more closely related to the academic context. As already noted, to ensure an appropriate range of levels of difficulty, item writers are advised to target the first two at CEFR Levels B1 and B2 and the third and fourth at Level C1.

This compromise results from an attempt to address the needs of both the General Training candidate and the Academic one in a single test (as discussed by Taylor and Weir 2012). It is surely hard to defend offering a combined test of this kind for listening when there are separate ones in reading and writing. Enough has been quoted here to illustrate the high importance accorded to listening in certain professional domains; while, even in an academic context, the inclusion of everyday conversation both reduces overall test difficulty and limits the opportunity to focus on major routes for the transmission of information in the form of lectures and seminars. The compromise also results in a situation whereby nurses and other skilled workers are tested on more abstract lecture-style material which may fall outside the type of listening in which they need to demonstrate their competence.

If, indeed, test designers were to separate out general and academic listening, a stronger case could certainly be made for the relevance of the test a) for immigrants b) for the initial screening of professionals and even c) for university applicants. A General Training Listening test could be devised in which the relevant listening demands genuinely progressed from B1 to C1, thus offering greater scoring validity in cases a) and b). The same would apply to an Academic Listening version which would enable academic content to be adequately represented at all levels targeted. The situation has not passed entirely unrecognised. Since 2015, examiners have offered an IELTS Life Skills test, designed to meet specific visa requirements laid down by the UK authorities. The test is targeted at a very basic A2 level, to meet the anticipated needs of three quite limited groups: those applying for 'family of a settled person' visas, indefinite leave to remain and (curiously) citizenship. Significantly, it only tests listening and speaking; applicants do not need to demonstrate any competence in reading and writing.

A second possible way of strengthening the representation of listening would be to take fuller account of the interactive nature of the skill so far as these two major groups of candidates are concerned (namely, immigrants and health professionals). Here (see Comment 21 above, reported by Berry et al 2013), it might make good sense to reconfigure the IELTS Speaking test as one of Spoken Communication and to add new descriptors on listening proficiency (including the listener's ability to test their own

Test taker characteristics: Experiential and behavioural

understanding and use confirmation checks) or possibly a separate score for listening. This would make the General Training version of the test much more relevant to the needs of those who make use of it, whether professionals or immigrants.

Long term, the IELTS test providers may need to consider larger-scale solutions to the present situation. The most radical would be to introduce three different and more specifically targeted versions of IELTS: i.e. Academic, General and Professional. Granted, the last of these would remain a Pandora's box; but the policy might perhaps be to highlight the test's screening function ahead of a second test focusing on more precise professional demands (a situation as noted already pertains in some medical administrations).

Even so, this still leaves open the question of what the initial screening operation entails. A number of respondents in Berry et al's study (and indeed the researchers themselves) represent the IELTS test as serving a gate-keeping function, with successful candidates then being further put to the test in the UK GMC's own, more context-oriented PLAB test. However, it is important to add two riders to this version of events. Firstly, PLAB is not intended as a further, more advanced test of language, though it does require candidates to engage in role plays. Secondly, it is primarily aimed at doctors, so that the language and contexts specific to nursing are not represented.

This suggests a more radical approach. Test providers might perhaps consider offering to use their considerable expertise and experience in the field in order to assist certain large and distinct groups of stakeholders in developing post-screening tests that fully represent the type of content (in the case of listening, the language, the discourse patterns and the interactions) which applicants encounter in real-world professional contexts. This kind of cross-professional approach may sound somewhat idealistic, but it would strengthen the argument that a test like IELTS can indeed serve multiple purposes.

Psychological characteristics

Building on O'Sullivan (2000), O'Sullivan and Green (2011) highlight a number of psychological characteristics pertaining to candidates taking a language proficiency test. These include: cognitive factors such as working memory, cognitive style/development and attention span, as well as affective factors such as personality, affective schemata and emotional state. Elliott (2013:38–41) discusses some of these factors as they relate specifically to general listening skills, and Chapter 5 in Section 2 will explore in greater detail some of the cognitive factors implicated in listening primarily for academic purposes. In this section, the focus will be on two particular affective characteristics which can impact directly on test taker behaviours in listening tests – *anxiety* and *self-monitoring*.

The impact of anxiety

While there has been considerable interest in the communicative needs of IELTS candidates, there has been relatively little exploration of candidates' personality traits and how they might impact on test performance. One reason may be that there are limited implications for those concerned with test design. A study described earlier (Winke and Lim 2014) briefly addressed the issue of *anxiety*. The researchers concluded that anxiety (whether as a test taker or more specifically as an L2 listener) did not seem to be alleviated by practice-based instruction and greater familiarity with the test but was more clearly associated with level of proficiency (cf. also Golchi 2012). A rather more nuanced interpretation (Lu and Liu 2011) holds that anxiety is heightened where a listener lacks the strategic competence with which to resolve problems of communication.

In the general ELT literature, the phenomenon of listening anxiety (Horwitz 2001) has been quite widely discussed. There has been particular interest in the relationship between anxiety and performance, in both classroom and test settings. In'nami's (2006) study apparently showed that test anxiety, measured through two questionnaires and using a structural equation modelling approach, did not affect listening test performance; he concluded that test anxiety seems to work differently compared with communication apprehension and fear of negative evaluation. Zheng and Cheng (2018) examined the relationships between Chinese students' foreign language classroom anxiety and cognitive test anxiety and their performance on the College English Test Band 4 (CET-4) to understand the nature and degree of the examined relationships; their findings confirmed the cognitive test anxiety factor as a significant negative predictor of language achievement, though questionnaire (N = 921) and interview (N = 12) data suggested that most students did not perceive themselves to be very anxious in either classroom or testing situations. Zhang (2013) suggested that anxiety is often the cause rather than the outcome of failed comprehension. Much anxiety is reported to originate at the level of word and phrase recognition, which then goes on to weaken the listener's confidence in the overall comprehension of the recording (Bekleyen 2009). In a testing (or indeed instructional) context, an important contributory factor appears to be the use of comprehension questions to which responses have to be found in the real-time conditions of listening. The level of anxiety is also considerably heightened when, in addition, test candidates are only allowed a single hearing of the recording in order to derive those answers (Field 2015).

The ability to self-monitor

Phakiti (2016) focuses attention upon another aspect of L2 listener psychology: the ability to self-monitor. Awareness of how accurately a piece of speech has been processed plays an important part in the listening process. It determines to what extent the listener can rely upon the information extracted – and what steps may need to be taken to deal with lacunae that have occurred. In other words, accurate and realistic self-monitoring is an important part of strategic competence. In a testing situation, it also entails weighing possible responses against each other. This is most obvious in the case of multiple-choice formats, where the test taker has to match three or four possible propositions against a stretch of speech and decide which inspires most confidence. It especially plays a role where a second play of the recording is permitted and a test taker is able to double-check those responses about which they may have a criterial level of doubt.

Phakiti's study examined the *appraisal calibration* (i.e. the relationship between level of confidence and accuracy of performance) of test takers of mixed L2 backgrounds and proficiencies. Participants (N = 376) were asked to undertake four representative sections drawn from retired IELTS Listening tests. Sections 1 and 2 were monologues, while Sections 3 to 4 were dialogues; Sections 1 and 3 were informal, while Sections 2 and 4 related to academic contexts. Participants had to perform under timed conditions, and, after choosing each answer, to indicate their level of confidence in its accuracy. Confidence was reported on a 6-level scale ranging from 0% (extremely low confidence) to 100% (absolute confidence), with intervals at 25%, 50%, 75% and 90%. The study found that the test takers tended to be consistently over-confident as to the accuracy of their responses, confirming a similar finding by Stankov and Lee (2008). There were small differences of gender, with female participants assessing their performance more accurately in certain sections than male. However, the main issue addressed was the possible relationship between accuracy of self-monitoring and either level of proficiency or level of difficulty (of content and question).

In relation to proficiency, Phakiti divided the participants into six ability levels. He found that those at the highest level were generally accurate in their judgements, which only exceeded their scores by 5.71%. The lower groups were less so, and the lowest was extremely over-confident (with a gap of 33.48%). All proficiency groups displayed considerable over-confidence in relation to the most difficult items in Section 4 (academic monologue). One conclusion drawn was that the ability to judge one's own listening performance broadly increases with the accuracy of one's responses. This might well be a two-way process. On the one hand, increased proficiency enables a listener to be more confident as to whether an answer is right or not.

On the other, greater accuracy in detecting a problem alerts one to the need to adopt specific strategies to circumvent difficulties. Phakiti found that the ability to judge the likely correctness of an answer was closely associated with self-reports of strategy use.

An incidental finding of the study was a large difference in scores across the four sections of the test. Participants performed well in Section 1 (informal dialogue) with 63% accurate responses and Section 3 (formal dialogue) with 58%. But they did poorly in Sections 2 (46%) and 4 (32%), suggesting that the monologues were more difficult to process, particularly when they involved lecture-listening. At all events, there seemed to be no clear relationship between appraisal and performance, with 20% over-estimating their accuracy in Section 1 and only 10% in Section 4. The most realistic assessment was in respect of Section 2 (only 6.5% over).

A rather different finding was achieved when the relative difficulty of *test items* was taken into account. It became clear that, with the easiest (highest scoring) of the items, participants were capable of assessing the accuracy of their responses in a way that diverged from reality by 5% or less. However, as items became more difficult, the appraisals deviated more and more from performance, until, with the most difficult of all, participants showed themselves to be up to 25% over-confident. Appraisal scores were especially inaccurate in relation to the most difficult items of Section 4 (the lecture).

Self-monitoring is an important and under-researched area in L2 listening studies – and one with particular relevance to testing. Phakiti argues that over-confidence can explain why some test takers fail in the IELTS test and recommends the inclusion of performance appraisal training as part of test preparation courses. As he puts it (2016:51): '… when they do not know that they are *not* performing a test task well, they cannot use strategic problem-solving skills to address the given test task. On the other hand, if they do not know that they have already performed well, they may spend too much time attempting to complete a task over and over again …'

Physical/physiological characteristics

Shaw and Weir (2007), Khalifa and Weir (2009), O'Sullivan and Green (2011) and Elliott (2013) all provide helpful discussions of the issues associated with the physical/physiological characteristics of test takers such as age, gender, short-term ailments and longer-term disabilities. Elliott, in particular, describes and discusses the special arrangements in listening tests that may need to be made for candidates with special requirements, e.g. visually or hearing impaired candidates, those with special educational needs such as dyslexia or autism, etc. Kormos and Taylor (2021) provide an up-to-date overview concerning the L2 assessment of learners with specific learning

Test taker characteristics: Experiential and behavioural

difficulties. With regard to IELTS, it is the responsibility of IELTS test centres to make appropriate arrangements for test takers with accessibility requirements. Details of the IELTS partners policy and procedures for this are available from the IELTS website, together with examples of modified test arrangements.

Section 2
Cognitive and contextual issues in assessing academic listening

The chapters that follow examine a number of features of the current IELTS test, with a view to matching them against research findings and current thinking on L2 listening in general and L2 academic listening in particular. They provide a concrete example of a validation exercise that can be extended to any other test of academic or professional listening.

Precedents for the approach to be adopted can be found in a series of monographs in the SiLT series, which investigated in turn the validity of the writing, reading, speaking and listening components of the Cambridge English Qualifications (for listening, see Geranpayeh and Taylor (Eds) 2013). The approach applied here adopts a cognitive angle, with due attention given to the target skill and to the type of test taker behaviour elicited by the materials. The procedure is firstly to present in Chapter 5 an empirically supported model of the listening construct, which serves to define the perceptual and conceptual processes that underpin the skill. One can then move on (Chapters 6 to 10) to examine:

- the *contextual validity* of the test: i.e. whether its content is representative of the type of material to which an L2 EAP listener is exposed in real-world conditions – and is thus likely to generate representative behaviour;
- the *cognitive validity* of the test: i.e. whether the materials used and the tasks set elicit behaviour from the test taker which resembles the behaviour that would be required by real-world performance.

The analysis in Chapters 6 to 10 highlights certain aspects of the IELTS Listening test which could be revisited and improved as part of the routine test review and revision cycle which the test providers undertake periodically. Practical suggestions for improvement are developed and discussed more fully in Section 3 of the volume.

5 A cognitive profile of academic listening

Introduction

The chapters that follow examine a number of features of the current IELTS test, with a view to matching them against research findings and current thinking on L2 listening in general and on L2 academic listening in particular. They represent a partial exercise in validation. A precedent for the approach to be adopted can be found in a series of monographs in the SiLT series which investigated in turn the validity of the Writing, Reading, Speaking and Listening components of the Cambridge English Qualifications (for Listening, see Geranpayeh and Taylor (Eds) 2013). Part of the approach applied there embraces a cognitive element, with due attention given to the target skill and to the type of test taker behaviour elicited by the materials. The procedure is firstly to present a model of the listening construct, which serves to define the perceptual and conceptual processes which underpin the skill. One can then move on to examine:

- the context validity of the test: i.e. whether its content is representative of the type of material to which an L2 EAP listener is exposed in real-world conditions;
- the cognitive validity of the test: i.e. whether the materials used and the tasks set elicit behaviour from the test taker which resembles the behaviour required by real-world performance.

It is worth commenting briefly at this point on other possible approaches to validation. Aryadoust (2013) offered what he describes as a novel, comprehensive and rigorous validity argument with specific reference to the IELTS Listening test. His data collection was impressively extensive. Two groups of students (N = 209/N = 467) undertook a retired IELTS test under test conditions. Members of the second group were asked to complete a self-assessment questionnaire; and members of a sub-group (N = 63) also took a TOEFL-related Educational Testing Service (ETS) test in order to check scoring validity across tests. In addition, Aryadoust and two fellow raters went on to analyse the items employed in the IELTS test in the study in order to determine a) what 'subskills' they elicited, b) what strategies might be used to answer them, c) what difficulties test takers might experience in answering them, and d) any construct-irrelevant factors. This provided the researchers with indications as to the demands imposed upon the participants.

After some complex factor analysis, the findings reported (2013:228–229) focused quite heavily on data at item level. The test items studied were found to relate to low-level targets and not to entail sufficient inference-making. Differential item functioning, it was concluded, might well be shaped by test takers' use of guesswork. Item difficulty arose, in part at least, from the propositional density of the wording; and test method partly accounted for the variance in item scores. So far as the scoring validity issue was concerned, IELTS scores and those obtained in the ETS test were found to be moderately correlated. The final verdict on IELTS by Aryadoust was a negative one (2013:229): 'Overall, the findings from this volume's examination of the tests' validity inferences ... refute its validity argument'.

However, this conclusion is partly arrived at by linking a set of scores to the mental processes that are taken to underlie performance. Its reliance upon differential item functioning does not make allowance for the view (see e.g. Buck 2001:59, Weir 2005:100–102) that a statistical analysis of scores cannot of itself substantiate the claim that a test fully represents the construct being targeted. Even where a test is found to discriminate well between candidates, the result might well be the consequence of factors that are extrinsic to the skill being tested or that do not adequately represent how the skill would be employed under real-world conditions. Some of the findings reported by the study arguably fall within this concern: not least, the conclusion (2013:224) that, because many test items fit the Rasch model observed scores are closely associated with what is termed 'the listening comprehension trait'.

One might argue instead that construct validation should ideally be supported by a) a well-supported model of the skill in question against which to match what the test targets in practice; and/or b) verbal reports by test takers which demonstrate that, in taking the test, they are or are not employing processes central to the skill. Weir's (2005) argument was that ideally the first should be taken into consideration before a test was designed.

To be fair, Aryadoust's analysis of the sub-skills elicited by individual items does make use of a self-assessment questionnaire to provide insights into performance. But self-assessment is an approximate tool at best (see Ingram and Bayliss (2007) quoted above). And though questionnaires have been very widely used in listening research as a solution to the internalised nature of the skill (see e.g. Vandergrift, Goh, Mareschal and Tafaghodtari 2006), they are very susceptible to over-reporting. They can also be found to be unreliable if participants are asked to comment on their use of cognitive as against metacognitive processes. A major characteristic of the former is that they become increasingly automatic for higher-level L2 listeners and thus unavailable or difficult to report.

There is undeniably a need for research into the academic listening construct and how validly it is represented in test material. However, some caution is perhaps necessary where construct validation studies closely link inferences about test taker behaviour to the statistical analysis of scores. More informative (and more current) approaches might entail interpreting data by reference to a widely supported model of the processes that contribute to the skill and/or to protocols from the test taker obtained immediately after having taken the test[1].

A cognitive approach to test validation

Previous chapters have reviewed a range of research studies exploring different aspects of the relationship between the IELTS Listening module and its stakeholders. The chapters that follow take some tentative steps towards providing validity evidence in respect of its content and of the test taker behaviour that it elicits. A central consideration is the role of the candidate for whom the test is principally designed – the academic L2 listener. The purpose of the exercise is twofold. It is firstly to outline for the benefit of future test designers some recent insights into L2 listening which may be relevant to the future development of their own formats and content. A second goal is (by way of example) to apply some of these criteria to the current version of the IELTS test (and potentially other listening tests used for similar purposes), with a view to identifying certain aspects of assessment which could potentially be adapted to ensure greater construct validity.

As a point of departure, the present chapter presents a detailed account of the listening construct. This serves to define the perceptual and cognitive skills that an experienced listener commands and that an L2 learner is in the process of acquiring. The account is based upon extensive research by speech scientists and draws upon empirical evidence in a way that conventional 'subskills' lists or even the CEFR descriptors do not. It provides a framework for considering the ways in which L2 listening diverges from this model, and serves to identify those operations which might be particularly important to an academic listener.

This systematic analysis of what constitutes listening has relevance for the way in which the skill is represented in test guidelines and specifications. It might provide for example, a more concrete representation of the skill in the IELTS instructions to item writers. There, listening is characterised in

---

1 Even this kind of support may not provide reliable insights unless it is used meaningfully. There have been one or two recent examples of listening researchers using questionnaires and verbal reports as evidence that L2 participants employ basic perceptual processes like word recognition. This makes no sense: listening (and for that matter reading) cannot exist without such processes so it is relatively meaningless to establish that participants are employing them.

terms of general 'listening for' categories which are differentiated in terms of content:

Section 1: 'Listening for main idea and detail'
Section 2: 'Listening for detail and stated opinion'
Section 3: 'Listening for opinion/attitude/feeling directly stated or implied'
Section 4: 'Listening for main idea, detail and stated opinion' (IWGs:6)

and which do not accord with any empirical body of evidence as to what listening entails.

A model of listening

The model below (a simplified version based on Field 2008, 2013) represents the listening skill as entailing five distinct operations:

Figure 1   A simplified cognitive model of the listening process

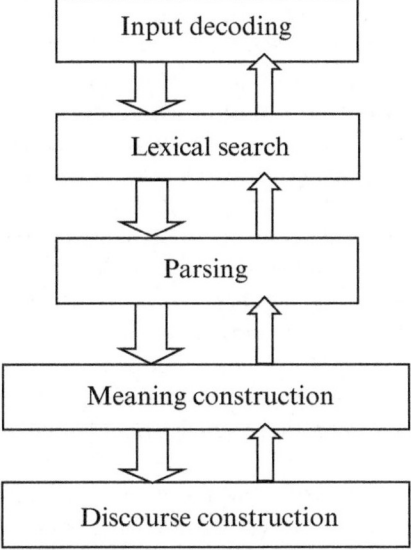

The downward arrows show a progression from smaller to larger units of language and from linguistic information to more abstract representations based upon meaning. However, the reverse arrows serve to remind us that listening is not a purely linear progression. Listening, even in L1, is a hit-and-miss operation which often has to draw upon multiple cues as to the words that are present. In this, larger units can influence the recognition of smaller ones in a 'top-down' way. To give two examples – knowledge of the spoken form of a complete word can influence perception at phoneme level, while awareness of the general context can enable a listener to fill gaps in understanding or correct mis-hearings. In short, listening must be recognised to be a highly interactive process.

The first three operations are largely perceptual. Listeners have first to *decode* the input – linking sensations reaching their ears to the sounds of the language being spoken. A problem here is that the exact form taken by any phoneme is shaped by the phonemes that precede and follow it. It may well be that listeners normally analyse speech at the level of the syllable instead.

They then have to make a *lexical search* – matching groups of syllables to known words. Again, this is more demanding than one might suppose because of the way in which word forms change in connected speech (Brown 1990, Field 2008:Chap. 9, Gimson 2008:Chap. 12). Speakers take the easiest articulatory route – with the result that the words they produce often diverge markedly from the citation forms that feature in L2 vocabulary instruction. To give two common instances: *half-past* might become *huppast* and *don't know* might become *dunno*. Two further obstacles to word recognition are a) that certain words within an intonation contour (especially function words) are less prominent than others; and b) that there are no consistent spaces between words in connected speech, so that it falls to the listener to determine where one ends and the next begins.

Once a content word has been identified, it opens up a connection to its place in the listener's lexical store. This *lexical entry* releases information about the item in question – not simply its meaning (and/or range of meanings), but also its word class, the way it inflects and the words with which it commonly co-occurs. There may be links to other words bearing similar or associated meanings and links to particular patterns of syntax ('put' for instance, signals the likely pattern '+ object + location').

Following recognition, words then have to be retained in sequence in the listener's mind until such time as a syntactic pattern (e.g. Subject – Verb – Object) becomes evident and the string of words can be *parsed* into a phrase or clause. As the pattern evolves word by word, the process may well involve a degree of anticipation based upon the syntactic or lexical likelihood of what will come next.

The linguistic form of the signal is then converted into a unit of information – in other words an abstract notion rather than a piece of language. To make it meaningful, it has to be embedded into some kind of context. *Meaning construction* draws upon the listener's world knowledge, recall of the current topic of conversation and impression of the speaker's apparent intentions. The listener may also have to infer ideas that the speaker has not explicitly expressed and to interpret anaphors such as *she, they, it, this, what I said*.

At a final stage (*discourse construction*), the new piece of information is added to what the listener has understood of the exchange up to now. This may entail using discourse markers (*then, but, so, on the other hand*) to make connections between points or simply relying on intuition to determine how a new point seems to fit the current line of argument. It may be necessary to establish the point's relative importance, and in due course the point may need to be integrated into a wider pattern based on all that has been said previously by the current speaker or by all parties in a conversation.

A number of processes contribute to each of the operations just identified. These are distinct from the earlier notion of 'sub-skills' (Richards 1983), which were useful in focusing attention on the component parts of the skill but were mainly intuitive. Instead, they represent cognitive processes that have been investigated by researchers and demonstrated to be psychologically real. For example, the processes supporting word recognition might include:

- building syllables into words;
- using the stressed syllable of a word as a cue to its identity;
- recognising words that occur in reduced form;
- recognising groups of words that often occur together;
- identifying in connected speech where one word ends and the next begins;
- mapping from the form of a word to its range of meanings.

The L2 listener

Clearly, the behaviour just described is that of a fully competent listener. Individuals listening to a second language find their own performance constrained by a number of factors. Those on which materials writers and syllabus designers tend to focus relate to limitations of knowledge, either linguistic or pragmatic. But L2 listeners are also hampered by a lack of *expertise* at handling unfamiliar spoken input. For many, the L2 listening experience differs qualitatively from L1 listening, with a greater possibility of failures of decoding and a consequent reliance upon remedial strategies.

While knowledge of vocabulary and grammar is clearly important, the effectiveness with which it is employed depends critically upon how accessible the information is to the user and how *automatic* is the connection made between what is heard and the corresponding meaning. The L2 listener's performance at word level again provides a useful example. There may at first be a simple problem of recognition. Once a word can be confidently identified, the listener then has to map from its sound to a set of information in the mind which includes the word's syntactic status, collocates, synonyms and range of senses. A major stumbling block in the early stages is the

A cognitive profile of academic listening

listener's lack of experience in undertaking the mapping process in relation to L2 words. However, with time and experience, the word/meaning connection becomes less effortful and more and more *automatic*.

The role of automaticity is critical (Styles 2006:Chap. 7, Segalowitz 2016). Human working memory resources are limited. So, if a basic operation like matching a set of speech sounds to a word requires an effort of attention, it limits how much working memory is free to engage in wider thought processes (Gathercole and Baddeley 1993, Pashler and Johnston 1998). Limited vocabulary and inexperience in listening to the target language mean that early L2 learners have to focus heavily on perceptual processes (input decoding, lexical search and parsing). So long as this is the case, they have insufficient attention free for handling the meaning-based operations described above, such as making inferences, interpreting a speaker's intentions, recognising a line of argument and so on (Field 2013:106–107). Evidence from learner transcription (Field 2019:17) suggests that, just before CEFR B2 level, a threshold is reached when processing at lexical level becomes markedly more accurate and more automatic. The effect of this is to free up attention, enabling learners to report on deeper and wider aspects of meaning.

The growth of automatic processing in the novice L2 listener is accompanied by an increasing awareness of recurrent chunks of language (Wray 2002), both lexical (*on the other hand*) and syntactic (*might've done*). This supports the B1+ breakthrough and provides an important indicator when designing performance descriptors.

The academic L2 listener

Let us now consider the specific case of the academic L2 listener. As early as 1983, Richards viewed academic listening as very distinct from listening for general purposes and provided a separate taxonomy for it, which appears in the panel below.

Sub-skills associated with academic listening (Richards 1983)

1. ability to identify purpose and scope of lecture
2. ability to identify topic of lecture and follow topic development
3. ability to identify relationships among units within discourse (e.g. major ideas, generalisations, hypotheses, supporting ideas, examples)
4. ability to identify role of discourse markers in signalling structure of a lecture
5. ability to infer relationships (e.g. cause, effect, conclusion)
6. ability to recognise key lexical items related to subject/topic

Insights into Assessing Academic Listening: The Case of IELTS

> 7. ability to deduce meaning of words from context
> 8. ability to recognise markers of cohesion
> 9. ability to recognise function of intonation to signal information structure (e.g. pitch, volume, pace, key)
> 10. ability to detect attitude of speaker toward subject matter
> 11. ability to follow different modes of lecturing: [face-to-face], audio, audio-visual
> 12. ability to follow lecture despite differences in accent and speed
> 13. familiarity with different styles of lecturing: formal, conversational, read, unplanned
> 14. familiarity with different registers [i.e. spoken vs written, colloquial]
> 15. ability to recognise relevant matter: jokes, digressions, meanderings
> 16. ability to recognise non-verbal cues as markers of emphasis and attitude
> 17. knowledge of classroom conventions (e.g. turn-taking, clarification requests)
> 18. ability to recognise instructional/learner tasks (e.g. warnings, suggestions, recommendations, advice, instructions)

It should be stressed once again that this group of 'sub-skills' simply represents the intuitions of a well-informed commentator. As Buck (2001:59) puts it, commenting on a similar exercise by Buck and Tatsuoka (1998): '[Taxonomies] based on theory are only lists of what scholars think are likely to be important ... They give no indication of the relative importance of individual skills, nor do they provide guidance on how they should be sampled for test construction'. We still lack a sufficiently detailed account, fully underpinned by research, of precisely what the academic listening experience entails. However, Richards' taxonomy is more comprehensive than many sets of criteria developed since. What is striking is that 17 out of its 18 terms (the exception is no. 7[2]) correspond to the higher levels of the psycholinguistic model of listening outlined above (i.e. to meaning and, above all, discourse representation). They signal the importance of ensuring that test items that are designed for academic candidates focus on these interpretive areas.

In relation to evidence-based cognitive accounts of the skill, it is clear that successful L2 academic listening requires the learner to have developed a

---

2 This is a rather ambivalent category – something between an L1 technique for dealing with an unfamiliar word and an L2 strategy for compensating for one that has not been recognised.

comfortable degree of competence at lower levels. This is not just a matter of recognising items of vocabulary, syntactic patterns and common word clusters of all kinds (*must have done, on the other hand, contrary to popular belief*). It is also a matter of processing many of these linguistic features with a high degree of automaticity. As noted earlier, effortful processing at lower levels (pronunciation, lexis and syntax) makes heavy demands upon working memory and thus limits the extent to which a listener can engage in the higher-level operations of processing (namely, meaning construction and discourse construction) which are critical to tracing patterns of meaning in a lecture, a talk, a broadcast or a seminar.

Within the stages of the psycholinguistic model presented above, one can identify a number of higher-level functions that are central to the academic listening experience:

At parsing level:
- anticipating upcoming words: the 'garden path effect' (Sanz, Laka and Tanenhaus 2013);
- recognising formulaic chunks (Wray 2002).

At meaning construction level:
- identifying the current main point;
- resolving anaphors (e.g. linking pronouns to their referent);
- making necessary inferences where information is incomplete or not explicit;
- drawing on topic knowledge, speaker knowledge and world knowledge;
- judging whether a new piece of information is central, secondary or irrelevant;
- monitoring the accuracy of comprehension.

At discourse construction level:
- linking points of information (including where links have to be inferred);
- distinguishing macro-propositions from micro-;
- integrating new information into a developing discourse representation;
- monitoring the developing discourse representation for consistency;
- building an overall discourse structure which represents the lecturer's line of argument.

Despite its obvious importance, processing at the levels of meaning and discourse can be under-represented in the testing of L2 academic listening. Although some tests of academic listening do include items that require a listener to identify the main point or to link points of information, item writers are often tempted to focus on interesting single points of information, with the consequence that their items target a set of isolated facts, without requiring test takers to report the wider argument that links them. Sometimes the key to an item will be as small as a single word. In due course, this concern will be examined in relation to sample IELTS tests.

Strategy use[3]

Given the developmental pattern outlined above, there will quite often be gaps of understanding in the language and information that an L2 listener, even at quite an advanced level, extracts from a recording. Indeed, because of the variability of the signal, listening appears to be the most dependent of the four language skills upon the use of strategies to fill such gaps. Strategy instruction usually forms part of the training which learners receive when preparing for academic tests of listening. However, it is important to make some distinctions here which are not always fully recognised by instructors. Firstly (Field 2000), one needs to distinguish between:

- *processes* intrinsic to normal listening such as those profiled in Figure 1, which constitute what a language learner needs to acquire for long-term performance;
- *strategies*, deliberate expedients used periodically when an individual's listening competence cannot match the demands of a listening task.

Admittedly, there are grey areas between the two. Even an expert listener may still need to make occasional use of strategies (e.g. to identify words in noisy conditions); while some strategic techniques (e.g. checking understanding against what has been heard so far) also form part of competent listening at discourse level. Nevertheless, it is useful for commentators to distinguish between activities which hopefully, long term, will become fully integrated into the behaviour of a listener and highly automatic; and others which are short-term expedients to overcome an inadequate grasp of the second language. In any testing context, we also need to distinguish between:

- *compensatory strategies*, used to fill gaps of understanding;
- *test-wise strategies*, used to exploit loopholes in test method (Cohen 1998:219). For concrete examples in relation to IELTS Listening, see Field (2012a) and Badger and Yan (2012).

The latter need to be minimised by controlling those aspects of test design that enable them to be used; regrettably, the present reality for many listening

---

3 The strategies considered here are principally compensatory strategies: Cohen's *strategies of use* (1998).

tests is that they play a central role in much of the examination preparation that takes place in advance of taking the test. Li's (2014a, 2014b) account of the training received by Chinese IELTS candidates illustrates this quite well but the same criticism could easily be made of examination preparation and training for other tests in the marketplace.

There has been considerable research on listening strategies in recent years. However, as Macaro, Graham and Vanderplank (2007) acknowledge in a perceptive review of the literature, it is hard to draw clear conclusions from it. This is partly attributable to the fragmented nature of the field in terms of research goals, criteria applied and populations studied. In addition, the research methods adopted in investigating strategy use are not always entirely sound. There has been much reliance on questionnaires, which are open to over-reporting and heavily based on the assumption that the strategies listed are easily identifiable and psychologically real. The use of verbal report has given us more accurate and detailed insights into learner and test taker performance (Badger and Yan 2012, Field 2012a, Goh 2000, Graham 2011).

Early attempts to classify listening strategies more systematically in terms of their purpose (e.g. Dörnyei and Scott 1997, Faerch and Kasper 1983) do not seem to have been followed up. However, there is widespread use of O'Malley and Chamot's (1990:44) classification of three strategy types: metacognitive, cognitive, and social-affective. There has been particular interest in metacognition (e.g. Vandergrift and Goh 2012). By contrast, cognitive and socio-affective strategies are less represented in the literature, which seems unfortunate, given the needs and likely behaviour of lower-proficiency learners. One reason for the preference may be that metacognitive activities involve intentionality and are therefore more accessible to report by test takers. Unsurprisingly, this means that they feature disproportionately in verbal reports or questionnaires aiming to quantify frequency of use, which can give a distorted impression of their relative importance.

There is a tendency by commentators (e.g. Chung 1999) to focus heavily on a single type of metacognitive strategy: namely, 'advanced organiser' techniques such as reflecting on topic before listening to the recording. These represent an interesting grey area. In terms of strict construct validity, they are not options available to the L2 listener in many real-world situations. However, they do play a role in academic contexts, where the student might use prior knowledge of a topic to anticipate what the lecturer will say and even formulate questions in advance, to which the lecture may provide answers. Reading the rubrics and thinking ahead about the content of the recording can thus be argued to be an entirely valid strategy to practise in relation to a test of academic listening in a way that more narrowly test-wise strategies such as identifying 'key words' in test items are not. More recently, eye-tracking methodology has begun to provide another valuable source of additional evidence for an understanding of listening strategies (Holzknecht et al 2017).

One angle surprisingly little investigated has been the extent to which strategy use varies according to individual temperament or is culturally determined. It may be that the educational formation of learners from certain parts of the world encourages speculative thinking, while the formation of others restrains them from making guesses until sufficient evidence is available (Braxton 1999).

A major topic of discussion has been the effectiveness of strategy training in improving listening proficiency. Macaro et al (2007:182) report largely unclear results concerning the impact of training on performance. This may partly be because many studies have employed a longitudinal methodology based on control groups and pre- and post-testing – an approach that, in listening research, is susceptible to variables such as participants' degree of exposure to L2 sources during the trial period (especially if they are living in an L2 environment).

6 Test content as text

Having established a profile of academic listening, we now move on to consider the implications for test design. The account will focus on the IELTS test, but has relevance to all tests that aim to assess L2 listening in an academic context. The chapters that follow examine various characteristics of such tests, with a view to matching them against the account given so far of the nature of the listening construct.

This chapter and the next explore the nature of the listening passages to which the candidate is exposed, and compare them to their real-world equivalents. The concern will be one of content: how representative are these passages of the type of material to which the candidate would be exposed in a real-world academic context? But behind this lies a question that is essentially cognitive: Can the listening behaviour demanded of a candidate be compared with that of a real-world encounter? The present chapter will focus on linguistic and discoursal aspects of the material; the following one on the material as recording. Chapters 8 to 10 will then go on to examine aspects of the test that relate to how it is delivered – again, with a view to comparing it to the type of behaviour that might be demanded by a real-world context.

Observations made and concerns raised in Chapters 6 to 10 will be revisited in the final chapter of this volume. This section will draw upon the extensive review and discussion of IELTS and its Listening test throughout this volume to offer a summary of general and specific recommendations, relevant not just for future versions of IELTS but for any test designed to assess academic listening skills.

General content

Mention has already been made of attempts to differentiate between the requirements of certain broad academic domains when determining the content of ELTS and of the first version of IELTS. The thinking behind this (Davies 2008), well in advance of its time, was that content, discourse patterns and above all the student's interaction with the information provided might vary markedly from one discipline to another (see similar arguments about non-academic candidates in Chapter 3).

The initiative clearly ran into major logistical problems in the need to produce multiple versions of the test, to control for difficulty across versions and to administer a range of different papers in the same exam centre. It was also untenable for another reason. In principle, the arrangement permitted the use of content which was close in detail, discourse patterns and terminology to what might actually be studied in a particular area of specialism. In practice, however, it could not be so specific for fear of biasing a test in favour of those already possessing an informed background in that field. The advantages conferred upon L2 listeners by previous topic knowledge are well attested (Chiang and Dunkel 1992, Jensen and Hansen 1995, Schmidt-Rinehart 1994).

The present version of IELTS (and indeed that of other academically oriented tests such as TOEFL iBT) does not attempt to represent discipline-specific differences: 'IELTS Academic testing reflects some features of academic language but does not aim to simulate academic study tasks in their entirety' (IELTS 2015:12). The consequences of a non-specific approach of this kind are that:

- The issue of bias becomes even more critical. The topics employed (particularly in reading and listening) have to be as neutral as possible, so as to avoid favouring certain candidates by referring to their specialism. In effect, this potentially distances the test from real-world circumstances, where a student's interpretation of a lecture may benefit from knowledge (even if rudimentary) of the terminology and issues in their chosen field.
- The processes engaged also have to be as neutral as possible so as to avoid incorporating cognitive or language demands specific to certain disciplines and not to others. Examples might be the types of highly abstract reasoning that feature in philosophy or the types of diagrammatic information that feature in engineering or computer science.

A rather different issue concerns whether a test should take account of the specific contexts in which an academic listener is likely to have to operate. As part of their study, Ingram and Bayliss (2007) provide a valuable insight into what academic listeners actually do during the course of their studies – valuable because it is underpinned by reports obtained from learners. The researchers asked participants across several different disciplines to specify the types of academic activity in which they principally engaged. Of the 14 pursuits the participants mentioned (2007:7), seven directly entail listening:

- Listening and note-taking
- Following spoken instructions
- Group discussions/tutorials
- Attending and giving oral presentations
- One-to-one meetings

- Working with others in a laboratory
- Practical experience working with L1 speakers

They suggest a range of different roles for the listener, both individual and interactional. Clearly a test cannot represent all of these contexts, and some are in any case quite specific to certain disciplines. In order of importance, Field (2019) proposes the following activities as critical to most academic experience:

Lectures > seminars > interactions with tutor > advice and instructions > social activities

The present situation, as noted earlier, is that, in principle, the IELTS test is now available in two versions: one which is said to represent more general uses of English, and one which is more related to an academic context. In practice, however, there is only a single version of the Listening test, one which thus has to cover both targets. Half of the recorded material in the test relates to everyday contexts while only half represents the type of encounter that might occur in a place of higher study.

Although there are historical reasons for this situation (see Taylor and Weir 2012:1–23) it is not ideal. It means that candidates seeking to use IELTS for immigration purposes are tested against academic-style material while those aiming to display readiness for academic entry are tested on two passages out of four that represent informal conversational material rather than academic discourse. An argument in favour of the latter is that overseas students might well need a level of conversational English in order to integrate into the host community; but that consideration is outweighed by the consequence that only 50% of the material is at a level of linguistic and discoursal complexity that fits their purpose in sitting the test. For stakeholders, this must certainly raise questions of ecological validity. More importantly: as already noted, the inclusion of accessible material targeted at B1–B2 level risks lowering the overall difficulty of the test while nevertheless making it suitable for institutions that wish to use it for entrance to pre-sessional programmes and may require band scores of 5/5.5.

The effect upon scoring emerged as an incidental finding in a study by Field (2015). For the purposes of the research, participants were tested on Section 4 of the IELTS paper, which featured a lecture presentation. Their band scores after a single play of the recording were found to be significantly below their previously recorded IELTS scores on a complete listening test – arguably demonstrating the extent to which the latter had been inflated by their performance on the more informal Sections 1 and 2. Depending upon the formulae used, reliability can of course be strengthened where there is a broad range of difficulty. However, an alternative conclusion could be that mixing conversational listening with academic weakens a test's scoring validity and its ability to discriminate between candidates at higher levels. Other evidence to this effect has already been cited in reviewing some of the literature on criterion-related validity (Cotton and Conrow 1998, Lim et al 2013, Picard 2007), which suggests a degree of disparity between the proficiency levels targeted by the Academic Reading module and those targeted by the Listening test.

Topic

As just indicated, the issue of topic is a potential headache for a general academic test such as IELTS or TOEFL iBT. It is important not to favour particular candidates by featuring subject-specific information and terminology with which they are already familiar. A fine path has to be trodden which entails devising content and discourse patterns that are representative of general academic discourse, without venturing too deeply into detail.

The IELTS *Item Writer Guidelines* (2018b) do not offer advice about controlling the level of specialist detail and terminology. Indeed, the document appears to endorse material that is subject-focused by providing (2018b:9) a list of academic disciplines ranging from Agriculture to Theatre Studies that can feature in lecture-based sections. The only indirect reference to possible bias is a mention (2018b:15–16) that draft tests may be rejected if they have 'content which is likely to be already known to some candidates'.

Despite these reservations, it is apparent, once one turns to actual samples, that item writers are sensitive to the need to generalise. Section 4 tests in the *IELTS 7* collection of past papers cover some ingeniously neutral topics: lectures on rock art, handedness in sport, criteria for holiday accommodation and monosodium glutamate in cooking. Just occasionally, however, a topic in the samples reviewed seems to slip through the net. A Section 3 text on a robotic float project (2009:144–145) is conceptually difficult to follow and heavily loaded with topic-specific lexis (*robotic, float data, ozone depletion, search and rescue missions, sustainable fishing practices*). This provides a good illustration of content rendered relatively impenetrable by terminology that a non-specialist would have difficulty in handling.

Concerns relating to the content could also be extended to the tutor–student dialogues that feature in Section 3 of the test. A list is provided (IWGs, 2018b:9) of various aspects of study that could form the focus of discussion: among them, receiving oral feedback on different types of written work. One can understand the rationale behind including the type of interaction that a student might have with an academic staff member, but the situations represented do not seem to reflect real-world conditions very closely:

- A tutor–student interaction is one where the student is normally a participant rather than an overhearer.
- In this kind of interaction in the real world, a student would have prior knowledge of any written documents and/or time to prepare for the meeting.
- The section extends to including between-student conversations involving study planning; this entails an entirely different, more informal conversational style, making comparability difficult between different versions of the test.

To this one can add, from a socio-cultural perspective, that the tutor–student relationship may be unfamiliar to a pre-admission test taker, and only fully experienced post-admission.

Overall, an opportunity seems to have been missed in these sample papers of modelling a type of interaction that is likely to be central to the student's later experience – namely, the exchange of views in a seminar. Differentiating between speaker views is an important discourse-level function, and one that seems little represented in this admittedly small sample – though it features quite importantly in some other tests designed for academic admission, such as TOEFL iBT.

A brief comment on the more informal Sections 1 and 2. Here, the topics and types of interaction cover a wide range of settings, but their purpose in assessment terms is relatively unclear. One of a selection of five published exam practice volumes (*IELTS 7*) was chosen as representative of typical test content over past years. Almost all of the Section 1–2 papers featured there were found to fall into the simplest types of listening activity: receiving personal and factual information, following an orientation talk and understanding instructions. Their original purpose seemed to have been to test how well equipped the candidate was to deal with everyday encounters on campus. However (perhaps with immigrant and professional candidates in mind), the current IWGs (2018b:8) now explicitly warn item writers to avoid college/university settings. It could also be argued, of course, that the types of interaction described are unlikely to vary greatly across the different contexts/domains.

Discourse types

Real-world academic lectures and seminars embrace a range of discourse types. Expository and discursive are the most frequent, and the most closely associated in the public mind with the notion of 'lecture'. However, the general term 'discursive' does not really do justice to the various types of discourse that an academic listener might need to handle. After reviewing a range of recordings used in higher-level tests, Field (2012b) proposed the following categories – with the proviso that a given piece of academic discourse is not restricted to one of these types but may well alternate between two or more. There will also inevitably be variation between disciplines as to whether or not particular types are employed.

- Expository (including cause-and-effect and counterfactual relationships)
- Discursive (weighing evidence 'for and against')
- Argumentative (putting forward a single viewpoint)
- Persuasive (trying to win the listener over)
- Analytical/interpretive (deconstructing data or ideas)
- Critical (evaluating – common in humanities subjects)
- Process-descriptive (Brown and Yule 1983), featuring (e.g.) objects that potentially change their form as part of a process

In addition, of course, there are simpler conventional categories, representing argument structures that are less complex and widely used to test general listening at lower proficiency levels:

- Narrative
- Instructional (giving instructions and directions)
- Descriptive
- Informational (providing facts)

At the risk of over-generalising, one important reason why these four types tend to be easier for listeners is that the connections between points of information are often relatively transparent: they are indicated by the chronological sequence of the text, by cause-and-effect or by clear markers of change of topic.

Using these 11 categories, samples of the four retired Listening tests in *IELTS 7* were examined further to gain an impression of the range of discourse types used across the different sections of the test. In Section 1 and 2, all eight recordings were informational. In Sections 3 and 4, six were expository (one of them with elements of instruction). One was argumentative. The final one fell loosely into the category of 'discursive', with two participants making and rejecting suggestions.

This was only the smallest of samples, but it does suggest that item writers tend to represent the academic lecture quite narrowly in terms of information content, and maybe do not exploit a wide enough range of types of argument.

Greater use of discursive, argumentative and analytical material would surely be appropriate for the type of candidate being targeted. Clearly this was only a very random sample but cross-checking four other collections of retired IELTS papers suggested it was relatively typical.

Language

The IELTS IWGs do not contain specifications on grading vocabulary and grammar; and the general approach appears to be unprescriptive in terms of the language used. This makes sense in a test that aims to cover a range of levels; and, again, there is evidence in the sample materials that the item writers are capable of using their own experience to determine what is likely to be within the test takers' linguistic repertoire.

Vocabulary

So far as vocabulary is concerned, there need be no hesitation about including a limited number of low-frequency items in a recording designed for the academic candidate. One can assume that, at the higher levels targeted, test takers would not be fazed by an unfamiliar item and will have sufficient strategic competence to decide whether to a) ignore the word, b) derive a general meaning, or c) work out the word's meaning from context. However, an important proviso that bears repeating is that, so far as possible, the candidate's understanding of an item key in the recording should not be critically dependent upon a low-frequency word.

Another reason for avoiding a prescriptive approach to listening vocabulary is that certain long-term preconceptions about vocabulary grading have recently been challenged. One issue relates to the use of frequency bands (K1, K2 etc.) to narrowly determine vocabulary content in tests. Field (2019:33) makes the point that most corpora record the frequency of word *forms*, ignoring the fact that the sense attached to a word may be dependent upon its co-text and may be complicated by the existence of homonyms and homophones. It has also become apparent (Milton 2009:55) that, until recently, much research into oral vocabulary acquisition and use relied upon inappropriate sources based on the recorded frequency of written, not spoken forms. There is also the issue that L1 can play a significant role in vocabulary acquisition and knowledge (Schmitt, Dunn, O'Sullivan, Anthony and Kremmel 2021).

An important issue in recent L2 vocabulary studies has been whether a learner's listening vocabulary is likely to be similar in size to the reading one. Research (Milton and Hopkins 2006) has suggested that knowledge of the spoken forms of words lags behind that of written, even in the early stages of L2 acquisition; and that the gap between the two becomes wider as learners become more proficient[1]. This is understandable, given the fact that a reader can fix attention on a new word form in a way that the transitory nature of speech does not allow a listener to do. Milton (2009:183) proposes a minimum spoken vocabulary of around 3,000 to 3,500 words at B2 level and about 4,500 at C2, as compared with suggestions from commentators such as Nation (2001) that the base for reading may be around 6,000 or more. Milton (2009:179) partly attributes lower vocabulary needs in listening to the different content of written and spoken texts. In this regard, academic listening material occupies an anomalous position as it is likely to contain a certain amount of lexis that is either subject-specific or is closely related to academic discourse. This vocabulary may not be part of the everyday oral repertoire of the listener but may have to be accessed by a process of *matching a form known through reading to an oral one that may never have been heard before.*

This illustrates, once again, the importance of monitoring the proportion of specialist vocabulary in a recording and ensuring that responses to items are not critically dependent upon esoteric terms being understood. Indeed, an issue much raised in the vocabulary literature is *coverage*: i.e. the relationship between familiar and unfamiliar words in a text. How many unknown words is it reasonable for a test writer to include in a recording without compromising the learner's ability to make sense of it? Researchers investigating reading suggest coverage of around 95% (Laufer 1989) or 98% (Nation 2001:147). These figures sometimes get cited quite categorically, so designers of academic tests need to understand their limitations. Firstly, 'comprehension' is conceived by some commentators purely in terms of correct answers to factual questions, and without allowing for the fact that the figures are likely to vary with different text content (e.g. narrative versus discursive) or different styles (formal versus informal). It is also worth noting that 'coverage' figures tend to ignore the distinction between content and function words. Function words not requiring lexical access make up nearly 48.5% of all word tokens (McCarthy and Carter 1997). This means that, leaving aside the other concerns, the figure of 98% coverage is not as restrictive for item writers as it might appear. In effect, in a test designed for a higher proficiency level, 4% of the content words included (30 in a text of 750 words) could be allowed to fall outside the range of what one would expect a test taker to know.

---

1 This is obviously not the case with learners already resident in an L2 setting, with extensive exposure to spoken language outside the learning context.

Grammar

Controlling grammar in a test of academic listening could be argued to be a low priority[2]. If the test is aimed principally at C1 level, there is a reasonable assumption that the learner has quite an extensive repertoire in terms of knowledge. However, sight should not be lost of the fact that behind the processing of syntax by a listener is the need to hold a gradually increasing group of words in the mind until such time as a grammatical pattern becomes apparent. An important (and often overlooked) variable in test difficulty is thus the *length of utterance* of the speaker. Field (2013:122) demonstrates that a gradual increase in this measure is intuitively used by item writers as a means of calibrating difficulty across the tests of the Cambridge English Qualifications.

That said, there is some evidence that utterance length is not always such an important factor for a student processing real-world lecture material. A competent lecturer will often modify their delivery, using relatively short utterances in order to make the content more accessible to the audience. Here is an extract from an authentic source (Lynch 2004:164):

> *Earlier in previous reports from the IPCC + there was some doubt about + whether um temperature change of this magnitude had actually occurred + because people said they were biased + there was bias in the temperature records + primarily coming from the urban island effect + that is + that many of the temperature measuring stations are close to cities.*

The complexity here lies not in the syntactic parsing of the utterances by the listener; but in the conceptual links that the listener has to trace between one utterance and the next. This type of delivery is too little represented in the recordings used in test materials, where there is a heavy reliance on studio scripts employing sentence-level punctuation conventions.

Academic discourse

Perhaps the most important consideration when examining the language of an academic listening test is whether it can be said to be representative (linguistically and perceptually) of the type of discourse that a candidate would actually encounter in a real-world lecture, seminar or tutorial.

There is a growing literature examining the nature of academic discourse. For recent reviews, see Snow and Uccelli (2009) and Gilmore (2015); and,

---

2 Mecartty (2000) found that grammar was not a significant factor in listening test scores but that knowledge of vocabulary accounted for about 15% of success. Nevertheless, he also found, with Milton, that 'lexical knowledge appears to be more crucial to reading than it is to listening' (2000:340).

from a listening perspective, Rogers and Webb (2016) and Deroey (2018). However, a great deal of work in this area has focused on written forms of language. A collection of papers on academic discourse edited by Flowerdew (2012) is typical in containing very few references to oral forms as distinct from written, except in Flowerdew's own contribution. This has led at times to an implicit assumption that the types of text encountered in writing – information-dense, formal in style, dependent upon abstract nominalisation and explicitly signposted by markers – are representative of all academic discourse.

Recent attempts have been made to define precisely what it is that best characterises academic discourse. Snow and Uccelli (2009:119) propose a widely quoted set of five major characteristics: detached interpersonal stance, concise information load, organisation of information, lexical diversity and grammatical embedding and nominalisation. Even here, however, the authors seem at times to fall into the trap of generalising from written style to spoken. Their initiative was extended by Patterson and Weideman (2012), who apply the characteristics to the specific circumstances of testing – but again do not distinguish the two modalities as much as one might hope.

Much of the early research and analysis relating specifically to discourse in L2 academic listening concerned itself with macro-structure. There was discussion (Olsen and Huckin 1990) as to whether a clear distinction could be drawn between two lecture types – one point-driven and one information-driven. Dudley-Evans (1997) concluded that, if such a distinction is at all valid, it may well be discipline-specific. There was also speculation about the extent to which the language content of a lecture reflected lecturer style (read-aloud, note-driven or informal); and much attention was given to the part played by discourse markers.

More recently, research has taken a refreshingly concrete turn by comparing the type of discourse represented in EAP coursebooks (often reflecting received assumptions about the nature of oral discourse) with what is actually present in real-life conversation, talks and lectures. Clearly this line of research has important implications, not simply for materials writers but also for test designers with concerns about context validity.

Gilmore (2015), who has a long-term interest in this area, identifies four major possible sources of information: corpus data plus the findings from discourse analysis, genre analysis and conversational analysis. He then goes on to list 44 published sources which discuss mismatches between the content of ELT coursebooks for general study and what we know about natural speech. His conclusions are that much useful research has been ignored: 'For a wide range of discourse features (including lexico-grammatical items, speech acts, generic structure and interactional features of contingent talk), ELT course books often provide learners with distorted or partial representations of the target language to work from …' (2015:515).

Gilmore makes clear that a major problem in ELT textbooks lies in the incorrect representation of spoken as against written models. On listening dialogues, he comments that 'native speaker intuitions about language and speech behaviour are notoriously unreliable' and cites Burns (1998) in support of this view. Field (2013:111) extends this comment to testing, reporting evidence that Cambridge test writers at lower levels sometimes succeed better at emulating natural speech than those at higher levels, where there are pressures to increase the density of the information and the complexity of the links between it.

A study by Deroey (2018) relates specifically to an academic context, and reinforces Gilmore's findings. Deroey examined 25 EAP lecture listening coursebooks and compared the language represented within them to examples retrieved from the British Academic Spoken English (BASE) corpus of 160 authentic lectures (2005, Thompson and Nesi 2001). She focused initially on a single aspect: the use of signposts marking the importance of a point. She found that the lecturers used a wide range of such markers and that they were less explicit than those that featured in the teaching materials, and more dependent upon context. A contrast might be found between casual markers such as *remember that ...*/*bear in mind that* widely used in actual lectures and more explicit ones such as *The key point is ...*/*what I'm stressing is ...* favoured in the materials. The recordings used in the materials were mainly scripted and (confirming Gilmore's 2015 finding) it appeared to be rare for coursebook authors to consult corpora of Academic English speech or findings from discourse analysis. However, Deroey reports positively (2018:63) on two authors who did bother to do so. Speech content in the BASE corpus alerted Campbell and Smith (2012:7) to the need to reflect 'a substantial use of informal and idiomatic language by lecturers' – thus challenging received ideas about the formality of lecture-style delivery. The same commentators also mention 'less use of (and consistency in the use of) discourse markers to organise information than we might have expected'.

In a study covering a similar area to Deroey's, Martinez, Adolphs and Carter (2013) examined how new terms are introduced and defined by lecturers. They too discovered that the discourse markers used were not always as explicit as materials writers tend to assume. One method of communication was indeed transparent and entailed the use of verbs such as *mean, call* or *define*. More commonly, formulaic phrases were used which did not contain such key words. The most opaque approach was to engage in a long discussion of the term in question with little signalling at all to indicate that it was being glossed.

These studies underline a need to ensure that the patterns of discourse featured in the lecture simulations of any academic listening test correspond more closely to those employed in real-world contexts. One means of ensuring this would be for IWGs to stress the importance of consulting authentic sources such as BASE more carefully before choosing recordings or writing scripts. This might dispel prevailing false assumptions about analogies between the characteristics of academic writing and those of academic speaking.

The following speaker turns are taken from an IELTS script of a tutorial, which forms part of the materials examined in this review. They provide an example (admittedly, quite rare in the sample) of the difficulties of emulating natural academic speech.

PHILIP: ... On the positive side, exposure to such diversity helps encourage creativity, which is generally *an asset* to a company. But unfortunately individual differences are also *the root of* conflict between staff and they can lead to difficulties for management, which can sometimes be serious.

JANICE: Well, currently teamwork is *in fashion* in the workplace and in my opinion the importance of the individual is generally neglected. What managers should be *targeting* is those employees who can *take the lead* in a situation and are not afraid to accept the idea of responsibility.

TUTOR: That's true Janice but unfortunately many managers think *the entire notion of* encouraging individuality amongst their staff is far too hard.

JANICE: Yes that may be true but I think one of the most important tasks of managers is to consider the needs of the individual on the one hand and group co-operation on the other. It requires *creative thinking* on the part of management to avoid tension.

(*IELTS 7,* 2009:132–133)

The excerpt illustrates the challenges faced by an item writer when composing a script for a test that features a discursive exchange. There is an uneasy relationship between the need to make the text sound interactional but at the same time to represent what are thought to be the principal characteristics of academic style. The result is a not entirely convincing mix, where low-frequency idiomatic expressions unlikely to be used in a conversation with an L2 listener (italicised) sit uncomfortably with formal characteristics such as nominalisation (underlined). The latter feature is indeed widely encountered in *written* academic discourse. However, it is reasonable to assume, from evidence in the BASE corpus and elsewhere, that it is not as consistent or as frequent in spoken discourse. It seems especially less likely to occur in a tutorial context like the one represented in the extract, where a more concrete alternative to the opening assertion is available: i.e. 'being exposed to diverse points-of-view helps to encourage staff to be creative'.

In addition, the writer has felt the need to insert some very explicit markers (highlighted in the text) of the type that are often taught in EAP materials – markers which the research just cited indicates are much less commonly used than is supposed.

To summarise, the writers of academic listening test materials need to distance oral academic style more clearly from written. In particular, they might take on board two findings reported above: the more informal style that is often adopted, even in lectures, and the more limited use of explicit discourse markers.

Interest in the issues associated with generating spoken texts for L2 listening assessment has increased in recent years and it is worth noting here the outcomes from some recent research in this area. Wagner, Liao and Wagner (2021) examined the process of 'authenticating' scripted texts, i.e. making changes to scripted texts to give them more of the lexico-grammatical, phonological and speech rate characteristics of unscripted spoken language. They compared test taker performance on tests that had been 'authenticated' with performance on scripted spoken texts, and observed higher scores on tests with scripted texts than with 'authenticated' versions. Rossi and Brunfaut (2021) explored the effectiveness of an item writing training course to produce authentic-sounding listening texts for use in L2 listening assessment. Their findings suggested that item writers can indeed be trained to be aware of spoken language features and to reproduce these so as to develop more authentic-sounding listening texts.

With permission, sample extracts from the BASE corpus might perhaps be made available to writers to serve as examples. Access to corpora as a resource for item writing is becoming increasingly widespread, especially as large-scale corpora are made available to a wider audience. The BASE corpus, for example, can be accessed through Sketch Engine, a repository for 600 ready-to-use corpora in over 90 languages and thus a valuable resource for practising item writers.

A further notion about academic discourse that merits discussion is that it is more likely to represent 'abstract' ideas. This is of course not necessarily the case: a great deal depends upon the discipline and the lines of argument associated with it. Assumptions about the role of abstractness no doubt derive partly from the tendency for academic writing to make extensive use of nominalisation. However, a wider concern is that the term 'abstract', often used when referring to the content of higher-level listening tests, tends to be extremely vaguely defined in IWGs (a point made some time ago in Field's 1999 internal review of the Certificate of Proficiency in English (CPE) test, now known as C2 Proficiency). There is always a danger that item writers will try to represent abstractness in terms of the kind of theoretical line of argument that even a native listener might have difficulty in following – thus taking a test into cognitive areas beyond those that characterise normal academic listening competence. It is also worth bearing in mind that the most abstract propositions in real-life academic contexts are generally supported by exemplification and explication. That said, a device that certainly does not serve to make them more accessible to a listener (especially an L2 listener) is the use of metaphorical analogies. By way of example, Field (2013:123–124; italics in original) quotes the following extract from a CPE sample test. The topic is memory and imagination:

> When we imagine, we *create* the future out of *fragments* from the past. And when we remember, we construct *pathways in our brain* to *remake* the experience and, at a certain moment, it's as if *a jigsaw comes together*, and we'll accept that as the truth.

It could, of course, be argued that metaphorical analogy is an important part of academic discourse and there is some research suggesting that metaphor is prominent in lecture discourse (Low, Littlemore and Koester 2008). The question then becomes to what extent tests of Academic English should reflect this, even if such use of metaphors may sometimes hinder rather than help listeners.

Length and information density

Word length as specified in the IELTS IWGs is as follows:

Section 1 (dialogue): 650–750   Section 2 (monologue): 700–850
Section 3 (dialogue): 800–950   Section 4 (monologue): 750–850

It is difficult at higher proficiency levels to be precise about running time, given the higher number of multi-syllabic words; one might also expect a slower speech rate in the lecture presentation of Section 4. However, at a medium conversational speaking rate of 200 words per minute (Calvert 1986) and allowing for longer words, the figures above suggest recording lengths which range from around 3.5 to 5 minutes. Despite the specifications, a glance at the sample materials reviewed suggests that considerable flexibility is allowed in the relative lengths of the sections: the shortest recording in one test is a Part 3 and the longest is a Part 1. The overall timings (including instructions etc.) range widely from just over 5 minutes to just over 9.

Length is especially an issue for the lecture-based section; a 5-minute recording clearly cannot emulate the experience of listening to a 45-minute presentation. Some commentators (e.g. Rogers and Webb 2016:171) argue the need to expose academic listeners to much longer stretches of recording. This is obviously not a practical option for an international test. Instead, what appears to happen is that an item writer feels constrained to include a great deal of information in a small space – partly as an attempt to replicate the content coverage of a real-world lecture and partly to provide sufficient material for 10 items. It is then not the duration of the recording that creates difficulty but the density of the information that it includes. A short passage with tightly packed information can place particularly heavy cognitive demands upon a learner because of the speed at which the detail has to be integrated into an overall picture. A number of the participants interviewed in Field's (2012a) IELTS study reported their concern about parts of the recordings they heard which were either dense in terms of the detail they contained or complex in terms of the links between propositions.

The following extract from the sample materials is one that even an L1 listener might find difficult to process without visual support such as accompanying gestures. The item writer was wise enough not to base an item on this part of the recording but its information density must have fazed many test takers. The various information units are numbered.

> (1) Anyway, his team measured the hands, feet and eyes (2) of 2611 players and (3) found that there were really three main types of laterality: (4) mixed – you work equally well on both sides – (5) both hand and eye – (6) single – you tend to favour one side but (7) both hand and eye favour the same side – and (8) cross-laterality – (9) a player's hands and eyes favour only one side (10) but they are opposite sides.

One way of dealing with issues of information density is to allow a second hearing of the recording – something that is increasingly possible in academic institutions through the practice of recording lectures and making them available to students online. Allowing a second hearing – or even multiple hearings – in assessment contexts therefore becomes more defensible in terms of real-world conditions.

Density of information in a listening passage may also be reduced (and the pressure on the listener lightened) by including elements in the text which add nothing to the task in hand. It quite often happens that a lecturer includes information peripheral to the task, repeats points in order to emphasise them or backs up a point by providing a concrete example. This is a particular characteristic of skilled speakers, who are sensitive to the demands they are placing upon listeners and deliberately pace the introduction of new points of information or reinforce points already made. It gives the listener an opportunity to take stock of the information conveyed so far. Here is an example from one of the authentic lectures featured in Lynch (2004:149), with the emphasised material in bold and the italics denoting low-key delivery:

> Our second problem is obesity / obesity brought about by **an overindulgence in certain foods** / **especially saturated fats** / and a lack of exercise / our Victorian ancestors had few of the labour saving devices that we enjoy today / *that we that we profit from today* / of which the car is the perhaps the chief offender / lack of exercise / overindulgence in saturated fats / bringing about obesity / and obesity leads to heart disease / back problems and so on ...

That said, item writers also need to bear in mind that, in certain circumstances, redundant material can actually increase test difficulty. A speaker who repeats a point by paraphrasing it might seem to be assisting the listener; but it can result instead in the listener having to make a decision as to whether the paraphrase represents a repetition or a new point of information. In addition, of course, including these digressions can add significantly to the length of a recording without adding any testable content.

It is evident that a test of academic listening has to rely upon recordings of at least 4 to 6 minutes because of the need to represent a reduced version of the kind of discourse structure that candidates will encounter in a real-world situation. However, testers tend to overlook the fact that failures of understanding in lecture situations sometimes originate at a local level, where mishearing a key word or failing to comprehend a discourse marker may lead to wider misunderstanding. On these grounds, a case can perhaps be made for adding a new section to the conventional L2 academic listening test: one that supplements longer texts with short clips of 15 to 30 seconds of the kind that feature very often in general listening tests. These texts might be derived from an authentic source such as BASE and, for example, feature instances of the less explicit discourse markers that lecturers have been shown to employ. Clips such as these can be relatively neutral in terms of specialist content. They are also time-economic: a section consisting of 5 to 10 clips might enable the length of a subsequent lecture-based section to be extended somewhat so as to thin out its information load.

Monologue vs dialogue

As noted earlier, the IELTS Listening test has a four-part structure:

Section 1: informal + dialogue   Section 2: informal + monologue
Section 3: more formal + dialogue   Section 4: formal + monologue

This may appear to ensure a neat and progressive balance between different interactions and speech styles. However, as commented previously, it leaves the academic listener with only two of the four sections representing the type of input that they are likely to find challenging in real-world conditions – while the immigrant candidate has to handle academic discourse as well as that of everyday.

Furthermore, the content of Section 3 (dialogue in an academic context) is quite loosely profiled. It is described in the IWGs (2018b:6) as follows: 'The focus involves the development of ideas and/or the exchange of opinions related to an academic topic, with meaning being negotiated between the speakers. It is not purely factual'. In practice, judging by the sample materials reviewed in this study, it seems that it can range between:

- an exchange of views in a seminar
- a one-to-one tutorial
- a discussion between two students of a lecture they have heard or a project they plan

The cognitive demands of each are quite distinctive and must surely lead to important divergences between test versions in terms of the demands they make and the processes they tap into.

An indication of this is provided by some incidental figures in Coleman and Heap's 1998 study of responses to IELTS rubrics. Participant responses to three versions of the IELTS Listening test were examined. In two of the three, the highest level of error occurred in Section 3 (59.7% in one version, 68.5% in another) while, in the third, Section 3 recorded the *lowest* level of error at 28%. Yet the instructions for the whole test specify: 'Four sections in increasing levels of difficulty'.

There is sometimes an assumption in testing circles that dialogue material is necessarily less demanding than monologue (see e.g. the lack of monologue material in Cambridge Young Learners tests). There is some logic in this: information in dialogues is often more thinly distributed and/or repeated between speakers. However, particularly in an academic context, a great deal depends upon the nature of the speech event. It can be considerably more demanding in a seminar setting to switch between two speakers and to follow two distinct lines of argument than to listen to a single lecturer whose presentation includes well-placed signposting (Papageorgiou, Stevens and Goodwin 2012). The former situation should ideally be specified more precisely within the test profile to ensure that candidates are indeed tested on this type of listening.

7 Test content as speech

Authenticity

Chapter 6 discussed the nature of academic discourse from a linguistic perspective; equally if not more important when reviewing a test of L2 listening is to enquire whether the recorded spoken material used represents an adequate simulation of the spoken input that test takers would encounter in a real-world context.

Materials writers and test producers have four possible sources for the recordings they choose, differentiated by their level of authenticity (Field 2008). They can script them; they can ask actors to improvise a situation in the studio; they can use recordings of real-life speech events; or they can make use of **semi-scripted** materials, where an authentic event is transcribed and re-recorded under studio conditions. Test producers and publishers often find the fourth option attractive as it avoids the complications associated with reproduction rights. It also enables them to manipulate the original text by editing its language and even by introducing MCQ distractors (sometimes with unfortunate consequences for information density).

By way of contrast, the use of fully authentic materials is increasingly a possibility open to EAP classroom instruction, given the wide availability of such materials both on the internet and in corpora. This (and the increasing use of guest lecturers on university pre-sessional courses) means that many academic test candidates will have previously been exposed to actual lecture material, delivered naturally. Research into the effects of authenticity upon learner comprehension and motivation is limited but generally positive. Herron and Seay (1991) reported improvements in learners' listening skills as a result of supplementing conventional materials with authentic ones. Wu and Stansfield (2001:196) constructed tests based on improvised material; but compromised spontaneity by recording a target conversation multiple times 'until it was determined to be wholly authentic'. Gilmore (2011) reports on the positive effects of exposure to authentic listening materials upon Japanese learners' communicative competence.

Elsewhere, discussion has focused on the formal differences between authentic and scripted speech. In an interesting study that compared material within a single genre, Gilmore (2004) identified a predictably higher prevalence of false starts, repetitions, overlaps and back-channelling in authentic sources; and very large differences in relation to fillers and pauses (he did not distinguish between hesitations and planning pauses). This suggests that a real-world presentation is likely to differ quite radically in rhythm and pace from one recorded or re-recorded by an actor in a studio.

Lynch (2011:81) also mentions these larger-scale prosodic effects. Citing findings by Thompson (2003), he comments on the way experienced lecturers use metadiscoursal and intonational signals to put across their points more transparently: 'the use of textual/prosodic cues reflects the existence in the speaker's mind of a coherent cognitive map which he/she wishes learners to recreate as they listen, whereas the prosodic cues given by speakers/readers of simulated lectures in some EAP materials may not provide such help to second language listeners.' The consequent lack of sensitivity to these cues may affect later performance: Pickering (2004) compared the performance of native and non-native listeners when listening to lecture-style material, and found that the former made sensitive use of pitch and pause cues to create 'paragraphs' whereas the latter did not.

Repeated below are some of the comments on the IELTS test obtained by Berry et al (2013) – in this case, provided not by academic candidates but by medical practitioners:

- *It's a good test of listening ability but it's too clean, it's not listening in the real world and some of it is too artificial and structured.* (AHP)
- *I found it to be forced, unnatural conversation. It wasn't like natural conversation where it was flowing quickly and you had to pick things up fast.* (AHP)
- *The audio is a lot easier to understand than a lot of hospitals ... And people don't speak in such neat sentences.* (D)
- *It's all actors, makes it very stilted. There's no variety really in what we are asking them to do.* (N)

Given the increasing online availability of real-world samples of lectures and other types of specialist interaction, test takers' judgements about the naturalness of test recordings are only likely to become better informed. It has become an important issue for listening test designers to demonstrate that the recorded material they employ adequately reflects some of the more important characteristics of actual listening events. There are implications for any test's ecological validity; there are also implications in terms of cognitive validity (how representative are the listening processes elicited from candidates when speech in a recording varies greatly in pace, rhythm and intonation from that of a real-world event?).

At present, intending candidates receive some rather mixed messages from the IELTS designers, who assure them (*Guide for Teachers*, IELTS 2018a:1) that 'test questions are based on authentic materials sourced from all over the world'. The unavoidable fact is that any attempt at drawing upon authentic sources is quite difficult to achieve in the case of sections like IELTS 1 and 2 which represent typical everyday exchanges. It is perhaps for this reason that the first source of ideas for recorded content suggested in the IWGs (2016:10–11) consists of *written* material in the form of information leaflets and internet sites aimed at the general public; the suggestion is even made that it may provide material for Sections 3 and 4 as well as the first two. To be fair, other more relevant sources are subsequently mentioned: namely, 'recordings and transcriptions of talks and interviews', 'online materials' and 'real-life events such as lectures, seminars, talks or conversations'. However, much of the emphasis in what follows is on the need to adapt and edit these original sources. It is only at the end that item writers are exhorted to make the text reflect features of natural spoken English, without specifics as to what might be required.

A review of recording scripts for the sample tests discussed earlier suggested that most of them were based upon written sources or had been specially written. This may be unavoidable in interactive contexts; but is harder to justify where sections aim to simulate lectures and seminars. As already noted, it can result in scripts which diverge markedly from the delivery of normal academic discourse or do not manage to pace information in the way an experienced lecturer might. To be fair, relying heavily upon written sources has long been common practice among test writers. As long ago as 2005, Salisbury reported that, of 10 experienced item writers studied, only one regularly used oral material as their point of departure, with the remainder often generating text from written sources such as magazine interviews.

An important additional consideration is the nature of the delivery. Close listening to the recordings that accompany the IELTS tests under review reveals that most show traces of their studio origin. They lack certain features of natural speech, including some of those identified by Gilmore (2004). Speaker delivery is noticeably fluent (few or no hesitations, false starts, fillers or pauses to plan content ahead). It tends to be shaped by punctuation on the page and to be regular in pace and rhythm.

Due allowance has to be made for the difficulties experienced by high-stakes test boards in getting permission to use authentic recordings of broadcasts etc. However, there are other expedients available for dealing with this situation. It makes sense to:

a. Include in IWGs some sample extracts from natural lectures to be studied as models (good models are to be found in the BASE corpus or Campbell and Smith 2012). These should ideally be accompanied by actual recordings which can be used as models when training writers.
b. Make much greater use of improvised lectures, where studio actors speak to a set of lecture notes or to PowerPoint slides.

c. Encourage item writers trying to replicate academic presentations or interactions to explore real-world spoken sources as their point of departure (the internet offers many freely available examples of natural presentations).
d. Persuade item writers to design their scripts for the studio (whether specially written or transcribed from authentic sources) in ways that represent the content as spoken rather than read-aloud material. Conventions might be adopted from the way in which discourse analysts transcribe speech: scripts can give guidance to voice actors on the location of utterance boundaries and on hesitation and planning pauses (+ for hesitation and clause boundary, ++ for long hesitation, +++ for a planning pause). Punctuation should be limited to question marks. Bold type can be used to mark words carrying focal stress. A reduced italic font can be used for asides. See the sample below from Field (2019:52).
e. Ensure that item writers are present at studio recordings to monitor how their scripts are delivered.
f. Ensure that voice actors maintain a normal speech rate to avoid an unnaturally slow speed of delivery.

> M: The first time + I realised I'd got a **problem** + was when I went along to a **college** ++ At that time I wanted to be a **plumber** + and they **said** to me + you need to go to **night** school + and they gave me a **pen** + and a **form** to fill in ++ That's when I **realised** + I went **what** does it say? + hey I **can't** + is there anybody that can **help** me? + they said **no** ++ so I said **no** I don't want to **do** this + I said I'm a man who works with his **hands** + I don't need this **night** school
>
> *B2 level semi-scripted.*

Visual support

Test providers have proved reluctant to embrace recent technological advances that have made video material much more widely available and supported by soundtracks of high enough quality for use in assessment. Intuitively, it would seem that video material is more representative of real-world listening. It provides a visible context for the speech event; it enables speakers to be identified physically; and it gives access to their gestures and facial expressions. The much-quoted McGurk effect (McGurk and McDonald 1976) demonstrates that phonetic judgements are influenced by lip movements; there is also neurological evidence (Green 1998) that visual information becomes integrated into the listening process at a very early stage. By contrast, audio material can represent only a small range of real-world circumstances (phone conversations, radio broadcasts).

Curiously, the evidence that visual information enhances L2 listening comprehension is more mixed than might be assumed. Sueyoshi and Hardison (2005) reported improved results from participants when they had sight of the speaker's face and gestures. By contrast, Coniam (2001) found no difference between scores on a video version of a test as against an audio one; strikingly, 80% of the video group reported that the visual support had not assisted their comprehension. Gruba (2004) also interviewed learners, this time after they had watched news clips; and concluded that visual information can bring benefits to higher proficiency listeners but potentially distract weaker ones. Yet another result was reported by Suvorov (2009), who directly compared performance on audio recordings with performance on recordings supported by still pictures and by video. The scores for the video-assisted material were significantly lower than those for the other two conditions. By contrast, in a study into using video tasks on English as a second languge (ESL) test taker performance, Wagner (2010) compared the performance of two groups of learners on an L2 listening test: one group was presented with video tasks while the other group received audio-only tasks. The video group were found to score 6.5% higher than the audio-only group, a difference which was statistically significant. Results suggested that the non-verbal information in the video texts contributed to the video group's performance.

Perhaps the best way of interpreting these conflicting findings is to envisage visual material as imposing increased cognitive demands upon the listener, who has to integrate an extra source of information into the mental model being constructed. This may be especially difficult for early-stage listeners, given (see above) their need to focus much attention on auditory processing. Recent research, some of which uses eye-tracking methodology, has sought to address the limitations of earlier studies and provides some interesting counter-points to orthodox beliefs about video in listening assessment (Batty 2018, 2021).

The situation is rather more clear-cut in relation to the use of *still images* to support comprehension. Research findings have generally supported Ockey's conclusion (2007:533) that listeners are not usually helped or motivated by these stimuli. Ginther (2002) cites evidence that test takers benefit from 'content' images which complement the information provided by the recording but not from others that just provide background context. This suggests that pictures of lecturers and students of the kind used in, for example, TOEFL iBT, probably do not assist the test taker or add significantly to the test-taking experience.

However, one important aspect of the still image merits closer and more sustained research interest in EAP contexts. This is the part played by PowerPoint slides during oral presentations. Competence in real-world lecture listening (whether in L1 or L2) includes a complex process of mapping between written words on a PowerPoint slide and the points that the speaker is making. This operation is not as easy for the aspiring L2 listener as it might appear. Most experienced lecturers avoid simply reading aloud what is shown on the slides. Instead, they use the text as a trigger to their own memory and then go on to paraphrase it and/or to elaborate on it. An important mark of academic listening competence is thus the ability to *map from written words to paraphrase and vice versa*. Yet this is something that is rarely if ever tested within tests, whether international or local. Some tentative evidence of the interaction between slides and voice is provided by an eye-tracking study by Suvorov (2015).

Long term, a move towards the use of video materials in listening tests seems likely, particularly where the tests in question are computer-delivered. A strong case can certainly be made in relation to tests of listening for academic purposes. The technology is now widely available to create a split-screen presentation that represents more closely the reality of the lecture context; indeed in recent times we have become familiar with this format for the transmission of live conferences. One might show, for example, PowerPoint slides on one side of the screen and the lecturer (complete with facial expressions and gestures) on the other. As computer-based testing becomes more common, this type of presentation seems likely to become more widespread and even the norm.

Speaker characteristics

Voice

An aspect of listening which tends to receive very little attention in the L2 literature is the process of adjusting to an unfamiliar voice – something that happens repeatedly if a test features several audio recordings. In their first language, listeners make rapid and highly automatic judgements about the pitch of an individual's voice, the speed at which they speak, the range of their pitch movements and the precision of their articulation (Pisoni 1997). This is a necessary first step in decoding what is being said. Improbable as it may seem, even the listener's ability to recognise the vowels of a language is heavily dependent upon early judgements about the fundamental frequency of the speaker's voice (Peterson and Barney 1952). Some idea of the important role that this process of *normalisation* plays in all speech events can be gathered from our extraordinary capacity to recognise speakers' voices when we hear them again, even those that have only been heard once or twice. For the effects of familiarity upon accuracy of processing, see Nygaard and Pisoni (1998).

Normalisation does not come as readily to listeners when the voices in question are using a second language, with its own distinctive pitch ranges and rhythms. The demands are even greater when the input is in audio form, with no visual information to help differentiate speakers. Two voices in a dialogue do not pose a major challenge to the test taker, especially if the convention is observed of making one male and the other female and they are clearly distinguished by pitch. But where there are three or more voices, the level of difficulty is inevitably stepped up – partly because of the need to distinguish speakers of the same gender, but also because of the demands of adjusting to multiple voices at the beginning of a recording.

The recorded material used in the IELTS Listening test covers monologues, dialogues and sometimes three-way exchanges. Normalisation is therefore much less of an issue than in some other tests. However, in view of the fact that only one play is permitted, item writers still need to make some allowance for the need to adjust to unfamiliar voices by avoiding questions which target (say) the first 15 seconds of a recording.

It is well established in auditory phonetics (Laver 1994) that word forms in connected speech are highly variable. Within a single speaker, they vary according to speaking style, context, speech rate, importance in the utterance and so on; they also vary between speakers of the same variety of a language, let alone between those who speak with different accents. Listeners thus need to store not a single form for each word but a set of variations. The most convincing cognitive account of how we achieve word recognition in L1 or in L2 suggests that it is an accretional process. *Exemplar theory* (Bybee 2001:Chap. 1, Goldinger 1997, Hawkins 1999:255–260, Nygaard 2008:405–408, Pisoni 1997) holds that listeners store traces of a range of different voices speaking at different times in different contexts and from them extrapolate points of reference that enable them to identify phonemes, syllables and whole words. In short, what is required to achieve word recognition (even within a single variety of English) is time and exposure. For a discussion in relation to L2 listeners, see Field (2014).

Speech rate

The speed at which a piece of speech is delivered is widely cited by L2 listeners as a major cause of processing difficulty. It will be recalled that in the Ingram and Bayliss (2007) study of predictive validity, the learners interviewed reported speed of speech and the use of colloquial expressions as obstacles to comprehension. In fact, the notion of fast delivery is somewhat of a simplification. Early work by phoneticians (Goldman-Eisler 1968) demonstrated that a major contributory factor in the impression of 'slow' vs 'fast' speech is the extent to which a speaker pauses. More frequent pausing (even of brief duration) serves an important function in marking out word boundaries in connected speech.

Commentators such as Calvert (1986:178) and Griffiths (1992) agree on a mean conversational rate across different speakers of around 200 words per minute (wpm) or 3.3 words per second. However, particularly in academic contexts, it is important to bear in mind that speech rate is often determined by the nature of the event and the role of the speaker. In this context, a study by Tauroza and Allison (1990) is often quoted, which records the mean speech rates in words per minute of different types of audio material: radio broadcasts (160 wpm), conversations (210 wpm), interviews (190 wpm) and lectures (140 wpm). Some caution has to be exercised about these categories, as they were rather loosely represented. Radio broadcasts included read-aloud news alongside monologues and documentary material, on the assumption that all three were scripted. Conversational material was not controlled for familiarity of interlocutors; and the lecture results were for lectures aimed at largely non-native speaker audiences. The result is that the rates are rather slower than one might recommend in a language test. That said, they provide a useful reminder of the way in which speech rate varies by genre and by speaker style. They illustrate two sets of conditions that determine speech rate across various types of academic discourse: monologue vs dialogue in terms of interaction and conversational to formal in terms of style.

The figures indicate that the monologue presentational material analysed by Tauroza and Allison (1990) was much more slowly paced than the dialogue conversational material. This is unsurprising: presenters and lecturers weigh their words, plan more carefully what to say and how to say it, deliver it in accessible intonation contours and do not have to respond to sudden interventions. Testers sometimes ignore this: they attempt to ramp up the difficulty of a recording for C-level learners by greatly increasing the speed of delivery without reference to what might happen in a real-world context.

The lecture-style tests in the IELTS sample were studio-recorded, but reflect an appropriate pace of delivery, with mean speaking rates (articulation + pauses) ranging from 158 wpm to 197. In this respect, they contrast markedly with some very fast-paced presentational material in samples from TOEFL iBT.

Accent

There is an apparent assumption in some L2 contexts (see e.g. Canagarajah 2006:237) that achieving a high level of listening competence enables an individual to decode speech in a range of varieties of English, including unfamiliar ones that may be encountered later on. Listening competence seems to be perceived as flexible, with skilled listeners readily capable of adjusting their processing in new directions in order to accommodate to unfamiliar patterns of speech.

These views of listening are unsubstantiated. It will be obvious that even L1 listeners sometimes find difficulty in adjusting to dialects among their fellow citizens that they have not previously encountered. There is ample research evidence of the effects of accent familiarity on general understanding. Major, Fitzmaurice, Bunta and Balasubramanian (2005) investigated how strongly accents of different degrees of familiarity (standard taught forms, regional and international varieties of English) affected comprehension by both native and non-native listeners. The results showed that the more familiar the accent, the better the level of understanding – an effect that was considerably greater in the case of the non-native group.

IELTS information documents (ielts-academic.com/2015/10/31/ielts-listening-english-accents) make clear that the recordings used in the Listening test employ a range of standard native-speaker accents, principally British, Australian/NZ, US and South African. The documents urge candidates to familiarise themselves with them by listening to material (e.g. broadcasts) which employs these varieties. This requirement seems not unreasonable at the levels targeted; but it is by no means as easy or as rapid as commentators sometimes assume to develop this familiarity. A large-scale project by Ockey and French (2016) found that unfamiliar international accents (British and Australian) impacted adversely on the comprehension of candidates studying for the mainly US-accented TOEFL Listening test. This study also demonstrated a significant correlation between accent familiarity and the score achieved.

A few researchers have investigated the effects of accent training. Floccia, Goslin, Girard and Konopczynski (2006) and Floccia, Butler, Goslin and Ellis (2009) monitored the gradual recognition by native English listeners of regional and L2 accents; and concluded that extensive exposure was necessary to ensure full adaptation. A study by Bradlow and Bent (2008), using L1 listeners and Chinese-accented varieties of English, suggested that listeners succeeded in generalising their accent training to new voices when they were exposed to multiple speakers; but not when they were exposed to a single one. A similar result was reported by Clopper and Pisoni (2004) in relation to regional varieties of US English.

Surveying the literature on L1 accent processing, Clopper and Pisoni (2008:327) conclude that 'representations [of accents] develop naturally through a person's experience with and exposure to [a speaker's] community and the world at large'. In short, there are two key elements in acquiring the ability to recognise words in an unfamiliar accent: exposure and time. This and other accounts appear to accord closely with the exemplar model of phonological and word acquisition (see the earlier discussion of voice), which represents the need for learners to lay down traces of a number of voices in order to achieve reliable word recognition.

It is important for both language instructors and test designers to be aware of this background. It would certainly appear possible during a relatively extended IELTS preparation course to introduce learners to sufficient examples for them to acquire some familiarity with standard versions of the four L1 varieties mentioned. They would also, of course, benefit from external exposure (particularly to US spoken English) through the media.

However, this leaves unaddressed the issue of local varieties. If the IELTS Listening test is to demonstrate the ability to follow lecturers in universities in (say) Scotland or Newcastle, should not the relevant local varieties also be included? The answer has already been given. It must not be assumed that accents can be understood by a simple conversion process. Featuring a distinctive L1 regional variety in a listening test also runs the risk of bias in that it favours candidates who by happenstance have encountered that particular accent or prepared for their examination in that area (see e.g. Taylor 2006, 2009b). Arguments in favour of exposing learners to a variety of L1 accents tend to confound two very different issues. One (particularly sensitive in Britain, where accent has social as well as regional associations) is the unacceptability of viewing one variety as 'correct' or 'prestige' and dismissing others as of lower standing. The other issue is the entirely distinct question of choosing an accessible and sufficiently widely dispersed variety of British or American English which can be used as a model for second language teaching and learning.

This kind of discussion inevitably leads on to the question of whether test content should acknowledge the role that English plays as a language of international communication. Is it not desirable to feature some non-native accents of English in a test such as IELTS, given that intending students will be mixing with others from overseas and almost certainly exposed to lecturers whose first language is not English? The view has been much aired recently and pressure put upon exam boards to include L2 accents in their recorded material. However, the issue has tended to be presented rather emotively (e.g. linked to avoiding L1 elitism), with little thought given to the practicalities (Elder and Davies 2006:296). Here are two concerns (Field 2019:60–63):

What is an L2 variety? The easy assumption is that it is a version of English with traces of L2 phonological features. But that fails to address a number of important variables. The precise form of English spoken by any L2 speaker must depend heavily upon: a) their level of proficiency and length of exposure to English; b) the L1 variety of English (American, Australian/NZ, British) that they have been taught; c) whether they have lived in an English-speaking community; d) which contexts they have used their English in. With this in mind, the idea that recorded material in a test can feature a 'representative' version of an L2 variety seems illusory. And that is without considering the possible impact of regional L1 varieties upon the way L2 English is delivered (European vs Brazilian Portuguese, Mexican Spanish vs Castellano).

Insights into Assessing Academic Listening: The Case of IELTS

Which L2 varieties should one choose in an international language test that is taken by L2 speakers representing a whole range of L1s? This is a complicated question, given the enormous number of Speaker L1–Listener L1 pairings that are possible[1]. A major issue is, once again, the possibility of test bias (Geranpayeh and Taylor 2008:4, Major, Fitzmaurice, Bunta and Balasubramanian 2002). In a large-scale international test, it is hard to avoid the likelihood that some candidates will be presented with a recording of speakers of their own L2 variety. There is also the likelihood that an L2 variety from a country adjacent to the test takers' own will be more familiar and easier for them to process than it would for candidates on the other side of the world. This question was addressed by Harding (2011), using L2 speakers of English rated as 'highly intelligible'. The results were mixed: there were strong effects of familiarity in relation to one of the nationality groups and one of the two recordings, but they were not consistent across all participants. Nevertheless, they echo results obtained by others (e.g. Major et al 2002) and are sufficient to raise concerns about the likelihood of bias.

Finally, when considering the role of accents in testing, it is important not to lose sight of the fact that any audio-based test of listening places considerable perceptual demands upon the candidate. As noted in previous sections, they have to normalise to a number of unfamiliar voices and variations in speech rate. By adding a wide variety of accents, the test designer considerably heightens the demands of the task. This is especially true when, as sometimes happens, a single dialogue features speakers of two different varieties, and the listener has to switch between the two.

Having argued strongly up to this point the case for selecting standard, so-called 'native speaker' accents in large-scale international tests of listening, such as IELTS, there are two further issues which may be worth considering in this regard.

First, it is certainly the case that not all EAP listening tests operate under the same set of constraints as IELTS or similar large-scale tests of English language proficiency. There are only a handful of big, international tests, but there are many more local/institutional EAP assessments (the developers of which may indeed be readers of this volume). This trend is likely to grow in the future as higher education systems develop at the national level and as language assessment expertise increases in more localised contexts. The specific practical constraints that guide IELTS development might therefore be contextualised as somewhat unique, rather than as the norm. If a locally developed EAP test, for example, is to be used in English Medium Instruction

---

1 Contrary to what is sometimes suggested, Jenkins' (2002) data does not provide a solution by specifying what features of L2 spoken English make it universally more or less intelligible. It is based on an extremely small set of paired participants, with no controls for the first language of speaker or listener.

(EMI) settings (such as Sweden or Lebanon), are British/Australian/US/Canadian accents still the most useful to include? There may indeed be room for more localised models of accent selection, and that approach is already being explored in practical and consultative ways (Motteram 2020).

Secondly, while practicality issues and constraints clearly cannot be ignored when it comes to making decisions about the inclusion of accented speech in L2 (or even L1) listening tests, there is clearly a growing body of useful research that is helping to advance our thinking and understanding in this area (see, for example, Dai and Roever 2019, Kang, Thomson and Moran 2019, 2020, Kang, Moran, Ahn and Park 2020, Shin, Lee and Lidster 2021). See also Ockey's chapter in Ockey and Wagner (Eds) (2018) investigating the extent to which strength of accent in recorded material can be reliably judged by L2 listeners.

The role of the recording

The major conclusion to be drawn from this chapter is that testers should never lose sight of the fact that it is the recorded material, not the script, which forms the input on which the test taker is assessed. Established practice within test development needs to acknowledge more widely that, alongside linguistic and informational content, phonological and phonetic aspects of the speaker's delivery play a major part in determining the difficulty of a recording. In practice, features such as speech rate or precision of articulation are often not monitored, partly because of a division of labour between the item writer, the test designer and the studio technician. It is good practice therefore to provide guidance within IWGs as to the kind of delivery that is to be required of the speaker. Similar instructions can then be added to the recording scripts produced by item writers, so as to assist the performance of studio actors.

When a test is in the course of being written, an item may appear to target very precisely what the writer has identified as a relevant point in the script. However, there always remains the possibility that this point will be downgraded in prominence by the speaker's delivery – making it harder for the test taker to detect and thus considerably increasing item difficulty. Before trialling a test, it is good practice to check items against recorded content, taking due account of the perceptual salience of the item keys within the recording and of any confusing signals provided by phenomena such as speaker back-channelling.

8 Checking understanding

Current conventions of delivery

A number of conventions are widely observed across L2 listening tests. While most of them can be regarded as inevitable by-products of the testing context, they potentially impact upon the cognitive validity of any test – i.e. the extent to which it manages to elicit listening processes from a candidate which resemble those that they will go on to employ in the real world. It is therefore worth examining them in relation to the specific populations targeted by IELTS. Some of the issues that arise were investigated by Field (2012a) and Badger and Yan (2012) when specifically considering the cognitive validity of IELTS Listening. What characterised both studies was that they included verbal reports elicited from test takers while actually taking a version of the test.

Questions in written form

Questions are conventionally presented in written form; and the comment is often made that this loads at least part of the test outcome on to reading skills. In fact, we have little alternative in current test conditions. The written form is durable in a way the spoken is not – candidates are able to look back and consult it. It would be unreasonable to ask them to commit 10 (or even five) spoken items to memory before listening; and it would engage memory effects if the spoken items were introduced afterwards.

However, the full implications of introducing a written component into a listening exercise are rarely considered. The fact is that a low-frequency word (e.g. a subject-specific term) is likely to be recognised more readily by an L2 user in written form than it would be in speech; it thus offers an important cue to what the speaker will say. In a real-world lecture, an important requirement upon any listener is the ability to map in the opposite direction: i.e. from subject-specific and possibly unfamiliar words used by a speaker to terms that have previously only been encountered in reading. Of course, against this, it can be argued that, in real-world lecture contexts, visual assistance of this kind is available to the listener in the form of handouts and PowerPoint slides. Perhaps a more important concern is that, when designing tests for higher proficiency levels, item writers quite often load the increment in difficulty on to the wording of the items (Field 2013) or (in the case of MCQs) on to fine distinctions between options. In this way the task becomes weighted even more heavily towards the candidate's reading skills.

Pre-set questions

In paper-based tests such as IELTS, it is common practice to provide candidates with a set of written questions *before* the recording is played, so as to provide advance warning of the information that is to be demanded of them. It is sometimes argued that this convention makes listening more purposeful in that candidates are not listening randomly. It also, however, leaves the way open to test-wise strategies, where listeners exploit the written content of the questions in order to second-guess what they will hear. They might, for example, identify key words among the items and listen out for those very words or for paraphrases in order to locate precisely where in the recording the answers occur. Drawing on candidates' verbal reports, Field (2012a:415) reports 'extensive evidence of participants adopting a procedure of matching information from the written task sheet against what was heard in the recording'. Even a successful candidate (8 out of 10 on a particular test) commented candidly: '*I mean my my method to + listen to to do the IELTS Listening + yeah I just look at the words not focus what it is about*'. This sharply distances the task from the type of activity that takes place during a real-world lecture.

Order of questions

Questions generally have to follow the order of points made in the recording. Again, there is a perfectly reasonable logic behind this. If there are 10 questions to be answered, it is patently unfair to require a candidate to listen out for a possible answer to any one of 10 at the outset and to mentally tick it off as recognised. However, the availability of this information provides the candidate in advance with a rough map of the recording and distances the task from the sort of discourse-building that would play an important part in real-world EAP circumstances. The sequencing of questions also imposes a little-acknowledged constraint upon how candidates behave. It would seem (Field 2012a:415–416) that they adopt a technique of holding up to three questions in their mind at any time in case the key to one of them is overlooked: '*er when I try to get this answer um + he he is already talking about the make cities cooler yes + so I missed the answer*'.

Rubric

In line with most other audio-only tests of listening (curiously, not PTE Academic), the IELTS format compensates for the lack of visual input and pre-established context by featuring an informative rubric in advance of listening (IWGs, 2018b:11–14). This identifies the topic, the situation and the speakers. The guidelines appear to have been quite closely adhered to in the sample tests that were examined. There then follows an instruction on how to handle the question format. An IELTS study by Coleman and Heap (1998) found that this last aspect of the rubric was generally clear and concise and led to few misunderstandings – except where the test format changed too often within a single section of the test, so that multiple instructions were needed.

Number of plays

Playing the recording twice is a well-established convention in many listening tests; but it remains a contentious issue. The principal argument in favour of this practice is that it compensates test takers for the fact that an audio presentation does not allow them the opportunity of seeing paralinguistic signals such as facial expression, gesture or lip movement or indeed the physical context in which the talk or conversation took place. There are also arguments related to (e.g.) the need for listeners to *normalise* to unfamiliar voices in the recording.

The current version of IELTS Listening allows candidates to hear the recordings only once. Several arguments are likely to have influenced the partners to adopt this format. They include:

- In the real world, a listener only has one opportunity to hear the speaker.
- Hearing a recording twice makes a test simpler and so advantages weak candidates.
- Double-play of listening material means a longer (potentially more costly) test.

The first assertion is not entirely true these days, given the playback facilities that exist for radio and TV programmes, university lectures, etc. Similarly, when a listener engages in interactive listening, there is usually the possibility of asking the speaker for clarification. Despite this, opponents continue to claim that the double-play convention reduces the difficulty of a test, and opinion remains divided as to its costs and benefits. A major concern is that weaker students may be unfairly advantaged if the recording is played twice. Thus, Henning (1990) reported that TOEFL scores from a single play discriminated better. However, this view has not been supported by subsequent evidence. Findings by Cervantes and Gainer (1992) suggest that learners benefit from a second hearing regardless of their level of proficiency; while data from Chang and Read (2006) suggests that higher-level learners benefit much more than lower-level ones (perhaps because of the latter's limited skills at a perceptual level).

There has been relatively little research on the effects of double play. However, a recent major study was undertaken by Ruhm et al (2016), involving over 1,250 low-level Austrian school learners and local tests. The recordings used were relatively short clips. Results on the shorter ones (25 seconds or less) generally showed an improvement on the second play; scores on the longer ones (over 60 seconds) sometimes increased and sometimes actually went down.

Like Ruhm et al, Field (2015) found that double play does raise scores but by a relatively small amount. Two approaches were employed. In one, participants were asked to listen to and answer a lecture-based section from a retired IELTS test which featured a particular test method (either MCQ or gap filling). They were not told in advance that they would be permitted a double hearing of the recording; but were allowed to assume that the task would follow the single-play format that is customary in IELTS. The second approach tested participants individually using the same tests, and asked them to provide verbal reports of the processes employed. On each play of the test, reports of their choice of answers and the reasons for any changes were elicited during pauses inserted in the recording. There was then a brief interview on the experience.

Results from the first group, operating under test conditions, indicated that scores for two-thirds of the population increased as a result of the second play, with only 27% whose scores remained unchanged. This confirmed similar findings by Berne (1995) and Cervantes and Gainer (1992). The study then went on to explore a number of issues concerning the increase in scores and the cognitive processes engaged:

a. *Does a second play mainly advantage candidates at particular levels of proficiency?*

The logic behind this question is that a low-proficiency candidate might not be able to decode a sufficient amount of the input to be able to make an informed response, even after hearing the recording twice. Conversely, a high-proficiency candidate might be able to obtain confident answers on a first hearing and not need to hear it again. In fact, level of listening proficiency proved not to be a factor. Scores were found to increase within each of three proficiency bands in a way that was roughly proportionate and that *heightened the distinctions between the bands*. Far from blurring the score differentials (for example, by unduly favouring weaker candidates), the effect of a double play was to increase them. However, there was a greater increase in the scores of middle-range participants, compared with others. This is of concern as this particular group may be at the borderline between refusal and acceptance for university study. One possible conclusion is that providing a second play might give these learners a greater opportunity to prove what they can achieve. Another might be that they are likely to struggle without some level of additional language support.

b. *Are certain test formats associated with greater score gains on a second hearing?*

In terms of score increases, candidates working with a constructed response format (gap filling) were assisted by a second play to a significantly greater degree than those working with a selective format (multiple choice). The result confirmed an earlier finding (Boroughs 2003). The major reason was that participants undertaking the gap-filling task achieved much lower scores after the first play, despite close parities between the two sample tests. The increase in scores after a second play thus derived largely from the very low base from which participants were operating. Rather than simply indicating that one format is greatly assisted by a double play while the other is not, it reflected the considerable cognitive and linguistic difficulty faced by test takers when choosing gap-filling responses on the basis of information obtained from a single play. The available evidence, in fact, seems to suggest that a second play is likely to increase scores regardless of test format.

c. *How does a second play affect test taker attitudes?*

When asked to compare the experience of a double play with an earlier test involving a single one, over 50% of the respondents freely volunteered the information that they felt less *nervous*, more *relaxed* or more *confident* when permitted a second play. Only three participants out of 36 (8.3%) reported little or no difference in their confidence level when undertaking the double-play test. It would seem that the availability of a second play serves to counteract listening anxiety in many test takers: permitting them to avoid some of the stress caused by the real-time nature of the recording or by the complex demands of the task.

d. *Do test takers behave differently when there is the possibility of two hearings?*

Both verbal reports and interview data suggested that the input was processed differently during the second play when compared to the first. In the most commonly adopted procedure, participants located provisional answers to questions during the first play; then checked them during the second, or sought missing answers or words that had been missed or misunderstood. A major factor shaping these processes (one mentioned by two-thirds of the participants) was the greater familiarity of the material during the second play. It would seem that a second play also enables test takers to engage in a type of listening that suffers from fewer of the local constraints associated with finding answers to questions; and approximates a little more closely to behaviour in a real-world presentational or broadcast context. This picture of what occurs during double-play listening largely supports the findings reported by Buck (1990) who suggested that the first play was characterised by more local listening while the second was more global.

The costs and benefits of double play are thus considerably more nuanced than earlier discussions have suggested. While the old arguments about the ecological validity of allowing a listener to hear a piece of speech twice remain to some extent relevant, one should perhaps weigh against them a factor that has been relatively little considered in the literature. The tasks set in tests of listening (MCQ, gap filling etc.) require the candidate to undertake a process of *checking or matching information*. This type of activity is an artefact of the testing situation (Field 2013:127) rather than a characteristic of real-world listening to a lecture or seminar. Indeed, these formats greatly increase the cognitive demands upon the listener. An investigation of the cognitive validity of the IELTS test (Field 2012a) found that nearly a third of participants reported a free note-taking task to be easier than answering formal questions, despite the cues that those questions provided.

Computer-based testing

Increasingly, national and international tests of listening are made available in computer-delivered as well as paper-based formats. The advantages of a computer-based testing (CBT) format are obvious: flexibility in the timing of tests, the possibility of reaching a much wider population, reduced costs. It would appear that the IELTS test designers have had this option in mind for some time. The first trials of a computer-based version of IELTS took place in 2001 and showed little effect of test format upon performance (Thighe, Jones and Geranpayeh 2001). Further trialling then took place in 2003, when candidates took both paper- and computer-based versions of the test, without knowing which would contribute to their final scores. In this second round, a strong correlation was found between Listening scores under the two conditions (Blackhurst 2005). The correlation coefficient for Listening (.764) was higher even than that for Reading; and there was found to be a 66.13% agreement in scores within a half IELTS band and an 88.17% agreement within a whole one. Reliability (Cronbach's alpha) was also actually higher for Listening at 0.893 than for Reading (0.816). In short, Listening results appear to be closely comparable regardless of the type of delivery.

The material used in these trials obviously needed to be identical across conditions (paper vs computer) in terms of the items and test methods used. However, it should not be overlooked that, in the case of Listening, CBT delivery offers the possibility of dealing with some of the problematic aspects of the test conventions discussed in the preceding sections, and thus increasing a test's construct validity. Critically, whereas test items on paper have, for logistical reasons, to be made available before the test takes place, computer delivery enables control over the point of presentation. This enables a test designer to sidestep the problem of providing candidates with extensive advance information in written form. In a single-play condition, a possible approach is to stop the recording after (say) each third has been heard, then to allow the test taker time to answer up to three on-screen questions before resuming listening. This replicates to some extent the real-world process of building up a mental model with limited preconceptions apart from those supplied by the rubric. By contrast, the single-play TOEFL iBT takes advantage of computer delivery by presenting up to six four-option multiple-choice questions after the entire recording has been heard (ETS 2007). This is open to question: posing so many questions post-hoc makes the task heavily dependent upon the test taker's short-term memory for what has been heard.

CBT presentation adapts especially well to a double-play format. Questions can be withheld until the pause between the two plays, and answers are only required during the second of them. An approach of this kind represents a major advance over the traditional pre-presentation. It eliminates the use of test-wise strategies, where candidates create expectations about what they will hear on the basis of items seen in writing. It also reduces the construct-irrelevant demands of committing a number of test items to memory in advance of listening. It enables test takers to listen, on a first pass, in a way that resembles much more closely the type of listening that takes place in real life, without the unnatural pressures of having to locate answers to questions. It thus encourages candidates to process the content of the recording in a way that takes account of wider issues at discourse level rather than simply local facts. In addition, the approach provides the listener with the opportunity of normalising to the voices in the recording before listening more carefully on a second play to check understanding. Interestingly, Sherman (1997) reports that presentation of questions between plays led to better candidate performance than presenting them pre-play.

CBT also permits an adventurous solution to the issue of whether to permit a double play or not, by leaving it up to the individual test taker. This approach is especially useful in tests that, like IELTS, cover two or more proficiency levels; it was adopted, for example, in the first version of the British Council's Aptis test. A weaker listener might take the opportunity to listen to a recording two or more times, whereas a stronger one would be capable of extracting answers on a single hearing and would advance faster. However, in order to ensure that the final score reflects this difference of proficiency, it may be necessary to measure the overall time taken by each candidate and factor it in to the scoring. Another caveat about this free-choice approach is that it takes no account of the test taker's personality. Far from reducing the pressure upon an individual lacking confidence, the decision-making on whether to replay or not seems likely to increase it.

CBT thus provides remarkable opportunities for increasing the construct validity of tests of listening and for overcoming some of the test-wise issues associated with current test formats. However, these opportunities also, of course, come with the drawback that, in processing terms, they serve to distance the computer-based version of a test from what is demanded by the paper-based one. This may make it difficult to sustain an argument for two different concurrent versions of the same test.

9 Test formats

Conventional formats

The most important formats used in tests of academic listening will now be reviewed – both in terms of how closely they elicit from the test taker processes that are comparable to those that would obtain in a real-world EAP context, and also in terms of their practicality and their impact upon reliability. The discussion of test formats covers the scoring validity of those items currently employed in IELTS Listening and there is also a brief overview of the internal consistency of the current test.

As before, the IELTS test will provide examples. In it, item writers are provided with a choice of formats at each level. A single section may feature two different formats. What is striking is the high prevalence of constructed response methods (indicated in italics). It seems to be left to item writers to ensure a balance between these and selected-response formats.

Table 8 Specified formats for the IELTS Listening test

Section 1	*Form completion – Table completion – Note completion*
Section 2	*Flow chart completion – Map/plan labelling*
	3-option MCQ – 5-option MCQ (2 correct) – matching
Section 3	*Flow chart completion*
	3-option MCQ – 5-option MCQ (2 correct) – matching
Section 4	*Note completion*

As noted earlier, the operations demanded of learners by these formats are highly specific to the testing context and may demand cognitive processes that are considerably more demanding than those that would apply in a real-world listening context. Selected response formats such as MCQ may make demands (sometimes heavy) on a test taker's reading proficiency, while constructed response formats like gap filling require raters to separate out evidence of comprehension from other features that reflect competence in reading or writing. Field (2012a:410–412) found relatively weak non-significant correlations between the ability to answer questions in an IELTS Listening test and the ability to accurately report the content of a recording without any such questions. He reports on one participant with a previous

IELTS Listening score of 5 who was, however, able to deliver an extremely detailed and accurate account of the recorded content.

There follow brief comments on the strengths and drawbacks of the formats most employed by current tests of academic listening. Though IELTS Listening provides convenient examples of the relative strengths and drawbacks of test formats, similar observations could be made about the formats employed in many other listening tests in the marketplace used for academic purposes.

- **Multiple choice.** The MCQ format has important advantages in terms of ease of computer marking and familiarity. However, it is important not to overlook its well-documented limitations (Freedle and Kostin 1999, In'nami and Koizumi 2009, Wu 1998). They include a heavy reliance upon reading items that may be quite complex and finely discriminated; and the provision of written information about the recording (some of it potentially misleading) in advance of listening. Often overlooked is the fact that the MCQ format requires the test taker to perform an operation that is considerably more cognitively demanding than what would happen in real-life listening. We tend to assume that the sole goal of the test taker is to identify the correct option out of three or four; but self-report protocols show that test takers feel themselves obliged not simply to seek a match for the correct option but also to disqualify the incorrect ones.
- **Gap filling.** Gap filling (form completion, table completion, note completion, map or diagram completion) might appear to be an ecologically sound method in that it resembles the real-world academic process of note-taking. However, the fact is that the notes to be completed are not the listener's own but have to be read with some care. The test taker has to co-ordinate reading, writing and listening and to do so under pressures of time. This is not only a complex metacognitive operation; it also runs the risk of divided attention effects (Pashler and Johnston 1998), with the test taker having to understand and produce written texts at the same time as listening. Field's study of experiences during the IELTS Listening test (2012a) provides testimony to the challenges faced by the test taker. On the other hand, gap-fill also provides candidates with a great deal of quite specific information about the content of the recording, before they have even heard a word. Field points out (2012a:413–414) that the type of note-completion task that features quite often in the lecture-based Section 4 of IELTS provides a strategically minded candidate with the following information before the recording is played:
    - An outline of what the lecture covers, with some lexical gaps
    - An indication of the order in which points will be made

- Key words by means of which to locate information
- Sometimes one constituent of a collocation

Relating this to the cognitive validity of the test, he comments that 'the candidate is not required to undertake certain critical meaning [and discourse] building operations that would normally play a central part in lecture listening'.

- **Multiple matching (MM)**. An advantage of this format is that the options given can be brief, thus limiting the quantity and complexity of the written material that the listener has to process. In addition, items do not need to follow the order of their mention in the recording. However, the listener has instead to hold a series of propositions in the mind which can occur in any part of the recording (or even not occur at all) and to match them against supporting evidence. Multiple matching therefore risks drawing upon competencies which fall beyond the listening construct and which relate to the test taker's working memory and ability to manipulate information. To deal with this potential problem, it may be desirable to limit the number of the options to be matched and to contemplate a second play of the recording.

A mix of task types is clearly desirable in any academic listening test. Standard language testing formats often draw upon cognitive skills (e.g. decision-making or holding multiple options in one's mind) that are independent of listening. Test takers vary markedly in the extent to which they possess these skills, so using a variety of formats eliminates the possibility of bias against those with particular mental sets (Brindley and Slatyer 2002). A second advantage is that, while most formats provide prior information about the recording, they do so in different ways. Varying them means that test takers cannot fall back on a fixed set of test-wise strategies.

However, two reservations should be expressed about the way in which test designers vary the formats they feature. Firstly, Coleman and Heap (1998) produced evidence quite some time ago that too many changes of format within a particular section of a test may lead to confusion on the part of the test taker[1]. In cognitive terms, the reasons can be easily understood: the test taker not only has to internalise a set of written points to be matched against the recording but at the same time has to take on board the varied ways in which they are presented and in which they have to respond.

---

1 They even mention (1998:63) a version of the IELTS Listening test in which there were four changes of format across eight questions.

Despite this, there seems to remain a tradition within IELTS practice of consistently switching test formats within the various sections of a test. In four retired tests examined (source: *IELTS 7*), three had one section that featured three different formats while the fourth had two such sections. Also of concern was the fact that in three cases (Test 2: Section 2, Test 3: Section 3 and Test 4: Section 3) a particular format was used for only two items before the test taker moved on to a new one. It is quite difficult to see the rationale behind this. It would probably be fairer to the test taker to switch formats between rather than within sections – or at least to restrict the formats used to a maximum of two.

The other reservation relates to the combination of formats that are used in a particular test. A recommended set of task types for each section is listed in the IELTS IWGs (2018b:6). It would appear that the choice of which from the list to use is left to the item writers, with no subsequent controls to ensure a balance between the formats that feature. The figure below (based upon the four sample tests) shows the considerable extent to which gap-filling tasks of various kinds are favoured over others – perhaps because of the ease with which they can be linked to keys within the recording. The figures are out of 40 items per test.

This is quite a serious issue worthy of further consideration. From a cognitive perspective, it is important for test designers to be sensitive to the fact that different tasks elicit different types of listening process; it would certainly be good practice to take account of this notion in item writer training. Certain selected-response formats, including MCQ and multiple matching, enable an item writer to tap into quite a wide range of functions: they can focus equally on local factual information, main point, inference, speaker attitude, links at discourse level and argument structure. This advantage is especially important at the higher levels targeted by an academic listening test. By contrast, the gap-filling format (however much it might be favoured for its loose resemblance to academic note taking) encourages item writers to target information at a local level, thus limiting the range of processes that can be represented. The method is particularly associated with processing at the level of the word – understandably, because it is word-level information that test takers have to provide in their answers. As Field (2013:131) concludes after analysing the content of sample tests in the Cambridge English Qualifications: 'The sentence frame may well paraphrase information from the text, but the words to be inserted are often to be taken verbatim from the recording and rarely from a larger unit than a lexical chunk'. See Buck (2001:82) for a similar comment. The issue will be revisited in Chapter 10 when considering test items, and it could perhaps be argued this is a test specification issue as well as an item writer training matter.

Figure 2 Formats across four sample IELTS tests

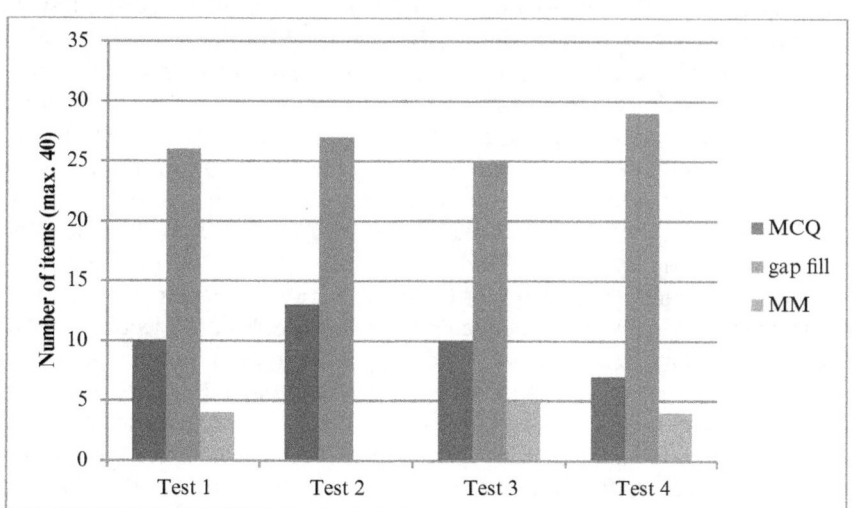

A note on scoring and scoring validity

Scoring validity within the socio-cognitive framework refers to the scoring system for any test, in terms of how test scores are arrived at (i.e. scoring criteria and marking approaches) and how reliable test results are for decision-making purposes.

As noted above, the IELTS Listening test uses mostly *selected-response* items, with a small number of items that are closer to a *constructed response* format, where the candidate is required to respond in up to three words. Selected-response formats are widely referred to as 'objective' to differentiate them from constructed responses which are dependent upon raters' judgements. However, one has to be cautious in applying the notion of objectivity too closely in any test of listening. The score obtained derives ultimately from subjective choices made by the item writer when determining which points of information to target and what questions to ask about them. Where (say) only seven major points of information can be easily identified out of the 10 that are required, they may even find it necessary to target peripheral points that a competent listener might normally skip.

For the multiple-choice and multiple-matching formats in IELTS, the test taker chooses the correct letter, word or number from a range of options given. In the case of a gap-filling format (e.g. form completion, table completion, note completion, map or diagram completion), the test taker provides a response of up to three words which may be penalised if poor or incorrect spelling or grammar is present. This raises the interesting question of whether or not awareness of correct spelling and grammar can justifiably be included as part of the marking criteria for a test of listening comprehension. One practical argument in support of this policy is that it helps to ensure marking consistency. Another might be that it is not unrealistic to expect correct spelling and grammar in a fairly high-level test of English proficiency designed to test communicative skills.

Centralised marking of the IELTS Listening test paper is undertaken on-screen by a team of trained markers and examiners, using MarkManager software. Markers are trained to understand the marking policy and required to demonstrate that they are marking to standard before they are accepted. Systematic monitoring and double marking of a proportion of answer sheets is carried out at each administration. Markers also undergo a re-certification process every two years to ensure that their marking is up to standard.

As mentioned at the outset, the IELTS Listening test contains 40 test items and every correct answer is awarded one mark. Scores out of 40 are then converted to the IELTS nine-band scale and these are reported in whole and half bands. Reliability of IELTS Listening is reported using Cronbach's alpha, a reliability estimate measuring the internal consistency of the 40-item test. Listening test material released in 2021 had sufficient test taker responses across 16 test versions to estimate and report meaningful reliability values between .877 and .932, with an average across all versions of .917.

The issues of test reliability and comparability across versions are obviously addressed with some care by test providers. But there is a limit to what even the most finely tuned statistical analysis can tell us. There are usually too many variables in a typical listening test for a commentator to say with entire confidence 'this low-scoring item entails demanding listening' and 'this high-scoring item is easy'. While some variations do indeed reflect the nature of the listening construct, others may be by-products of the method used, the questions asked and the relative importance and perceptual prominence of the information targeted. Statistical analysis may sometimes show up an item as too demanding for the level for which it has been designed; but it may simply be that a subset of test takers at that level have not fully mastered one of the basic processes that one might expect at that level (e.g. identifying the main point or reporting the speaker's goals).

10 Test items

Obviously, the wording of an item has to be unambiguous, transparent and within the assumed linguistic repertoire of the test taker. Some other familiar aspects of item design will be briefly reviewed, with particular reference to the academic context.

Issues of item design

Item length and complexity. Faced with the challenge of designing tests of sufficient difficulty for candidates at high CEFR levels, item writers sometimes resort to increasing item length and complexity. However, care needs to be taken with this expedient; the effect is often to increase reading demands without necessarily increasing the demands of listening. This comment particularly applies in the case of multiple-choice items, where there is a tendency for options to become longer as one moves up the proficiency scale (Field 2013:140), for them to become much more finely differentiated, and for a three-option MCQ to be replaced by a four-option one. This does, to be sure, increase the cognitive demands imposed upon the test taker; but they are cognitive demands created by the written input that the individual has to process rather than by the content of the recording.

A review of the retired IELTS tests used for this discussion suggests that, in general, the item writers involved were remarkably resistant to the temptation to increase the length and complexity of items at higher levels. This is particularly noticeable with multiple-choice questions, where the options are usually kept relatively short and propositionally distinct. It is standard practice in the IELTS Listening test to make use of three-option rather than four-option multiple choice, thus reducing the attentional resources that have to be committed to reading.

Item density. Keys that respond to items need to be quite widely spaced to counter-balance the unnatural situation whereby the items in a test provide the listener in advance with pieces of information that are to be matched against information in the recording. Dividing the duration of the recording in seconds by the number of items to be answered provides an indication of how intensive or well distributed are the responses required. Even so, there are more complex considerations. A combination of a *short recording* and *multiple items* increases the load upon the test taker because of the need to assemble answers under pressure of time. But a combination of a *longer recording* and relatively *few items* also does so since the recording provides many more points of information to choose between as possible item matches. General practice across tests seems to be to extend text length at higher proficiency levels rather than item density (Field 2013:139). Items in the IELTS samples appear well enough spaced to allow test takers to internalise their content, match it to the recording and identify a response. This is obviously important where only a single play is allowed.

Lexical overlap. A little-discussed factor determining an item's relative difficulty is the extent to which its wording follows that of the recording. This potentially provides the candidate with an easy indicator of where in the recording an answer is to be found – and thus rewards the type of strategic 'key word' technique that crammers are all too prone to recommend. To be sure, item writers often go to some lengths to paraphrase the speaker's words – a precaution particularly important in relation to constructed formats such as gap filling (Brindley and Slatyer 2002, Freedle and Kostin 1999). Even so (as already noted), gap-filling items conventionally follow the sequence of the main points in a recording, so that the constraints of the format still serve to provide some kind of written skeleton of the text in advance of listening.

Though paraphrase is widely used when formulating items, the IELTS materials sampled here quite often included instances with one or more of the key words appearing in both item and recording. Sometimes, the words serve as one-to-one keys to be reproduced in a gap-fill answer; sometimes, content they provide signposts to relevant information. Occasionally a complete phrase or clause from the spoken input is repeated in the written response. This renders the items in question easier than they might at first glance appear and it might be interesting to explore in a research study the degree to which test takers notice such occurrences and act on them.

Item targeting

In many L2 language tests, the test specifications and IWGs rely on very general behavioural goals. The result is that, in practice, items are often simply linked to pieces of factual information that offer obvious targets. One way of aligning test demands more closely to the real-world listening construct is by means of *item targeting* (Field 2013:136–139, 2019:87–91, 97–98) – i.e. designing items with a view to eliciting specific processes that are known to contribute to skilled listening. Items can be designed that target each of the five operations in the model of listening presented in Chapter 6 (decoding, lexical search, parsing, meaning construction, discourse construction). They can also be graded in terms of what a particular level of proficiency allows a candidate to achieve: e.g. by focusing principally on perceptual processes at lower levels and meaning-based ones at higher. As well as determining the content of an individual test, IWGs should perhaps specify the number of items in any version of the test that target particular types of process. This ensures greater comparability between different versions.

Here, a brief terminological explanation is called for. It is self-evidently wrong to assume that a given item draws upon a single level of processing. For example, one that tests a listener's ability to form an inference obviously has to rely upon other processes (input decoding, lexical search and parsing). If reference is made here to an item 'targeting' a particular type of processing, it relates to the highest level (on a gradient from decoding to discourse construction) at which the item is aimed.

We should expect tests at higher proficiency levels (particularly those aimed at an academic population) to elicit a variety of the more demanding processes which underlie meaning and discourse construction. They include (Field 2019:89):

- *Meaning construction*: placing a piece of information in a wider context, identifying the relative importance of a piece of information, noticing the connectives that link a speaker's points, interpreting speaker attitude, drawing inferences where a speaker is not explicit, inferring pragmatic and stylistic information, inferring links between a speaker's points, resolving anaphoric reference
- *Discourse construction*: linking new information to preceding, reporting the main point of a recording, distinguishing major and minor points, recognising signals of a change of topic, recognising the overall line of argument, reporting the speaker's overall goals, noticing inconsistency, evaluating the strength of the speaker's arguments

Field (2019:97–98) provides the following examples of processes that should if possible be elicited from candidates if a test is to adequately represent the academic listening construct:

- identifying the current main point;
- judging whether a new piece of information is central, secondary or irrelevant;
- distinguishing macro-propositions from micro-;
- linking points of information (especially where the links have to be inferred);
- integrating new information into a developing discourse representation;
- monitoring the developing discourse representation for consistency;
- building an overall discourse structure which represents the lecturer's line of argument.

Test items

To these can be added the ability to process certain discourse types: correctly identifying speaker opinions, attitudes, intentions and conclusions.

Item targeting and the IELTS test

In an early cognitive validation exercise, Field (2013:137–139) attempted to assess how closely the tests of the Cambridge English Qualifications tap into the various processes that constitute listening. The approach adopted was to match the keys that were targeted against the five phases of listening identified in Chapter 6. In effect, the challenge to the candidate was classified as phonological, lexical, factual, employing contextual meaning or covering an extended pattern of discourse. The sample was a small one; but the change in processing demands across different levels was found to conform to a clear developmental pattern. For example, at A2 and B1 levels, the focus was entirely on perceptual processes (decoding, lexical search and parsing).

Two unexpected findings are worth mentioning in relation to higher proficiency levels.

a. There were lexical-level targets at all levels, even at C2. Field concluded that this seemed to be a by-product of widespread use of the gap-filling format, which requires word-based responses that may sometimes be taken verbatim from the recording.
b. At Level B2, there were items requiring meaning construction (i.e. inference and interpretation of speaker intentions), and also some more demanding items requiring the test taker to connect information across a speaker's entire set of turns (i.e. to engage in summative analysis at discourse level). Curiously, items of the latter kind were entirely absent at Cambridge Advanced level (C1), though well represented in tests at Cambridge Proficiency level (C2). This suggested that discourse-level processing is sometimes largely or wholly overlooked in major tests.

A similar exercise was conducted in relation to the four sample IELTS tests that have been discussed here. The nature of the key was classified in terms of whether it was a) lexical, b) factual, c) indicative of speaker meaning or attitude or d) related to a wider discourse pattern. An additional step was to examine the extent to which the test items did or did not provide verbatim cues as to where in the recording the relevant information occurred. Across the set of 160 items, three major categories emerged:

- *Lexical + verbatim*: a lexical-level key recognisable in the recording a) because the same word or phrase occurred in the item or b) because the item included words from the recording that provided a reliable clue to where the information was located.

- *Lexical paraphrase*: a lexical-level key which has to be processed as a paraphrase at word or phrase level of what appeared in the item.
- *Fact + fact inference*: a propositional-level key based on retrieving from the recording a complete unit of information that constituted an item paraphrase.

These categories were derived by means of a grounded approach to the samples; and one can argue about how watertight they are. However, they do provide insights into the different types of elicited information that feature across the four tests; see Figure 3 below.

The most striking discovery was that the material targeted by the items did not extend beyond single units of factual information. Though some of the items were demanding because of the type of paraphrasing that they contained, none of them appeared to tap into the more demanding processes identified in the previous section. No item was found that clearly required the listener to undertake any type of meaning construction other than the conventional operation of mapping from paraphrase to text. Nor was there any type of discourse construction that engaged anything more than a discrete unit of information. In sum, apart from the extraction of facts, these general tests of listening did not elicit many of the higher-level processes that might be expected to play a critical role in competent listening in an academic environment. This is presumably of less concern in the general Sections 1 and 2 of the IELTS test; but the same lack of opportunity to elicit meaning interpretation and engage in discourse assembly was also to be seen in the 'academic' Sections 3 and 4.

Figure 3 Item targets

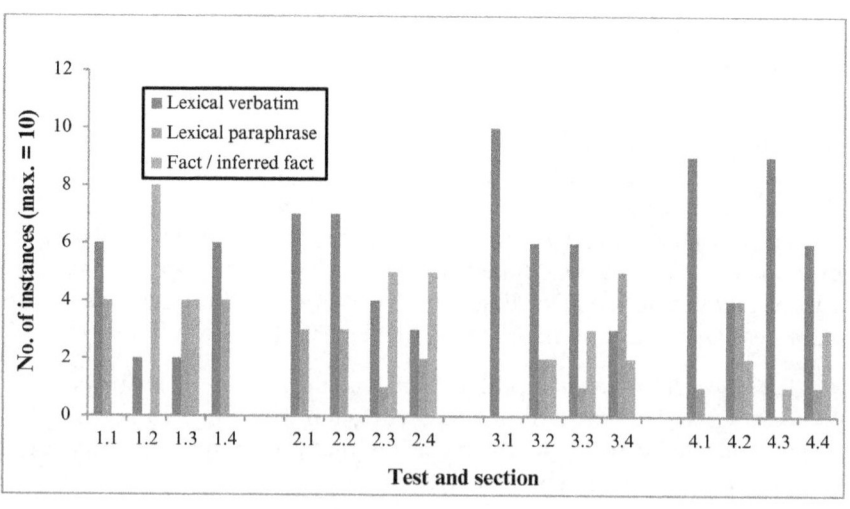

To be fair, the IWGs do actually mention (2018b:6) some of the processes that characterise academic listening: 'Listening for detail and stated opinion', 'Listening for opinion/attitude/feeling – directly stated or implied', 'Identifying relationships between ideas', 'Identifying agreement/disagreement between speakers – directly stated or implied', 'Listening for main idea, detail and stated opinion'. However, the importance of these specifications has perhaps not been prominently enough signalled to item writers and they have therefore not always been followed in practice. Field was more accurate than perhaps he realised when he offered the generalisation (2019:98) that: 'Processing at the levels of meaning and discourse is often curiously under-represented in the testing of L2 academic listening. Item writers tend to focus on interesting points of information, with the consequence that their items target a string of isolated facts, without requiring test takers to report the wider argument that links them'.

Granted, the IELTS sample quoted was a small one and the tests in question were retired ones from several years ago. But the problem must be viewed as systemic to testing at this level in that it is without doubt a by-product of the very extensive use of gap-fill formats within tests of academic listening. These formats may appear to loosely replicate certain academic activities such as note-taking; but, as already noted, their chief limitation is that they focus the listener's attention at lexical level, or at best elicit single facts. A strong case can be made for restricting the use of gap-filling tasks in academic Listening papers precisely because of their narrow frame of reference. For all their unfortunate reliance on the reading skill, the multiple-choice and multiple-matching formats have a far greater degree of flexibility in terms of the type of processing at which a question can be aimed. Alternatively, one possible way of adapting the conventional gap-fill to fit academic needs more closely is to present the task in the form of a 'Table of Contents' outline of the recorded material, in which occasional headings or sub-headings are provided. Test takers can be asked to supply the missing entries – in effect building a summary of what they have heard and showing how accurately they have been able to trace discourse-level patterns of argument.

In sum, it is advisable to considerably raise the profile within any set of IWGs of the processes that are central to academic listening (Field 2011). This might take the form of concrete examples of the types of question that can be asked, so as to shift the focus away from the word and the single information unit. Suggestions might even be made as to how many items in a test should target a given process; this would ensure consistency between versions of the same test. These steps are necessary if tests are to demonstrate that they do indeed assess actual preparedness for listening in an academic domain rather than simply the ability to extract random facts from a recording.

Footnote: Are the targets necessarily met?

A case has been put for designing test items that aim to elicit particular listening processes from test takers; but how sure can we be that these items do indeed produce the expected outcome? In some cases, the target can be clearly specified as part of the question: *What is the main point? What is the speaker's attitude? What is the connection between [flooding] and [house building]? What two reasons does the speaker give for believing that ...? Fill in the missing parts in this summary.* In other cases, one has to be certain when trialling test material that the wording of a question has been correctly interpreted and/or that the item writer's intention has been realised in the behaviour adopted by the candidate. This might particularly relate to items where the candidate is required to form an inference on the basis of evidence in the text or to infer an unexpressed connection between two pieces of information.

All of this signals the need for an additional strand in the process of trialling academic tests: one where we do not simply fall back on statistical evidence but try to tap into what is going on in the mind of a test taker when faced with a draft set of items. Obtaining this kind of evidence is neither easy nor always 100% reliable; but it can provide valuable insights into test taker behaviour. It also enables insights into (e.g.) the use of test-wise strategies that thwart the intentions of the item writer. An obvious method for checking whether items are hitting their targets (and more generally for investigating test taker behaviour) is to obtain verbal reports. This kind of approach to validating the content of a text can provide useful insights into test behaviour (see the cognitive reviews by Badger and Yan (2012) and Field (2012a) of the IELTS lecture-listening module). A recent example of verbal reports used to investigate whether specific items do or do not elicit expected behaviour can also be found in a study of the Aptis Listening test by Holzknecht et al (2017).

Section 3
General applications and conclusions

In this final section of the volume, Chapter 11 explores the practicality and scoring implications of employing tests of academic listening that link the skill to productive outcomes in speaking and writing, while Chapter 12 outlines the main points that have emerged in analysing IELTS and other widely used tests of academic listening. Hopefully, these chapters lay the ground for others to consider possible future directions that the testing of academic listening might take and especially the role of technology in this endeavour.

11 Integrated skills: The way ahead?

One of the major differences between IELTS and some of the other tests used for university admission nowadays is that its Listening test focuses solely on the target skill. TOEFL iBT, PTE Academic and OET all feature integrated-skills activities alongside more conventional tasks. This raises the question of whether at some point in the future other test boards and/or EAP tutors should follow suit when testing L2 listening. The rationale might be a) that this increases ecological validity (in that integrated-skills tasks resemble, at least superficially, those that commonly occur in academic contexts); and b) that it increases cognitive validity (in that listening in real-world academic contexts often has to be combined with other skills, including note-taking).

Cumming (2013) reviews the arguments for and against integrated-skills testing. He points to the value of simulating 'the cognitive, communication, and literacy demands of real-life academic or vocational tasks'. Alongside these more obvious authenticity arguments, he also draws upon theories of communication that would appear to endorse the approach and argues that it potentially counters some of the flaws of conventional test formats. On the other hand, he frankly acknowledges that this format produces major headaches for testers in terms of measurement, test design, and candidate performance.

In a general review of the research literature on integrated writing, Cumming, Lai and Cho (2016) identify several issues which have empirical support but need further investigation. One is that L2 students do indeed experience difficulties with the process of integrating sources into a piece of writing; but that with practice and training they can develop strategies to deal with them. The research has indicated marked differences between L2 and first-language students in terms of their understanding of how to make use of sources. (Here, a big issue must surely be whether these differences derive from educational culture or from language limitations.) In addition, with relevance to test design, the nature of the tasks that are set when candidates are both sourcing and producing texts appears to have an important effect upon performance. In a companion volume to this volume, Weir and Chan (2019) provide a useful discussion in Chapter 8 of the use of reading-into-writing tasks to assess academic reading skills. They look closely at the nature of reading-into-writing and how it is different from reading comprehension in general. They go on to argue that the reading-into-writing task type could improve the cognitive validity of an academic reading test such as IELTS, specifically because it is capable of eliciting higher-level reading processes.

In contemplating possible revisions to more conventional formats such as the IELTS one, a first consideration must obviously be the effect of mixed-skills testing on score reporting. Combining listening with another skill inevitably reduces the extent to which one can testify confidently to a candidate's listening proficiency alone. This may seem subsidiary when weighed against the need to demonstrate a candidate's ability to engage multiple skills in a real-world context. But accepting institutions often depend heavily on such evidence in the form of a skill-specific IELTS score when determining how to plan remedial practice for L2 students on pre-sessional courses. In addition, the issue of domain specificity arises again. The precise mixture of skills in a real-world academic context and the way in which they are integrated may vary considerably according to the discipline that the individual proposes to study. They may also vary as between academic and professional needs. To what extent, then, should a language tester be attempting to tap into this integrative behaviour; and to what extent should it be the domain of a study skills coach (maybe working within the target field of study)?

In terms of the type of listening that takes place in an academic context, the most obvious combination is 'listening into writing', reflecting the need to take notes in lectures and rework them later. Of concern here is that listening and writing are cognitively very complex but very different activities. The need to combine the two skills in this way must inevitably give rise to divided attention effects, with the candidate having to co-ordinate two modalities and three sets of processes (listening, note-taking and writing). As for scoring, how can a test designer provide descriptors that reliably separate out the multiple skills that contribute to these three operations? How to distinguish the candidate's ability to decode words and utterances in a spoken modality from their ability to render them accurately in a written one? To give an example, how should one treat evidence of unclear processing of discourse markers? Should it be assessed as a failure to trace a logical argument in the recording or a failure to use the right words to represent it?

Another relevant academic activity is integrating or comparing information from an oral source (e.g. a lecture) with information from a written one (study reading). Here, the compiled information might be tested by means of conventional comprehension questions that draw upon both sources. However, again there are cognitive concerns. There might well be memory effects if a time-constrained listening activity was followed by a time-rich reading activity. If note-taking were used to compensate for this, the candidate would then be switching between three skills and four operations. This task might well be felt to measure a degree of study-skill competence that, though relevant to an EAP candidate, goes beyond language-based performance.

A further configuration is 'listening into speaking', as currently featured in TOEFL iBT. This task (reporting orally in detail on the content of lecture-style material) does not seem to represent very closely the reality of academic experience. If a student needed to import information from a lecture into a class presentation, they would surely win few points by simply repeating point by point what had been heard. And there is a further scoring issue here. How to rate somebody who produced a version that repeated verbatim the language of the original without demonstrating clearly that it had or had not been understood?

With all these caveats in mind, the safest solution for testing specialists is perhaps to wait and see. Fortunately, there is a growing body of empirical research which seeks to explore and provide some answers to the sorts of questions highlighted above. In relation to use manipulation of content input, Frost, Elder and Wigglesworth (2012) conducted a discourse-based analysis to explore how test takers incorporated stimulus materials into their speaking performances on an integrated listening-then-speaking summary task, while Westbrook (2019) investigated the impact of audio versus video input on an integrated EAP listening-into-writing test. Rukthong and Brunfaut (2020) investigated the listening construct underlying integrated tasks with oral input (both listening-to-speak and listening-to-write), while Inoue and Lam (2021) examined the effects of extended planning time on candidate performance, processes and strategy use in the TOEFL iBT lecture listening-into-speaking tasks.

As the body of research literature in this area continues to grow, it is to be hoped that more sophisticated 'listening into ...' models will be developed in due course, and sets of well-constructed and proportionate descriptors to go with them. For the moment, the best one can say is that the versions of integrated listening tasks in current use do not seem to represent real-world processes of information transfer as closely as one might at first imagine. They seem likely to add to the cognitive demands that our present admittedly artificial formats impose upon the candidate, and thus to increase listening anxiety. And they give rise to ambivalent scores, which result in exam boards having to rely upon raters, rating scales and subjective assessments.

However, two important riders should be added to this discussion. The first is that the case as presented here relates specifically to listening. Clearly, a much more persuasive argument can be made for reading-into-writing tasks (Chan 2018, Knoch and Sitajalabhorn 2013) in that the two skills operate a) within the same modality; and b) under extended time periods which give the user some autonomy to plan[1]. The process of mapping directly from

---

1 Though test specifications might well control this by determining the relative amounts of time allowed for reading and for writing.

read text to written distillation is also one that resembles much more closely what might occur if (say) a student were writing an assignment in a library. This may explain why there has been quite a lot of research interest in the integrated processes involved in reading-into-writing (Weir and Chan 2019); but very little on how the more elusive listening and speaking skills interact with the written word.

The second point is that, while a convincing case has yet to be made for the suitability of integrated-skills formats for the testing of listening in academic contexts, there can be no doubt that the approach is highly appropriate to testing in many *professional* areas. One thinks particularly here of the comments of the medical professionals studied by Berry et al (2013) and Sedgwick et al (2016), who were of the view that the listening in which they engaged professionally was very much embedded in specific types of encounter (e.g. interactional and requiring a response, informative and requiring note-taking) and was not adequately represented by the tasks that feature in the IELTS test. Similar comments apply to the use of IELTS to test other types of professional (e.g. early years teachers, engineers) and to test the ability of an immigrant to integrate into the host community. In all these cases, it might be worthwhile to contemplate a role for integrated-skills formats that would more closely represent real-world contexts and real-world behaviour.

12 Summary of main recommendations and final remarks

The following recommendations and remarks draw upon the earlier review and discussion of IELTS and its Listening test. However, it is important to see the points made as having direct relevance to and implications for ALL listening tests which are used for academic or professionally oriented purposes, not simply IELTS.

The discussion can be framed against recent thinking to develop the original socio-cognitive framework which has guided the approach in this volume. In their recent volume entitled *Validity: Theoretical Development and Integrated Arguments*, Chalhoub-Deville and O'Sullivan (2020:155) revisit the socio-cognitive approach, stressing that:

> ... the development model (which addresses the test-taker model, the test model and the scoring model) and the measurement model must be fully integrated ... Test tasks should meet the expectations of the development model and the measurement model, if they are to offer meaningful estimates of ability.

Chalhoub-Deville and O'Sullivan present the socio-cognitive model as a set of 'integrated arguments', consistent with the contemporary argument-based approach to test validation (see Figure 12 on p.155 in Chapter 5 of their volume). The model combines attention to principled test design and development with a concern for test consequences as a primary consideration and a commitment to communication engagement with all relevant stakeholder groups. This final chapter summarises some general and specific recommendations within precisely this sort of framework of reference with a view to strengthening the validity argument that underpins tests of academic listening.

General recommendations

1. Stakeholders in general need to be better informed about the goals, administration and scope of academic tests of language proficiency if they are to successfully fulfil their roles of setting entry requirements and interpreting scores. The range of individuals regarded as in need of

assessment literacy should ideally be extended beyond EAP specialists and the wider teaching profession to include groups such as members of examination boards, academic administrators (institutional and departmental), professional gatekeepers, immigration authorities and policy makers (Murray 2016, Taylor 2009a). A good step towards communicating with this wider audience might be through accessible online tutorials about the content of such tests and what it aims to measure (cf. O'Loughlin 2012).

2. The specific importance of listening is recognised in some of the domains in which academic and professional tests are employed (e.g. Medicine) but the relevance of the skill seems to be undervalued in others. Stakeholders arguably need to be sensitised to the part played by the skill so as to assist them in setting entry criteria.

3. At present, reading and writing tend to be regarded as central to academic success and/or more accessible to conventional EAP assessment (hence the separate Academic and General versions of these tests in IELTS), whereas listening and speaking are not. This may reflect a traditional historical perspective on what constitutes 'academic literacy', which was envisaged primarily in terms of reading and writing skills. However, most academic contexts nowadays require high-level skills in listening and speaking competency as well. The 'academic literacy' tradition is perhaps partially responsible for the current IELTS Listening test, which seeks a blended solution by including general material targeted at B1 and B2 levels plus academic material targeted at C1. This makes some sense if the B1+ level is seen as a departure point for academic/professional study; the test needs to contain some items at this level, given that it is a key area for decision-making. Evidence has been quoted suggesting that the test does not discriminate quite as well at B2/C1 levels, that the easier general sections may inflate scores and that users of the test, both professional and academic, regard it as easy and only loosely related to their area of interest. In terms of both construct validity and the test's future reputation, possible solutions would be that:

    a. it might be divided into at least two versions: one General and one Academic (the first to be used for immigration purposes and the second for educational);
    b. it might be made clear to those using the test for professional gatekeeping that it serves only as a seeding stage in accreditation and should be supported by further tests which reflect the content and the types of interaction that characterise the profession in question.

Summary of main recommendations and final remarks

It was suggested here that, given the expertise of the IELTS partners, they might offer to support stakeholders in the development of domain-specific tests of this kind. This would especially offer an interesting new initiative for the test providers in the case of Medicine, given the present high profile of IELTS in this field.

4. Attempts to align score bands of tests like IELTS with CEFR criteria have been widely challenged and can be potentially misleading to stakeholders. The descriptors that are published by test providers generally are often limited and barely profile Listening at all as a set of co-ordinated processes. One reason for the lack of precision may be that listening tests used for academic purposes are currently designed to be many things to many people. It would seem useful, at this point, for IELTS and other test providers to produce a clearer and more detailed set of descriptors which provide concrete information on what can be expected of test takers at each of their score bands. This would not only strengthen the credibility of the tests but would greatly assist gatekeepers in their present incompletely informed attempts to specify entry criteria. Initially, the descriptors might characterise performance across each of the four skills. A long-term aim might be to provide separate descriptors of performance for instructors and gatekeepers in each of the main domains where the test is used: i.e. general – academic – professional.

Important issues of test content

1. *Speech events.* As noted earlier, the types of context to be targeted in Section 3 of the IELTS Listening test are not always clearly profiled. On the basis of empirical data (reports by students in various disciplines), Ingram and Bayliss (2007) managed to identify a number of distinct types of interaction which occur in academic contexts: see p. 74 above. Future tests should perhaps aim to embrace a wider range of interaction types to those that currently feature so as to better represent the various types than interactive speech event that can occur in an academic setting. Particularly important is the seminar context and (currently left largely untested) the candidate's ability within a seminar to follow two different lines of argument.
2. *Discourse type.* Item writers should be advised of the need to cover a range of different types of discourse argument in Section 4 rather than relying mainly on expository material. This would better represent the higher-level demands of listening to academic lectures in different disciplines. The IWGs might specifically mention a range of discourse choices: expository (including cause-and-effect and counterfactual

relationships) – discursive (evidence 'for and against') – argumentative (a single viewpoint) – persuasive (winning the listener over) – analytical/ interpretive – critical – process-descriptive. These types have been listed in a sequence that loosely represents gradual increments in the likely cognitive and linguistic demands upon the listener.

3. *Authenticity of language and speech*. The language employed in current versions of many listening tests used for academic purposes diverges quite markedly from the forms observed and reported in real-world academic contexts. Item writers in training should be encouraged to examine widely available samples of academic speech such as the Warwick/Reading BASE corpus; and to note how real-world lecturers structure their information, provide signalling and link arguments. Better still would be to standardly include in IWGs a few excerpts from a database by way of example.

4. *Naturalness of speech*. The recordings used in tests of academic listening bear the marks of their studio origin and diverge quite markedly from real-world delivery. The difficulty of obtaining permission to use authentic material is obviously a problem. One solution is for item writers to make use of semi-scripted material, based upon an authentic source. At the very least, it is useful for writers to mark up their scripts for studio recording in a way that shows both tonic stress and natural patterns of pausing. It often happens that only voice actors and studio engineers are present at recording sessions, perhaps with an administrator from the exam board. Whatever the present arrangement, it makes good sense for the item writer to attend the sessions – or at the very least an adviser with a background understanding of natural connected speech.

5. *Accent*. The present IELTS reliance on relatively standard international varieties of English (Australian/NZ, US/Canadian, British, South African) seems a sound decision. On the basis of current theory and findings on how phonology and word forms are acquired, test providers would be well advised to resist pressures to include any localised regional varieties. Given the enormous number of possible speaker–listener combinations and the consequent likelihood of bias, they would also be well advised to resist any pressures to include L2-accented varieties.[1]

---

[1] Not all informed commentators would agree. Harding (personal communication, 2022) takes the view that this is a solvable problem: 'Recent research shows the way forward in selecting highly intelligible, diverse-accented speakers. A test that does not adequately model the TLU [target language use] domain – including the broad varieties of speech found therein – can only have a weak connection to that domain.'

Summary of main recommendations and final remarks

Important issues of test design

1. *Variety of method.* Different task formats require different types of cognitive operation, some of which may come more easily to a candidate than others. This indicates the desirability of employing a variety of formats. However, this review has also noted:
    a. that test materials sometimes switch too often between methods. Studies such as Gardiner and Howlett (2016) have indicated that this risks causing confusion amongst test takers.
    b. that, conversely, in the sample materials reviewed item writers had a tendency to rely excessively upon one single method – namely gap filling. There are two warning notes to be sounded here. Firstly, we should be cautious in treating gap filling as somehow closely related to real-world note-taking, since cognitively the conditions are quite different. Secondly, IWGs should emphasise the need to avoid excessive use of a single test format because it has important consequences for the type and length of key that can be targeted.
2. *Single play.* Recent research evidence suggests that a double play of the recording a) does not render a listening test disproportionately easier and indeed heightens scoring differentials rather than blurring them; b) reduces listening anxiety in the unnatural conditions imposed by conventional test methods; and c) results in a less test-constrained approach to listening on at least one of the plays. On these grounds, and bearing in mind that, with 21st century facilities, there are often real-world opportunities for rehearing academic material after it has been delivered, test providers may wish to consider the case for changing from a single to a double play. Additional advantages are mentioned in the section that follows.
3. *Test-wise strategies.* The formats commonly used in tests of listening employ items that are presented in *written* form and thus contain words that are easier to identify than when the same words occur in connected speech. This encourages the widespread use of test-wise strategies that map from the item to the recording rather than vice versa (Badger and Yan 2012, Field 2012a). Training in using such strategies has come to feature prominently in EAP instruction programmes at the expense of more constructive listening practice.

Greater efforts should certainly be made by test designers to reduce these test-wise effects. If, for example, a double play is used, we should not simply take the obvious line that it reduces the construct validity of a test (i.e. that the real-world listener usually only has one opportunity to hear what a speaker says). The fact is that it also allows the test designer to present the test items, not at the outset, but on a screen between the two plays (Sherman 1997). This limits the opportunity to draw upon written cues and fosters a style of listening during the first hearing which approximates much more closely to uncued real-world performance. At the outset, candidates would only be given a blank answer sheet on which to record their responses (e.g. the letter of the correct MCQ response or a suggestion for a word or words that might serve to fill a gap).

4. *Item targets.* One of the more striking findings of this review was the fact that, of 160 items sampled in retired IELTS tests, none focused on keys in the recording that extended to more than a single information unit. The items in question targeted lexical units (words and phrases) or single facts. Admittedly there was extensive use of paraphrase to test understanding; but no items elicited the higher-level processes of which listeners need to be capable if they are to perform adequately in academic contexts. These processes include: inferring information not explicitly expressed, inferring connections between pieces of information, interpreting speaker intentions, distinguishing speakers' points of view, distinguishing main points from subsidiary ones, summing up a line of argument, showing the ability to follow a larger pattern of discourse. It was suggested that the small-scale targets of the items in the tests studied were partly a by-product of the excessive use of gap-filling formats, which tend to focus attention at word and phrase level. Multiple choice and multiple matching lend themselves more readily to devising items that relate to conceptual processes.

   a. Future IWGs provided by test designers should ideally make it clear that a set percentage of items in any given test need to target higher-level listening processes. These processes should be clearly specified and sample item wording should be given.
   b. Item writers should be actively encouraged to use flexible formats (e.g. multiple matching) more frequently and more constructively.
   c. Alternatively, gap-filling tasks could be adapted to represent higher-level processes – for example, by featuring a simulated Table of Contents for recorded lecture-style material, in which some of the headings and sub-headings are supplied but others have to be filled in.

Future developments

1. *Computer-based delivery.* Providers currently reliant upon paper-based formats may at some point wish to replace the present customary sound

recording with a computer-delivered version of the speech input. This method of delivery brings obvious advantages in terms of administrative flexibility. It also offers the opportunity (see above) of reducing the extent to which test-wise strategies are used by candidates. However, if test items are indeed presented on-screen between two plays of the recording, it will have to be recognised that the CBT version will no longer be directly comparable with the paper-delivered one in terms of the behaviour elicited from candidates.

2. *Visual stimuli.* The evidence on visual support during tests of listening is ambivalent; it may be that visual input actually distracts the listener. The practice adopted by TOEFL iBT of providing still visuals to supplement recorded materials may not be a useful precedent to follow. Evidence suggests that they have no impact upon performance. However, the situation may be very different if and when tests switch to computer-led presentation. Lecture-style material in tests (e.g. in IELTS Section 4) would be brought closer to real-world cognitive experience if it took the form of a) sight of the speaker (including lip movements and gestures and with accompanying PowerPoint slides in a side panel); or even b) simply the PowerPoint slides. Students became familiar with both of these formats during the coronavirus pandemic; and they seem likely to form part of distance education in years to come.

3. *Integrated skills.* A possible future role for integrated-skills formats was discussed in Chapter 11. While a case can be made on ecological grounds for reading-into-writing tasks, it was not recommended that test providers should at this stage consider featuring a listening-into-writing one. This recognises that, though listening-into-writing does indeed play an important role in lecture-based instruction, a) the student's written output has to be judged for the accuracy of its content rather than its language, and b) there are many other academic contexts where the skills operate separately and under very different time pressures.

Future research priorities

As illustrated by this volume, IELTS and other tests of academic listening are significantly under-researched when compared with the coverage accorded to the other three skills. The main focus has been on issues of predictive validity; here, however, studies have relied on many different measures of 'progress' and have sometimes made unverified assumptions about the part that the skill might play across disciplines and teaching cultures. There have been attempts to map the scoring systems against external measures – most notably, the CEFR, where, however, a general conclusion has been expressed that the two sets of criteria represent goals that are not entirely compatible. There has also been an interest in stakeholder perceptions, well justified given the important role that instructors and administrators play in setting entry criteria based upon scores. In addition, this review has mentioned a number of washback studies, which have particularly concerned the effect of instruction upon test performance. There are lessons to be learned here for those contemplating research into similar issues in relation to the tests of other providers.

There are at least two areas where there is a current need for more research. Firstly, an aspect of washback that has been insufficiently explored (with the notable exception of Read and Hayes 2003) is the reverse of the one just mentioned: it concerns the role of the test in instruction. Two rather concerning (but by no means untypical) features of the IELTS courses studied by Read and Hayes were a low priority accorded to listening and a heavy reliance on test practice and associated strategies. Today, a major unresolved issue amongst instructors still remains the precise balance to be struck between sessions that involve test practice, those that involve skills development and those that focus on other EAP skills. It would be instructive to gain greater insights into the patterns of exam preparation that are most widely adopted – possibly supplemented with later feedback from learners about the extent to which the course content prepared them for academic study rather than simply the test. This would greatly strengthen the authority of the types of advice that test boards provide on ways of preparing for the test.

Another neglected research focus is the mind of the test taker. While much interest has been attached to the implications and impacts of scores, there has been remarkably little work on the processes that give rise to them. As pointed out earlier, this is particularly important for listening where no hard evidence is available of how candidates handle test material as it is in the cases of writing and speaking. Clearly, online speak-aloud reports are not possible when studying behaviour in a test of listening. However, a post-perceptual technique that has proved its worth is to pause the recording after every three items and to ask the individual to justify their responses and how they were arrived at. As well as shedding light on the nature of L2 academic listening, an important benefit of this stimulated recall approach is that it enables researchers and test designers alike to distinguish items that tap into processes central to the construct from those that simply generate test-wise strategies. More widely, it enables future claims to be made about the context and cognitive validity of any listening test, in a way that an approach based solely on scores cannot. Test taker protocols of this kind can and should contribute importantly to the trialling of any new versions of a test – providing insights into the variables underlying performance in a way that scoring evidence cannot. Other more recent methodologies such

Summary of main recommendations and final remarks

as eye-tracking and keystroke-logging are increasingly able to offer insights into the mind of the test taker and the nature of their behaviour.

Further considerations for test content

1. *Topic.* It is obviously necessary to avoid bias in an academic listening test by excluding specialist topics that are familiar to some test takers and not others. This may need to be more unambiguously signalled in the IWGs than it sometimes is at present.
2. *Length of recording.* Recorded input that aims to test lecture listening skills needs to emulate, on a small scale, the complexity of argument of a real-world lecture or academic discussion. This indicates a need for recordings of around 5 minutes. However, a case can also be made for some short clips alongside these longer texts, so as to test the candidate's ability to recognise discourse signals and local patterns of logic.
3. *Monologue/dialogue.* Greater opportunity should be taken to make use of dialogue material to represent the complex demands of following two opposed lines of argument.
4. *Speech rate.* Speech rate in the sample IELTS recordings examined was found to conform to what one might expect in the relevant contexts. However, given the apparently loose control over this feature by some examination boards, it might be useful for future test specifications to be able to claim that the provider has guidelines in place which specify a speech rate that falls within certain limits and to ensure a different, more measured delivery in lecture-style contexts than in (e.g.) conversation.

13 Issues addressed in this volume

The goal of this volume has been to re-examine thinking and practice in the assessment of academic listening. This first entailed examining research evidence and matching it against examples of current practice to support a more informed approach to designing, developing and validating future tests of listening in academic contexts. The discussion was largely aimed at those who are specialists in language testing, and engaged in constructing tests of the (sometimes elusive) listening skill. Specifically, it is hoped that it will help shape the decisions and the creativity of item writers striving to produce test components that are both demanding and fair. But there were important implications for many other stakeholders – including senior academics and professionals setting standards for entry or performance within institutes of learning. The issues discussed also have implications for language teachers, and hopefully will lead them away from the type of test-wise strategy that often features prominently in instruction and towards approaches that embrace the actual processes that underlie the listening experience. These are processes that will serve the candidate well if and when they succeed in obtaining a place on the course of their choice.

Two general approaches were adopted. The first part of the volume reviewed recent research findings relating to the Academic Listening paper which features in the current IELTS test. The findings in question served to exemplify the types of issue that have arisen in recent years in relation to testing in this area and are of relevance to all test providers worldwide and to their stakeholders. Concrete conclusions were drawn as to how we might ensure that tests of academic listening perform better in respect of various types of validity. There were suggestions as to how present and future versions of tests might benefit from the insights obtained. The general headings in Section 1 under which the different aspects of academic listening were grouped will hopefully provide a useful framework of reference for future thinking and research.

The second major line of enquiry approached the construct to be tested from a perspective based on research evidence of the cognitive operations central to the listening skill, with specific consideration given to the circumstances of listening in an academic context. A simplified psycholinguistic model of the skill was presented, and provides a yardstick against which the content of various present-day listening tests, including

IELTS, can be matched. Characteristics of the current IELTS Listening test were used to provide concrete examples of where and how a test may or may not fit the basic criteria. The expectation is that this example of a cognitively led and systematic approach to validation will provide a sustainable model of how <u>any</u> test of listening used for academic purposes might be more relevantly reviewed and validated in future. The exercise also serves indirectly to draw attention to certain features and conventions of current listening tests which may compromise their ability to represent the target construct in a way that reflects real-world conditions.

Epilogue

Barry O'Sullivan, British Council, UK

Nick Saville, Cambridge University Press & Assessment, UK

The aim of this epilogue is to extend Field's line of thinking about the construct of listening by suggesting ways in which the rapidly changing technological landscape in the digital age might offer new opportunities to transform the way that listening is assessed in future. As in the case of reading (Weir and Chan 2019:Chapter 9), the role that technology already plays in the ways that students now learn and access knowledge in higher education provides the backdrop for this discussion.

The sociocognitive framework as an integrated approach to validity

In the Series Editors' note for SILT 51 (2019:xiv), the Editors suggest that the volume makes important contributions to the field of language testing by supporting the evolution of the sociocognitive framework through its application to reading, and by contributing to the conceptualisation of validity more generally.

Weir and Chan argue that the sociocognitive framework supports Messick's original conceptualisation of validity as *unitary* (Messick 1989, 1995), but that the division into its various different aspects provides a useful way to operationalise the model, acknowledging 'the practical nature and quality of an actual testing event' (2019:ixv). Importantly, the framework provides the basis for mapping out an integrated agenda for argument-based validation and research, and in their concluding chapter, focusing on assessing reading in a digital age.

Similarly, in Field's concluding chapter, he suggests that in revisiting the sociocognitive approach, it is important to emphasise that the test development model and the measurement model must be fully integrated. Field's account also accords with the broader integrated arguments approach proposed by Chalhoub-Deville and O'Sullivan (2020), highlighting the need for the test developer to set out a clear vision of what the test is trying to achieve (a theory of change) and how this is to be achieved (a theory of action), in addition to then communicating interactively with key stakeholder groups to ensure they fully understand the approach taken (communication model or models). Field concludes by making a number of recommendations in using the framework of reference with a view to strengthening the validity argument that underpins tests of academic listening. His recommendations include ways in which the changing landscape of learning in the digital age might be better reflected in the construct of academic listening in the future.

How we learn: Changing constructs of academic language proficiency

Field draws attention to certain features and conventions of current listening tests that, in his opinion, do not adequately represent the target language construct 'in a way that reflects real-world conditions'.

In a previous publication (Field 2019), he claims that several listening activities are critical to most academic contexts and the experiences of students in higher education. In order of importance, he proposes the following: lectures; seminars; interactions with tutors; receiving advice and instructions; and social activities. The first four typically require the student to be a competent listener when other people are speaking and while they, and often others at the same time, are listening. The student may also need to read or write while listening in this way, e.g. in referring to key texts or in taking notes.

In socialising within the wider academic community, students need to participate in conversations and group-based tasks that require turn-taking on their part or in making contributions to an ongoing discussion. These activities are interactive and involve both listening and speaking on the part of the various participants.

Prior to 2020, many of these activities required the students to be physically present, in the lecture or seminar room or while socialising on the campus. However, universities have increasingly been using digital learning platforms (commonly referred to as learner management systems – LMSs) to distribute reading materials and manage online learning activities. This trend, in Higher Education (HE) as in all cycles of education, has provided opportunities for the learning content and supporting materials to be provided using a range of media. The impact of the Covid emergency was to accelerate the trend and especially the need for remote and hybrid models of teaching and learning, e.g. using video-based communication systems such as Zoom or Teams. The rapid shift saw new requirements for students to access a wider range of information on screen and to carry out their assignments and assessment tasks using digital devices. In HE at least, these ways of working have not been reversed and are now considered to be the 'new normal'. This means that many of the listening activities listed above now take place remotely, including lectures that are recorded and made available on LMSs. For some courses (such as Massive Open Online Courses) students only interact online.

While the integration of language skills has always been necessary in the academic domain, the use of digital platforms as a matter of routine is now impacting the ways in which learners expect to engage with the content of their courses and to communicate with their lecturers and peers. This in turn needs to be reflected in the ways in which they are assessed. There have been some recent innovations as a result, e.g. increasing focus on integrated skills, 'scenario-based' models and the wider uses of multimedia in task designs, and this trend is likely to continue in future.

Although their work was pre-pandemic, Weir and Chan in their final chapter discuss the evolution of academic reading in the digital age, including the changing attitudes and behaviours of the students as learners and test takers. They point out (2019:243), that research has shown that the current generation of young people (GenZ) is in transition between use of printed materials and digital usage, but the expectation is that the next generation of HE students born after 2010 (GenAlpha) will have higher levels of digital literacy and express a clear preference for digital formats.

They also argue that digital test delivery has several advantages in replicating academic reading in real life. As academic reading on screens and mobile devices becomes the norm, authentic assessment of academic reading should also involve online reading as part of the construct. Digital delivery also mirrors other aspects of the way students now learn, e.g. by allowing students greater autonomy in selecting and handling the texts they read or by enforcing time restrictions that require students to use expeditious reading strategies that are necessary when selecting the key sections of longer texts. In many ways the same claims can be made about academic listening activities that now form part of a more complex and multifaceted understanding of academic literacy in the 21st century.

In terms of specific innovations that address the cognitive/contextual dimension of the reading construct, Weir and Chan make the case for reading-into-writing assessment tasks, facilitated by the digital technology that is now widely used, as noted above (see also Chan 2018). However, unlike reading, it is far less clear what kinds of test format and assessment tasks can address weaknesses and deficits that Field is concerned about in the case of listening. He does not offer a clear pathway forwards or propose innovative task formats for listening, but his conclusions echo the questions raised by Weir and Chan (2019:53) in their final chapter:

- How might it be possible to explore the interactions between different components of the sociocognitive framework? Are certain interactions more critical/dominant than others?
- How might new technologies facilitate the collection and analysis of the data to achieve this?

Epilogue

Cognitive and context aspects of validity in the digital age

It seems likely that the changing nature of students' academic experiences will involve listening tasks that were not previously required or indeed possible. This in turn will have implications for the future construct of listening in terms of the interactions occurring between the contextual features and the mental processes activated while students are engaging with onscreen content. In other words, the cognitive aspects of validity that Field is particularly concerned about will need to be revisited.

As a cognitive scientist, Field is particularly interested in the patterns of thought and patterns of language that help the listener to deal with the transitory nature of the aural message. Skilled listeners, he claims, are not only able to recall the main points in what they have listened to but also to understand and explain the connections between them. So in order to decipher and retain the message, it is important to be able to:

- summarise information, distinguishing the relevant from the irrelevant
- synthesise information and incorporate it into a subsequent assignment
- relate prior knowledge and experience to new information
- determine major and subordinate ideas
- identify the evidence which supports or contradicts an argument
- anticipate the direction of the argument
- retain information while searching for answers to self-generated questions.

Field believes the last point to be particularly important in academic listening contexts given the transitory nature of the acoustic signal, which typically cannot be cross-checked or re-listened to in the same ways that a written text can. He has in mind listening in the context of lectures and seminars of the traditional, in-person kind. However, in modelling the learning contexts of the future, one can imagine ways in which these abilities will need to change or adapt to the multifaceted nature of academic literacy. Metacognitive abilities are likely to become more relevant as they will be needed for selecting suitable materials and engaging in activities to meet students' individual needs. With more material being pre-recorded, and so available to listen to at any time, students will need to draw on both their metacognitive and cognitive strategies to find and understand the information they need (see Luckin 2018:Chapter 7).

Emerging techniques offer researchers more sophisticated means of collecting learner data of various types, and as more data becomes available concerning an individual learner's listening behaviours and habits, it will be possible to develop assessments that adapt to a test taker's ability level and learning needs in more valid ways.

Field reminds us that: 'test taker protocols should contribute importantly to the development of any new versions of a test – providing insights into the variables underlying performance in a way that scoring evidence cannot'. In supplementing verbal protocols, research methodologies such as eye-tracking and keystroke-logging are increasingly able to offer insights into the mind of the test taker and the nature of their behaviours and cognitive processes. Suvorov (forthcoming 2024) agrees that that validation studies are 'sorely needed for understanding L2 listeners' cognitive processes and test-taking strategies underlying their performance'. Acknowledging that eye-tracking has been used to investigate test takers' cognitive processes during the completion of items in the IELTS Reading test (Bax 2013), he outlines two studies that illustrate the potential of eye-tracking research in the context of listening. His findings support the view that it is a viable methodology for obtaining evidence of cognitive validity based on response processes. Furthermore, he suggests that the methodology is particularly insightful when eye-tracking data is used in combination with verbal data.

This finding is generally confirmed by other researchers (Kwon forthcoming 2024, Owen forthcoming 2024). Schmidt and Pastorino (forthcoming 2024) concur, but in their research they combine eye-tracking with electroencephalography (EEG) to tap into cognitive processes in ways that verbal methods cannot capture. Their chapter provides a useful overview of the two methodologies, explaining which measures show which type of processing is happening, and demonstrating the value each can add to research in second language processing, and especially in addressing the cognitive validity of language tests.

Interestingly, Suvorov claims that if/when eye-tracking becomes a mainstream technology that is integrated into personal devices, new opportunities will be created for collecting eye-tracking data during high-stakes language testing. In other words, it can become an integral part of a computer-delivered assessment system and be used in real time as a source of cognitive validity evidence to support score interpretations.

A research agenda for the future

As noted above, the latest operational versions of the sociocognitive model enable the development of 'integrated validly arguments' that are consistent with contemporary argument-based approaches to test validation. The underlying model that supports the early frameworks was initially proposed by O'Sullivan (2016, 2019) and most notably by Chalhoub-Deville and O'Sullivan (2020). In the latter authors' most recent publications, O'Sullivan and Chalhoub-Deville (2021, in press 2023) set out to demonstrate how their version of the model now enables a future-oriented research agenda to be drawn up that brings together the contextual and cognitive aspects of academic listening and offers the potential for new formats and assessment models to be designed and validated in the digital era.

In reviewing and revising existing assessment systems, such as IELTS, the model enables the intended impacts, including washback on learning, to be incorporated as a design principle (see Chalhoub-Deville and O'Sullivan 2020, Jones and Saville 2016, Saville 2009, Saville 2021). In this respect, a commitment to communication and engagement with all stakeholder groups and concerns for test consequences are also primary considerations during the design and development phases.

Field highlights concerns related to washback and how the design of a listening test can influence how students understand the construct of academic proficiency and practise it in order to reach the required level in tests such as IELTS. Excessive cramming and other kinds of test practice, as opposed to the development of the necessary academic language and literacy, are clearly undesirable. Inauthentic listening tasks, including some discrete item formats, have the perverse effect of distracting rather than focusing the attention of the listener. They therefore do not develop the listening abilities needed and so have a negative washback effect on learning if they are focused on in test preparation courses. By designing the test to be a closer representation of the real-world behaviour this can be avoided.

Artificial Intelligence (AI) – integrating learning and assessment

During the pandemic, online and remote assessments were developed using existing educational technologies (e.g. to deliver video-based speaking) supplemented by more advanced technologies using artificial intelligence (AI) to automate rating processes and support digital delivery by providing remote proctoring. The uptake of these technologies during the pandemic was rapid and essentially unquestioned. Solutions were required as a matter of urgency and questions around issues such as bias, privacy or even accessibility were largely ignored (the single exception in language testing appears to be O'Sullivan, Breakspear and Bayliss (2023) who focus on the validation of an auto-scoring language model). In addition, the rapid changes which saw teaching, learning and assessment move online also happened with little or no apparent concern for the welfare of the teaching staff who had to rapidly build systems with little or no experience or training (see Montenegro-Rueda, Luque-de la Rosa, Sarasola Sánchez-Serrano and Fernández-Cerero 2021).

A recent Study.com survey (2023) reported that almost three quarters of all US college professors surveyed were concerned that Chat-GPT would have an impact on cheating, while almost 9 in 10 students reported using it to write a homework assignment. Interestingly enough, while the survey found that one third of professors indicated they would like to see Chat-GPT banned, three quarters of students felt the same. Misuse of large language models (LLMs), when combined with known issues around bias (e.g. Buolamwini and Gebru 2018), suggest that some caution should be taken when considering their use in assessment.

However, in terms of the testing of listening, it is difficult to imagine that LLMs might pose an existential threat. Certainly, concerns with speed and accent (Field from this volume) or comprehensibility (Isaacs, Trofimovich and Foote 2017) would appear to be relatively easy to address given that the technology exists to manipulate these aspects of the language, or in the case of comprehensibility, to actually offer an effective measure (Saito, Macmillan, Kachlicka, Kunihara and Minematsu 2023). With the introduction of LLMs there exists the possibility of real-time human-machine communication (HMC), particularly with regard to speaking/ listening. Here, the technology will allow for quite rigid control over such issues as speed, accent or comprehensibility, though some doubts remain over other features of the machine's voice, for example Fortunati (2023:131) argues that machines are 'so far unable to feel and thus convey emotion to their users.' This has significant implications around affect and the concept of gender in HMC.

Conclusions

Digital technology not only enables greater cognitive validity to be achieved in test design and delivery, but can also address longstanding issues related to contextual validity. The technologies now emerging for assessment purposes respond to 'new normal' conditions of multimedia learning in academic contexts, and also enable test developers to revisit the *general-specific dilemma,* and the questions related to the predictive validity of language tests. As Field suggests in this volume, it is critical to accurately define precisely what a test such as IELTS or TOEFL iBT is actually aiming to predict. Any study that focuses on indicators of academic success (e.g., grade point average) is bound to come unstuck, as language is just one of many variables that lead to such success. Instead, the claim needs to be targeted on the reality of what a language test like IELTS or TOEFL iBT can predict – the likelihood that the successful candidate will possess the communication skills necessary to participate in university or professional life.

The challenge of language for specific purposes (LSP) and how discipline-specific content can be built into the design of integrated language tests dates back to the era of ELTS (1970–1989), the predecessor to IELTS – see SILT Volume 23, *Assessing Academic English: Testing English proficiency,*

Epilogue

1950–1989 – the IELTS solution (Davies 2008). By predicting the academic context and content that students will encounter in their chosen academic institution, and by incorporating that into the test-taking experience, it should be possible to provide greater authenticity and better predictive information about future success in the chosen domain. However, if the disciplines are defined at a high level, the variations within the disciplines can be as wide as those between them. This has proved to be an intractable problem to date.

With regards the demands on student's listening for academic purposes, Field notes that:

- the nature and importance of auditory input varies across disciplines
- the importance of auditory input varies across educational cultures
- listening skill development varies widely between individuals once they are in an English-speaking setting, partly reflecting their social activities and other developing interests.

This poses a dilemma in determining the extent to which the content should be specific to particular domains and what compromise needs to be made in delivering assessment that provides practical solutions. This was one of the reasons why ELTS was revised following the validation programme of the 1980s, leading eventually to the format of IELTS in 1995.

Murray (2016) argues against the use of subject-specific content because of potential bias and because it is the institution's responsibility to train incoming students in the discourse of their area of specialisation *after* the students start their courses. This is particularly relevant for undergraduates entering directly from high school or for others beginning a new course in an unfamiliar discipline.

Validation and impact studies have confirmed that IELTS is useful in indicating readiness to begin a course of study, but does not address familiarity with the actual processes that accompany every type of study. In this respect IELTS continues to provide a successful test of academic readiness in terms of the general language proficiency of students at the proficiency levels that typically enables successful engagement in academic contexts. As learning and assessment processes become better integrated, supported by educational technologies that provide automated formative and diagnostic feedback, language test designers will have opportunities to address these issues through the *personalisation of the test taking experience*. In the next generation of IELTS it is therefore anticipated that a student's 'individual learning journey' – both as language learner and language user in academic contexts – will be built into authentic assessment experiences that meet their expectations about the uses of the technology in their daily lives and the ways they use it to communicate and to learn in their chosen academic disciplines.

References and further reading

Ahern, S (2009) 'Like cars or breakfast cereal': IELTS and the trade in education and immigration, *TESOL in Context* 19 (1), 39–51.

Alderson, J C (1991) Bands and scores, in Alderson, J C and North, B J (Eds) *Language Testing in the 1990s: The Communicative Legacy*, London: Modern English Publications/British Council, 71–86.

Alderson, J C (1997) Bands and scores, in Clapham, C and Alderson, J C (Eds) *IELTS Research Report 3: Constructing and Trialling the IELTS Test*, Cambridge: The British Council /UCLES/IDP: IELTS Australia, 87–108.

Alderson, J C and Clapham, C (1992) Applied linguistics and language testing: A case study of the ELTS Test, *Applied Linguistics* 13 (2), 149–167.

Alderson, J C and Wall, D (1993) Does washback exist?, *Applied Linguistics* 14, 115–129.

Alderson, J C, Figueras, N, Kuijper, H, Nold, G, Takala, S and Tardieu, C (2006) Analysing tests of reading and listening in relation to the Common European Framework of Reference: The experience of the Dutch CEFR Construct Project, *Language Assessment Quarterly* 3 (1), 3–30.

Allen, D (2016) *Investigating Japanese undergraduates' English language proficiency with IELTS: Predicting factors and washback*, IELTS Partnership Research Papers 2017/2, Cambridge: The British Council /UCLES/IDP: IELTS Australia.

Allwright, J and Banerjee, J (1997) Investigating the accuracy of admissions criteria: A case study in a British university, *Language Testing Update* 22, 36–41.

Arkoudis, S, Baik, C and Richardson, S (2012) *English Language Standards in Higher Education*, Camberwell: Australian Council for Educational Research Press.

Aryadoust, V (2013) *Building a Validity Argument for a Listening Test of Academic Proficiency*, Newcastle: Cambridge Scholars Publishing.

Badger, R and Yan, X (2012) The use of tactics and strategies by Chinese students in the listening component of IELTS, in Taylor, L and Weir, C J (Eds) *IELTS Collected Papers 2: Research in Reading and Listening Assessment*, Studies in Language Testing volume 34, Cambridge: UCLES/Cambridge University Press, 454–486.

Banerjee, J (2004) *Study of the minimum English language writing and speaking abilities needed by overseas trained doctors*, Report to the General Medical Council, July 2004.

Batty, A O (2018) Investigating the impact of nonverbal communication cues on listening item types, in Ockey, G and Wagner, E (Eds) *Assessing L2 Listening: Moving Towards Authenticity*, Amsterdam: John Benjamins, 161–175.

Batty, A O (2021) An eye-tracking study of attention to visual cues in L2 listening tests, *Language Testing* 38 (4), 511–535.

References and further reading

Bax, S (2013) The cognitive processing of candidates during reading tests: Evidence from eye-tracking, *Language Testing* 30 (4), 441–465.

Bekleyen, N (2009) Helping teachers become better English students: Causes, effects, and coping strategies for foreign language listening anxiety, *System* 37 (4), 664–675.

Bellingham, L (1993) The relationship of language proficiency to academic success for international students, *New Zealand Journal of Educational Studies* 30, 229–232.

Berne, J E (1995) How does varying pre-listening activities affect second language listening comprehension? *Hispania* 78 (2), 316–329.

Berry, V, O'Sullivan, B and Rugea, S (2013) *Identifying the appropriate IELTS score levels for IMG applicants to the GMC register*, London: Centre for Language Assessment Research (CLARe), The University of Roehampton.

Blackhurst, A (2005) Listening, reading and writing on computer-based and paper-based versions of IELTS, *Research Notes* 21, 14–17.

Boroughs, R (2003) The change process at paper level. Paper 4: Listening, in Weir, C J and Milanovic, M J (Eds) *Continuity and Change: Revising the Cambridge Proficiency in English Examination: 1913–2002*, Studies in Language Testing volume 15, Cambridge: UCLES/Cambridge University Press, 315–366.

Bradlow, A R and Bent, T (2008) Perceptual adaptation to non-native speech, *Cognition* 106 (2), 707–729.

Braxton, M A (1999) *Adult ESL Language Learning Strategies: Case Studies of Preferred Learning Styles and Perceived Cultural Influences in Academic Listening Tasks*, unpublished PhD dissertation, Ohio State University.

Breeze, R and Miller, P (2012) Predictive validity of the IELTS listening test as an indicator of student coping ability in English-medium undergraduate courses in Spain, in Taylor, L and Weir, C J (Eds) *IELTS Collected Papers 2: Research in Reading and Listening Assessment*, Studies in Language Testing volume 34, Cambridge: UCLES/Cambridge University Press, 487–518.

Brindley, G and Slatyer, H (2002) Exploring task difficulty in ESL listening assessment, *Language Testing* 19, 369–394.

British Academic Spoken English Corpus (2005) *Universities of Warwick and Reading*, available online (password protected): warwick.ac.uk/fac/soc/al/research/collections/base/lecturetranscripts.

Brown, G (1990) *Listening to Spoken English* (Second edition), Harlow: Longman.

Brown, G and Yule, G (1983) *Discourse Analysis*, Cambridge: Cambridge University Press.

Buck, G (1990) *The testing of second language listening comprehension*, unpublished PhD thesis, University of Lancaster.

Buck, G (2001) *Assessing Listening*, Cambridge: Cambridge University Press.

Buck, G and Tatsuoka, K (1998) Application of the rule-space procedure to language testing: Examining attributes of a free response listening test, *Language Testing* 15 (2), 119–157.

Buolamwini, J and Gebru, T (2018) Gender shades: Intersectional accuracy disparities in commercial gender classification, *Proceedings of Machine Learning Research* 81, 1–15.

Burns, A (1998) Teaching speaking, *Annual Review of Applied Linguistics* 18, 102–123.

Bybee, J (2001) *Phonology and Language Use*, Cambridge: Cambridge University Press.
Calvert, D R (1986) *Descriptive Phonetics* (Second edition), New York: Thieme.
Campbell, C and Smith, J (2012) *English for Academic Study: Listening* (Second edition), Reading: Garnet Education.
Canagarajah, S (2006) Changing communicative needs, revised assessment objectives: testing English as an international language, *Language Assessment Quarterly* 3, 229–242.
Cervantes, R and Gainer, G (1992) The effects of syntactic simplification and repetition on listening comprehension, *TESOL Quarterly* 26 (4), 767–770.
Chalhoub-Deville, M and O'Sullivan, B (2020) *Validity: Theoretical Development and Integrated Arguments*, British Council Monographs on Modern Language Testing, Sheffield: Equinox.
Chalhoub-Deville, M and Turner, C E (2000) What to look for in ESL admission tests: Cambridge certificate exams, IELTS, and TOEFL, *System* 28 (4), 523–539.
Chan, S (2018) *Defining Integrated Reading-Into-Writing Constructs: Evidence at the B2-C1 Interface*, English Profile Studies 8, Cambridge: UCLES/Cambridge University Press.
Chang, A C-S and Read, J (2006) The effects of listening support on the listening performance of EFL learners, *TESOL Quarterly* 40 (2), 375–397.
Chiang, C S and Dunkel, P (1992) The effect of speech modification, prior knowledge and listening proficiency on EFL lecture learning, *TESOL Quarterly* 26 (2), 345–374.
Chung, J M (1999) The effects of using video texts supported with advance organizers and captions, *Foreign Language Annals* 32 (3), 295–307.
Clopper, C G and Pisoni, D B (2004) Homebodies and army brats: Some effects of early linguistic experience and residential history on dialect characterisation, *Language Variation and Change* 16, 31–48.
Clopper, C G and Pisoni, D B (2008) Perception of dialect variation, in Pisoni, D B and Remez, R E (Eds) *The Handbook of Speech Perception*, Oxford: Blackwell, 313–337.
Cohen, A D (1998) *Strategies of Language Learning and Language Use*, Harlow: Longman.
Coleman, G and Heap, S (1998) The misinterpretation of directions for the questions in the American reading and listening sub-test of the IELTS test, *IELTS Research Reports* 4, 38–71.
Coleman, D, Starfield, S and Hagan, A (2003) The attitudes of IELTS stakeholders: Student and staff perceptions of IELTS in Australian, UK and Chinese tertiary institutions, *IELTS Research Reports* 5, 161–235.
Coniam, D (2001) The use of audio or video comprehension as an assessment instrument in the certification of English language teachers: a case study, *System* 29, 1–14.
Cotton, F and Conrow, F (1998) An investigation of the predictive validity of IELTS amongst a sample of international students studying at the University of Tasmania, *IELTS Research Reports* 1, 72–115.
Council of Europe (2001) *Common European Framework of Reference for Languages: Learning, Teaching, Assessment*, Cambridge: Cambridge University Press.
Criper, C and Davies, A (1988) *ELTS validation project report*, University of Cambridge Local Examinations Syndicate.

References and further reading

Cumming, A (2013) Assessing integrated skills, in Kunnan, A (Ed) *The Companion to Language Assessment*, New York: Wiley, Chap. 13.

Cumming, A, Lai, C and Cho, H (2016) Students' writing from sources for academic purposes: A synthesis of recent research, *Journal of English for Academic Purposes* 23, 47–58.

Dai, D W and Roever, C (2019) Including L2-English varieties in listening tests for adolescent ESL learners: L1 effects and learner perceptions, *Language Assessment Quarterly* 16 (1), 64–86.

Davies, A (2008) *Assessing Academic English: Testing English Proficiency, 1950–1989: The IELTS Solution*, Studies in Language Testing Volume 23, Cambridge: UCLES/Cambridge University Press.

Davies, A, Brown, A, Elder, C, Hill, K, Lumley, T and McNamara, T (1999) *Dictionary of Language Testing*, Studies in Language Testing volume 7, Cambridge: UCLES/Cambridge University Press.

Denham, P and Oner, J (1992) *Validation Study of Listening Sub-Test: IDP/IELTS Commissioned Report*, Canberra: University of Canberra.

Deroey, K (2018) The representativeness of lecture listening coursebooks: language, lectures, research-informedness, *Journal of English for Academic Purposes* 34, 57–67.

Dooey P (1999) An investigation into the predictive validity of the IELTS Test as an indicator of future academic success, in Martin, K, Stanley, N and Davison, N (Eds) *Teaching in the Disciplines/Learning in Context*, Perth: University of Western Australia, 114–118.

Dooey, P and Oliver, R (2002) An investigation into the predictive validity of the IELTS test as an indication of future academic success, *Prospect* 17 (1), 36–54.

Dörnyei, Z and Scott, M L (1997) Communication strategies in a second language: definitions and taxonomies, *Language Learning* 447 (1), 173–210.

Dudley-Evans, T (1997) Variation in the discourse patterns favoured by different disciplines and their pedagogical implications, in Flowerdew, J (Ed) *Academic Listening: Research Perspectives*, Cambridge: Cambridge University Press, 146–158.

Elder, C (1993) Language performance as a predictor of performance in teacher education, *Melbourne Papers in Language Testing* 2, 68–85.

Elder, C and Davies, A (2006) Assessing English as a Lingua Franca, *Annual Review of Applied Linguistics* 26, 282–304.

Elder, C and O'Loughlin, K (2003) Investigating the relationship between intensive English language study and band score gain on IELTS, *IELTS Research Reports* 4, 207–254.

Elliott, M (2013) Test taker characteristics, in Geranpayeh, A and Taylor, L (Eds) *Examining Listening: Research and Practice in Second Language Listening*, Studies in Language Testing volume 35, Cambridge: UCLES/Cambridge University Press, 36–76.

ETS (2007) *The Official Guide to the New TOEFL iBT* (Second edition), New York: McGraw-Hill.

ETS (2010) *ETS Linking TOEFL iBT Scores to IELTS Scores – A Research Report*, available online: www.ets.org/s/toefl/pdf/linking_toefl_ibt_scores_to_ielts_scores.pdf.

Faerch, G and Kasper, G (1983) Plans and strategies in foreign language communication, in Faerch, G and Kasper, G (Eds) *Strategies in Interlanguage Communication*, London: Longman, 20–60.

Feast, V (2002) The impact of IELTS scores on performance at university, *International Education Journal* 3 (4), 70–85.

Ferguson, G and White, E (1994) *A Predictive Validity Study of IELTS*, Edinburgh: University of Edinburgh Institute for Applied Language Studies.

Field, J (1999) Unpublished internal report and recommendations on Certificate Proficiency in English.

Field, J (2000) 'Waving, not drowning': a reply to Tony Ridgway, *ELT Journal* 54 (2), 186–195.

Field, J (2008) *Listening in the Language Classroom*, Cambridge: Cambridge University Press.

Field, J (2011) Into the mind of the academic listener, *Journal of EAP* 10 (2), 102–112.

Field, J (2012a) The cognitive validity of the lecture-based question in the IELTS listening paper, in Taylor, L and Weir, C J (Eds) *IELTS Collected Papers 2: Research in Reading and Listening Assessment*, Studies in Language Testing volume 34, Cambridge: UCLES/Cambridge University Press, 391–453.

Field, J (2012b) *The cognitive validity of the CAE listening test as a predictor of academic performance*, unpublished report: Project funded by Cambridge ESOL Research and Validation Unit 2011.

Field, J (2013) Cognitive validity, in Geranpayeh, A and Taylor, L (Eds) *Examining Listening: Research and Practice in Assessing Second Language Listening*, Studies in Language Testing volume 35, Cambridge: UCLES/Cambridge University Press, 77–151.

Field, J (2014) Myth: Pronunciation teaching needs to fix in the minds of learners a set of distinct consonant and vowel sounds, in Grant, L (Ed) *Pronunciation Myths*, Ann Arbor: University of Michigan Press, 80–106.

Field, J (2015) *The effects of single and double play upon listening test outcomes and cognitive processing*, London: British Council ARAGS Reports.

Field, J (2019) *Rethinking the Second Language Listening Test*, Sheffield: Equinox.

Fiocco, M (1992) *English proficiency levels of students from a non-English speaking background: A study of IELTS as an indicator of tertiary success*, unpublished paper, Centre for International English, Curtin University of Technology.

Floccia, C, Butler, J, Goslin, J and Ellis, L (2009) Regional and foreign accent processing in English: can listeners adapt? *Journal of Psycholinguistic Research* 38 (4), 379–412.

Floccia, C, Goslin, J, Girard, F and Konopczynski, G (2006) Does a regional accent perturb speech processing? *Journal of Experimental Psychology: Human Perception and Performance* 32 (5), 1,276–1,293.

Flowerdew, J (2012) *Academic Discourse* (Second edition), Abingdon: Routledge.

Fortunati, L (2023) Gender and Identity in Human-Machine Communication, in Guzman, A L, McEwen, R and Jones, S (Eds) *The Sage Handbook of Human-Machine Communication*, Thousand Oaks: Sage, 127–135.

Freedle, R and Kostin, I (1999) Does the text matter in a multiple-choice test of comprehension? The case for the construct validity of TOEFL's minitalks, *Language Testing* 16, 2–32.

Frost, K, Elder, C and Wigglesworth, G (2012) Investigating the validity of an integrated listening-speaking task: A discourse-based analysis of test takers' oral performances, *Language Testing* 29 (3), 345–369.

Gardiner, J and Howlett, S (2016) Student perceptions of four university gateway tests, *University of Sydney Papers in TESOL* 11, 67–96.

Gathercole, S E and Baddeley, A (1993) *Working Memory and Language*, Hove: Erlbaum.

Geranpayeh, A and Taylor, L (2008) Examining listening: developments and issues in assessing second language listening, *Research Notes* 32, 2–5.

Geranpayeh, A and Taylor, L (Eds) (2013) *Examining Listening: Research and Practice in Assessing Second Language Listening*, Studies in Language Testing volume 35, Cambridge: UCLES/Cambridge University Press.

Gernsbacher, M A (1990) *Language Comprehension as Structure Building*, Hillsdale: Erlbaum.

Gilmore, A (2004) A comparison of textbook and authentic interactions, *ELT Journal* 58 (4), 363–371.

Gilmore, A (2011) Authentic materials and authenticity in foreign language learning, *Language Teaching* 40, 97–118.

Gilmore, A (2015) The influence of discourse studies on language descriptions and task design, *Language Teaching* 48 (4), 506–530.

Gimson, A C (2008) *Gimson's Pronunciation of English* (Seventh edition), London: Hodder Education.

Ginther, A (2002) Context and content visuals and performance on listening comprehension stimuli, *Language Testing* 19, 133–167.

Goh, C C M (2000) A cognitive perspective on language learners' listening comprehension problems, *System* 28, 55–75.

Golchi, M M (2012) Listening anxiety and its relationship with listening strategy use and listening comprehension among Iranian IELTS learners, *International Journal of English Linguistics* 2 (4), 115–128.

Golder, K, Reeder, K and Fleming, S (2009) Determination of appropriate IELTS band score for admission into a program at a Canadian post-secondary polytechnic institution, *IELTS Research Reports* 10, 1–25.

Goldinger, S D (1997) Speech perception and production in an episodic lexicon, in Johnson, K and Mullennix, J W (Eds) *Talker Variability in Speech Processing*, New York: Academic Press, 33–66.

Goldman-Eisler, F (1968) *Psycholinguistics: Experiments in Spontaneous Speech*, London/New York: Academic Press.

Graham, S (2011) Self efficacy and academic listening, *Journal of English for Academic Purposes* 10 (2), 113–117.

Green, A B (2006) Watching for washback: observing the influence of the IELTS academic writing test in the classroom, *Language Assessment Quarterly* 3 (4), 333–367.

Green, A B (2018) Linking tests of English for Academic Purposes to the CEFR: The score user's perspective, *Language Assessment Quarterly* 15 (1), 59–74.

Green, K P (1998) The use of auditory and visual information during phonetic processing: implications for theories of speech perception, in Campbell, R and Dodd, B (Eds) *Hearing by Eye II: Advances in the Psychology of Speechreading and Audiovisual Speech*, Hove: Psychology Press, 3–25.

Gribble, C, Blackmore, J, Morrissey, A M and Capic, T (2016) Investigating the use of IELTS in determining employment, migration and professional registration outcomes in healthcare and early childcare education in Australia, *IELTS Research Reports Online Series* 2016/4, available online: www.ielts.org/-/media/research-reports/ielts_online_rr_2016-4.ashx.

Griffiths, R (1992) Speech rate and listening comprehension: full evidence of the relationship, *TESOL Quarterly* 26 (2), 385–390.

Gruba, P (2004) Understanding digitized second language videotext, *Computer Assisted Language Learning* 17 (1), 51–82.

Hall, G (2010) International English language testing: A critical response, *ELT Journal* 64 (3), 321–328.

Harding, L (2011) *The Use of Speakers with L2 Accents in Academic English Learning Listening Assessment: A Validation Study*, Frankfurt: Peter Lang.

Hawkins, S (1999) Re-evaluating assumptions about speech perception: Interactive and integrative theories, in Pickett, J M (Ed) *The Acoustics of Speech Communication: Fundamentals, Speech Perception Theory, and Technology*, Needham Heights: Allyn and Bacon, 232–288.

Hayes, B and Read, J (2004) IELTS test preparation in New Zealand: Preparing students of the IELTS academic module, in Cheng, L, Watanabe, Y and Curtis, A (Eds) *Washback in Language Testing: Research contexts and methods*, Mahwah: Lawrence Erlbaum, 97–112.

Henning, G (1990) *A study of the effects of variation of short term memory load, reading response length and processing hierarchy on TOEFL listening comprehension item performance*, ETS Research Report RR-90-18, TOEFL-RR-33, Princeton: ETS.

Herron, C A and Seay, I (1991) The effect of authentic oral texts on student listening comprehension in the foreign language classroom, *Foreign Language Annals* 24 (6), 487–495.

Hill, K, Storch, N and Lynch, B (1999) A comparison of IELTS and TOEFL as predictors of academic success, *IELTS Research Reports* 2, 62–73.

Holzknecht, F, Eberharter, K, Kremmel, B, Zehentner, M, McCray, G, Konrad, E and Spötti, C (2017) *Looking into listening: Using eye-tracking to establish the cognitive validity of the Aptis Listening Test*, London: British Council ARAGs Reports, available online: www.britishcouncil.org/sites/default/files/looking_into_listening.pdf.

Horwitz, E (2001) Language anxiety and achievement, *Annual Review of Applied Linguistics* 21, 112–126.

Hyatt, D and Brooks, G (2009) Investigating stakeholders' perceptions of IELTS as an entry requirement for higher education in the UK, *IELTS Research Reports* 10, 17–68.

IELTS (2009) *University of Cambridge ESOL Examinations: Cambridge IELTS 7*, Cambridge: Cambridge University Press.

IELTS (2015) *Ensuring Quality and Fairness in International Language Testing*, IELTS Partners.

IELTS (2016) *Item Writer Guidelines*, IELTS Partners.

IELTS (2018a) *Guide for Teachers*, IELTS Partners.

IELTS (2018b) *Item Writer Guidelines*, IELTS Partners.

In'nami, Y (2006) The effects of test anxiety on listening test performance, *System* 34 (3), 317–340.

In'nami, Y and Koizumi, R (2009) A meta-analysis of test format effects on reading and listening test performance: focus on multiple-choice and open-ended formats, *Language Testing* 26, 219–244.

Ingram, D and Bayliss, A (2007) IELTS as a predictor of academic language performance, Part 1, *IELTS Research Reports* 7 (3), 1–68.

Inoue, C and Lam, D M K (2021) *The effects of extended planning time on candidates' performance, processes, and strategy use in the lecture listening-*

into-speaking tasks of the TOEFL iBT® test, ETS Research Report No. RR-21-09, available online: onlinelibrary.wiley.com/doi/10.1002/ets2.12322.

Intersegmental Committee of the Academic Senates of the California Community Colleges, the California State University, and the University of California (2002) *Academic Literacy: A Statement of Competencies Expected of Students Entering California's Public Colleges and Universities*, available online: www.asccc.org/papers/academic-literacy-statement-competencies-expected-students-entering-californias-public.

Isaacs, T, Trofimovich, P and Foote, J A (2017) Developing a user-oriented second language comprehensibility scale for English-medium universities, *Language Testing* 35 (2), 193–216.

Jafari, K and Hashim, F (2012) The effects of using advance organizers on improving EFL learners' listening comprehension: A mixed method study, *System* 40 (2), 270–281.

Jenkins, J (2002) A sociolinguistically based, empirically researched pronunciation syllabus for English as an International Language, *Applied Linguistics* 23 (1), 83–103.

Jensen, C and Hansen, C (1995) The effect of prior knowledge on EAP listening-test performance, *Language Testing* 12, 99–119.

Jones, N and Saville, N (2009) European language policy: Assessment, learning, and the CEFR, *Annual Review of Applied Linguistics* 29, 51–63.

Jones, N and Saville, N (2016) *Learning Oriented Assessment: A Systemic Approach*, Studies in Language Assessment Volume 45, Cambridge: UCLES/Cambridge University Press.

Kang, O, Thomson, R I and Moran, M (2019) The effects of international accents and shared first language on listening comprehension tests, *TESOL Quarterly* 53 (1), 56–81.

Kang, O, Thomson, R I and Moran, M (2020) Which features of accent affect understanding? Exploring the intelligibility threshold of diverse accent varieties, *Applied Linguistics* 41 (4), 453–480.

Kang, O, Moran, M, Ahn, H and Park, S (2020) Proficiency as a mediating variable of intelligibility for different varieties of accents, *Studies in Second Language Acquisition* 42 (2), 471–487.

Kerstjens, M and Nery, K (2000) Predictive validity in the IELTS Test, *IELTS Research Reports* 3, 85–108.

Khalifa, H and Weir, C J (2009) *Examining Reading: Research and Practice in Assessing Second Language Reading*, Studies in Language Testing volume 29, Cambridge: UCLES/Cambridge University Press.

Knoch, U and Sitajalabhorn, W (2013) A closer look at integrated writing tasks, *Assessing Writing* 18, 300–308.

Knoch, U, May, L, Macqueen, S, Pill, J and Storch, N (2016) Transitioning from university to the workplace: Stakeholder perceptions of academic and professional writing demands, *IELTS Research Reports* 2016 (1), 4–37.

Kormos, J and Taylor, L (2021) Testing the L2 of Learners with Specific Learning Difficulties, in Winke, P and Brunfaut, T (Eds) *The Routledge Handbook of Second Language Acquisition and Language Testing*, New York/Abingdon: Routledge, 413–421.

Kwon, S K (forthcoming 2024) The impact of visual input in a video listening test on test takers' viewing patterns and listening performances, in Yu,

G and Xu, J (Eds) *Language Test Validation in a Digital Age*, Studies in Language Testing Volume 52, Cambridge: Cambridge University Press & Assessment.

Laufer, B (1989) What percentage of text is essential for comprehension?, in Lauren, C and Nordman, N (Eds) *Special Language: From Humans Thinking to Thinking Machines*, Clevedon: Multilingual Matters, 316–323.

Laver, J (1994) *Principles of Phonetics*, Cambridge: Cambridge University Press.

Li, J (2014a) *IELTS Listening Test Strategy Research*, MA dissertation, University of Warwick.

Li, J (2014b) *IELTS Listening Test Strategy Research*, Köln: LAP Lambert Academic Publishing.

Lim, G, Geranpayeh, A, Khalifa, H and Buckendhal, C (2013) Standard setting to an international reference framework: Implications for theory and practice, *International Journal of Testing* 13, 32–49.

Low, G, Littlemore, J, and Koester, A (2008) Metaphor use in three UK university lectures, *Applied Linguistics* 29 (3), 428–455.

Lu, Z and Liu, M (2011) Foreign language anxiety and strategy use: A study with Chinese undergraduate EFL learners, *Journal of Language Teaching and Research* 2, 1,298–1,305.

Luckin, R (2018) *Machine Learning and Human Intelligence: The Future of Education for the 21st Century*, London: UCL IOE Press.

Lynch, T (2004) *Study Listening*, Cambridge: Cambridge University Press.

Lynch, T (2011) Academic listening in the 21st century: Reviewing a decade of research, *Journal of English for Academic Purposes* 10 (2), 79–88.

Macaro, E, Graham, S and Vanderplank, R (2007) A review of listening strategies: Focus on sources of knowledge and on success, in Cohen, A D and Macaro, E (Eds) *Language Learner Strategies,* Oxford: Oxford University Press, 165–185.

Major, R C, Fitzmaurice, S F, Bunta, F and Balasubramanian, C (2002) The effects of nonnative accents on listening comprehension: implications for ESL assessment, *TESOL Quarterly* 36, 173–190.

Major, R C, Fitzmaurice, S F, Bunta, F and Balasubramanian, C (2005) Testing the effects of regional, ethnic and international dialects of English in listening comprehension, *Language Learning* 55 (1) 37–69.

Martinez, R, Adolphs, S and Carter, R (2013) Listening for needles in haystacks: How lecturers introduce key terms, *ELT Journal* 67 (3), 313–323.

McCarthy, M and Carter, R (1997) Written and spoken vocabulary, in Schmitt, N and McCarthy, M (Eds) *Vocabulary: Description, Acquisition and Pedagogy*, Cambridge: Cambridge University Press, 20–39.

McDowell, C and Merrylees, B (1998) Survey of receiving institutions' use and attitude to IELTS, *IELTS Research Reports* 1, 116–139.

McGurk, H and McDonald, J (1976) Hearing lips and seeing voices, *Nature* 264, 746–748.

McNamara, T (2000) *Language Testing*, Oxford: Oxford University Press.

McNamara, T and Roever, C (2006) *Language Testing: The Social Dimension*, Oxford: Blackwell.

Mecartty, F (2000) Lexical and grammatical knowledge in reading and listening comprehension by foreign language learners of Spanish, *Applied Language Learning* 11, 323–348.

Merrifield, G (2012) The use of IELTS for assessing immigration eligibility in Australia, New Zealand, Canada and the United Kingdom, *IELTS Research Reports* 13, 1–32.
Merrifield, G (2016) An impact study into the use of IELTS by professional associations in the United Kingdom, Canada, Australia and New Zealand, 2014 to 2015, *IELTS Research Report* 2016 (7), 1–35.
Messick, S (1989) Validity, in Linn, R L (Ed) *Educational Measurement* (Third edition), Washington DC: The American Council on Education and the National Council on Measurement in Education, 3–103.
Messick, S (1995) Validity of psychological assessment: Validation of inferences from persons' responses and performances as scientific inquiry into score meaning, *American Psychologist* 50 (9), 741–749.
Milanovic, M (2009) Cambridge ESOL and the CEFR, *Research Notes* 37, 2–5.
Milanovic, M and Weir, C J (2010) Series Editors' note, in Martyniuk, W (Ed) *Relating Language Examinations to the Common European Framework of Reference for Languages: Case Studies and Reflections on the Use of the Council of Europe's Draft Manual*, Studies in Language Testing volume 33, Cambridge: UCLES/Cambridge University Press, viii–xx.
Milton, J (2009) *Measuring Second Language Vocabulary Acquisition*, Bristol: Multilingual Matters.
Milton, J and Hopkins, N (2006) Comparing phonological and orthographic vocabulary size, *Canadian Modern Language Review* 63 (1), 127–147.
Montenegro-Rueda, M, Luque-de la Rosa, A, Sarasola Sánchez-Serrano, J L and Fernández-Cerero, J (2021) Assessment in Higher Education during the COVID-19 Pandemic: A Systematic Review, *Sustainability* 2021 (13), 10509.
Moore, T, Morton, J, Hall, D and Wallis, C (2015) Literacy practices in the professional workplace: Implications for the IELTS reading and writing tests, *IELTS Research Reports Online* 2015-1, available online: www.ielts.org/-/media/research-reports/ielts_online_rr_2015-1.ashx.
Motteram, J (2020) *Standard English as spoken by Singaporeans: Exploring language test localization and the impact of accent in listening comprehension*, paper presented at New Directions East Asia 2020, Singapore.
Murray, N (2016) *Standards of English in Higher Education: Issues, Challenges and Strategies*, Cambridge: Cambridge University Press.
Murray, D and Arkoudis, S (2013) Discussion Paper 1: Preparation and Selection, in International Education Association of Australia (Ed) *Five Years On: English Language Competence of International Students. Outcomes Report June 2013*, 23–51, available online: www.ieaa.org.au/documents/item/54.
Murray, J, Cross, J and Cruikshank, K (2014) Stakeholder perceptions of IELTS as a gateway to the professional workplace: The case of employers of overseas trained teachers, *IELTS Research Reports Online Series* 2014/1, available online: www.ielts.org/-/media/research-reports/ielts_online_rr_2014-1.ashx.
Nation, I S P (2001) *Learning Vocabulary in Another Language*, Cambridge: Cambridge University Press.
Nguyen, T N H (2007) Effects of test preparation on test performance: The case of the IELTS and TOEFL iBT listening tests, *Melbourne Papers in Language Testing* 12 (1), 1–24.
Nygaard, L C (2008) Linguistic and nonlingusitic properties of speech, in Pisoni, D B and Remez, R E (Eds) *The Handbook of Speech Perception*, Oxford: Blackwell, 390–413.

Nygaard, L C and Pisoni, D B (1998) Talker-specific perceptual learning in speech perception, *Perception and Psychophysics* 60, 355–376.
O'Loughlin, K (2008) The use of IELTS for university selection in Australia: A case study, *IELTS Research Reports* 8, 145–187.
O'Loughlin, K (2012) Developing the assessment literacy of university proficiency test users, *Language Testing* 30 (3), 363–380.
O'Loughlin, K and Arkoudis, S (2009) Investigating IELTS score gains in higher education, *IELTS Research Reports* 10, 95–180.
O'Malley, J M and Chamot, U (1990) *Learning Strategies in Second Language Acquisition*, Cambridge: Cambridge University Press.
O'Neill, T R, Buckendahl, C W, Plake, B S and Taylor, L (2007) Recommending a nursing-specific passing standard for the IELTS examination, *Language Assessment Quarterly* 4 (4) 295–317.
O'Sullivan, B (2000) *Towards a model of performance in oral language testing*, unpublished PhD thesis, University of Reading.
O'Sullivan, B (Ed) (2011) *Language Testing: Theories and Practices*, Basingstoke: Palgrave Macmillan.
O'Sullivan, B (2016) Validity: What is it and who is it for?, in Leung, Y (Ed) *Epoch Making in English Teaching and Learning: Evolution, Innovation, and Revolution*, Taipei: Crane Publishing Company Ltd, 157–175.
O'Sullivan, B (2019) Considering Validity, in Roever, C and Wigglesworth, G (Eds) *Social Perspectives on Language Testing: papers in honour of Tim McNamara*, Frankfurt: Peter Lang, 199–216.
O'Sullivan, B and Chalhoub-Deville, M (2021) Language Testing for Migrants: Co-Constructing Validation, *Language Assessment Quarterly* 18 (5), 547–557.
O'Sullivan, B and Chalhoub-Deville, M (in press 2023) Validity: An Integrated Arguments Approach, in Dobric, N, Cesnik, H and Harsch, C (Eds) *Festschrift in Honor of Günther Sigott*, Language Testing and Evaluation Series Volume 46, Frankfurt: Peter Lang.
O'Sullivan, B and Green, A B (2011) Test taker characteristics, in Taylor, L (Ed) *Examining Speaking: Research and Practice in Assessing Second Language Speaking*, Studies in Language Testing volume 30, Cambridge: UCLES/ Cambridge University Press, 36–64.
O'Sullivan, B and Weir, C J (2011) Language Testing and Validation, in O'Sullivan, B (Ed) *Language Testing: Theory and Practice*, Oxford: Palgrave, 13–32.
O'Sullivan, B, Breakspear, T and Bayliss, W (2023) Validating an AI-Driven Scoring System: The Model Card Approach, in Sadeghi, K and Douglas, D (Eds) *Fundamental Considerations in Technology-Mediated Language Assessment,* New York: Routledge, 115–134.
Ockey, G J (2007) Construct implications of including still image or video in computer-based listening tests, *Language Testing* 24, 517–537.
Ockey, G J and French, R (2016) From one to multiple accents on a test of L2 listening comprehension, *Applied Linguistics* 37 (5), 693–715.
Ockey, G J and Wagner, E (Eds) (2018) *Assessing L2 Listening: Moving Towards Authenticity*, Amsterdam: John Benjamins Publishing Company.
Olsen, L A and Huckin, T N (1990) Point-driven understanding in engineering lecture comprehension, *English for Specific Purposes* 9, 33–47.
Owen, N (forthcoming 2024) Investigating the cognitive validity of a reading test using eye-tracking technology and stimulated recall interviews, in Yu, G and

Xu, J (Eds) *Language Test Validation in a Digital Age*, Studies in Language Testing Volume 52, Cambridge: Cambridge University Press & Assessment.

Papageorgiou, S, Stevens, R and Goodwin, S (2012) The relative difficulty of dialogic and monologic input in a second-language listening comprehension test, *Language Assessment Quarterly* 9 (4), 375–397.

Pashler, H and Johnston, J C (1998) Attentional limitations in dual task performance, in Pashler, H (Ed) *Attention*, Hove: Psychology Press, 155–189.

Patterson, R and Weideman, A (2012) The refinement of the construct for tests of academic literacy, *Journal for Language Teaching* 47 (1), 125–151.

Pearson (2010) *Aligning PTE Academic test scores to the Common European Framework of Reference for Languages*, Pearson PTE.

Peterson, G E and Barney, H L (1952) Control methods used in a study of the vowels, *Journal of the Acoustical Society of America* 24, 175–84.

Phakiti, A (2016) Test takers' performance appraisals, appraisal calibration, state-trait strategy use, and state-trait IELTS listening difficulty in a simulated IELTS Listening test, *IELTS Research Reports Online* 2016/6, available online: www.ielts.org/for-researchers/research-reports/online-series-2016-6.

Picard, M (2007) English entrance requirements and language support for overseas postgraduate students, in Higher Education Research and Development Society of Australasia Inc. (Ed) *Enhancing Higher Education: Theory and Scholarship: Proceedings of the 30th HERDSA Conference, Adelaide, 2007*, New South Wales: Higher Education Research and Development Society of Australasia Inc., 439–449.

Pickering, L (2004) The structure and function of intonational paragraphs in native and non-native speaker instructional discourse, *English for Specific Purposes* 23, 19–43.

Pisoni, D B (1997) Some thoughts on "normalization" in speech perception, in Johnson, K and Mullennix, J W (Eds) *Talker Variability in Speech Processing*, San Diego: Academic Press, 33–66.

Read, J (2022) Test review: The International English Language Testing System (IELTS), *Language Testing* 39 (4), doi.org/10.1177/02655322221086211.

Read, J and Hayes, B (2003) The impact of IELTS on preparation for academic study in New Zealand, *International English Language Testing System (IELTS) Research Reports* 4, 153–206.

Read, J and Hirsh, D (2005) *English language levels in tertiary institutions. Export Education Levy Project E4*, Wellington: Education New Zealand.

Read, J and Wette, R (2009) Achieving English proficiency for professional registration: The experience of overseas-qualified health professionals in the New Zealand context, *IELTS Research Reports* 10, 181–232.

Richards, J (1983) Listening comprehension: approach, design, procedure, *TESOL Quarterly* 17, 219–239.

Rogers, M P H and Webb, S (2016) Listening to lectures, in Hyland, K and Shaw, P (Eds) *The Routledge Handbook of English for Academic Purposes*, New York/Abingdon: Routledge, 165–176.

Rossi, O and Brunfaut, T (2021) Text authenticity in listening assessment: Can item writers be trained to produce authentic-sounding texts?, *Language Assessment Quarterly* 18 (4), 398–418.

Ruhm, R, Leitner-Jones, C, Kulmhofer, A, Kiefer, T, Mlakar, H and Itzlinger-Bruneforth, U (2016) Playing the recording once or twice: Effects on listening test performances, *International Journal of Listening* 30 (1–2), 67–83.

Rukthong, A and Brunfaut, T (2020) Is anybody listening? The nature of second language listening in integrated listening-to-summarize tasks, *Language Testing* 37 (1), 31–53.

Saito, K, Macmillan, K, Kachlicka, M, Kunihara, T and Minematsu, N (2023) Automated assessment of second language comprehensibility: Review, training, validation, and generalization studies, *Studies in Second Language Acquisition* 45 (1), 234–263.

Salisbury, K (2005) *The edge of expertise: Towards an understanding of listening test item writing as professional practice*, unpublished PhD thesis, King's College London.

Sanz, M, Laka, I and Tanenhaus, M K (2013) *Language Down the Garden Path*, Oxford: Oxford University Press.

Saville, N (2009) *Developing a model for investigating the impact of language assessment within educational contexts by a public examination provider*, unpublished PhD thesis, University of Bedfordshire.

Saville, N (2021) Learning-Oriented Assessment: Basic Concepts and Frameworks in Using Assessment to Support Language Learning, in Gebril, A (Ed) *Learning-Oriented Language Assessment: Putting Theory into Practice*, Abingdon: Routledge, 13–33.

Sawyer, W and Singh, M (2012) Learning to play the 'classroom tennis' well: IELTS and international students in teacher education, *IELTS Research Reports* 11/2, available online: www.ielts.org/-/media/research-reports/ielts_rr_volume11_report2.ashx.

Schmidt, E and Pastorino, C (forthcoming 2024) Eye tracking and EEG in language assessment, in Yu, G and Xu, J (Eds) *Language Test Validation in a Digital Age*, Studies in Language Testing Volume 52, Cambridge: Cambridge University Press & Assessment.

Schmidt-Rinehart, B C (1994) The effects of topic familiarity on second language listening comprehension, *Modern Language Journal* 78 (2), 179–189.

Schmitt, N, Dunn, K, O'Sullivan, B, Anthony, L and Kremmel, B (2021) *Knowledge-based Vocabulary Lists*, British Council Monographs, Sheffield: Equinox.

Sedgwick, C, Garner, M and Vicente-Macia, I (2016) Investigating the language needs of international nurses: Insiders' perspectives, *IELTS Reports Online Series* 2016/2, available online: www.ielts.org/-/media/research-reports/ielts_online_rr_2016-2.ashx.

Segalowitz, N (2016) Automaticity, in Robinson, P (Ed) *The Routledge Encyclopaedia of Second Language Acquisition*, New York/Abingdon: Routledge, 53–57.

Shaw, S D and Weir, C J (2007) *Examining Writing: Research and Practice in Assessing Second Language Writing*, Studies in Language Testing volume 26, Cambridge: UCLES/Cambridge University Press.

Sherman, J (1997) The effect of question preview in listening comprehension tests, *Language Testing* 14, 185–213.

Shin, S Y, Lee, S and Lidster, R (2021) Examining the effects of different English speech varieties on an L2 academic listening comprehension test at the item level, *Language Testing* 38 (4), 580–601.

Smith, H and Haslett, S (2007) Attitudes of tertiary key decision-makers towards English language tests in Aotearoa New Zealand: Report on the results of a national provider survey, *IELTS Research Reports* 7, 13–57.

References and further reading

Smith, P A, Allan, H, Larsen, J A and Mackintosh, M M (2005) *Valuing and Recognising the Talents of a Diverse Healthcare Workforce*, Report from the REOH Study: Researching Equal Opportunities for Overseas-Trained Nurses and Other Healthcare Professionals, Surrey: University of Surrey/RCN.

Snow, C and Uccelli, P (2009) The challenge of academic language, in Olson, D R and Torrance, N (Eds) *The Cambridge Handbook of Literacy*, Cambridge: Cambridge University Press, 112–133.

Stankov, L and Lee, J (2008) Confidence and cognitive test performance, *Journal of Educational Psychology* 100 (4), 961–976.

Study.com (2023) *The Perception of Chat GPT in Schools*, available online: study.com/resources/perceptions-of-chatgpt-in-schools

Styles, E (2006) *The Psychology of Attention*, Hove: Psychology Press.

Sueyoshi, A and Hardison, D M (2005) The role of gesture and facial cues in second language listening comprehension, *Language Learning* 55, 661–699.

Suvorov, R (2009) Context visuals in L2 listening tests: The effects of photographs and video vs. audio-only format, in Chapelle, C A, Jun, H G and Katz, I (Eds) *Developing and Evaluating Language Learning Materials*, Ames: Iowa State University, 53–68.

Suvorov, R (2015) *Interacting with visuals in L2 listening tests: An eye-tracking study*, London: British Council ARAGs Reports, available online: www.britishcouncil.org/exam/aptis/research/publications/interacting.

Suvorov, R (forthcoming 2024) The use of eye tracking in validating L2 listening assessments, in Yu, G and Xu, J (Eds) *Language Test Validation in a Digital Age*, Studies in Language Testing Volume 52, Cambridge: Cambridge University Press & Assessment.

Tannenbaum, R J and Wylie, E C (2008) *Linking English language test scores onto the Common European Framework of Reference: An application of standard setting methodology*, TOEFL iBT Research Report RR-08-34, Princeton: Educational Testing Service.

Tauroza, S and Allison, D (1990) Speech rates in British English, *Applied Linguistics* 11 (1), 90–105.

Taylor, L (2004) IELTS, Cambridge ESOL examinations and the Common European Framework, *Research Notes* 18, 2–3.

Taylor, L (2006) The changing landscape of English: implications for language assessment, *ELT Journal* 60 (1), 51–60.

Taylor, L (2009a) Developing assessment literacy, *Annual Review of Applied Linguistics* 29, 21–36.

Taylor, L (2009b) Language varieties and their implications for testing and assessment, in Taylor, L and Weir, C J (Eds) *Language Testing Matters: Investigating the Wider Social and Educational Impact of Assessment. Proceedings of the ALTE Cambridge conference, April 2008*, Studies in Language Testing volume 31, Cambridge: UCLES/ Cambridge University Press, 139–157.

Taylor, L (Ed) (2011) *Examining Speaking: Research and Practice in Assessing Second Language Speaking*, Studies in Language Testing volume 30, Cambridge: UCLES/Cambridge University Press.

Taylor, L and Chan, S (2015) *Reviewing the suitability of English language tests for providing the GMC with evidence of doctors' English proficiency*, available online: www.gmc-uk.org/about/research/28134.asp

Taylor, L and Geranpayeh, A (2011) Assessing listening for academic purposes: Defining and operationalising the test construct, *Journal of English for Academic Purposes* 10 (2), 89–101.

Taylor, L and Saville, N (Eds) (2020) *Lessons and Legacy: A Tribute to Professor Cyril J Weir (1950–2018)*, Studies in Language Testing Volume 50, Cambridge: UCLES/Cambridge University Press.

Taylor, L and Weir, C J (2012) Introduction, in *IELTS Collected Papers 2: Research in Reading and Listening Assessment*, Studies in Language Testing volume 34, Cambridge: UCLES/Cambridge University Press, 1–33.

Thighe, D, Jones, N and Geranpayeh, A (2001) *IELTS PB and CB equivalence: A comparison of equated versions of the reading and listening components of PB IELTS in relation to CB IELTS*, Cambridge ESOL Internal Validation Report 288.

Thompson, P and Nesi, H (2001) The British Academic Spoken English (BASE) Corpus Project, *Language Teaching Research* 5 (3), 263–264.

Thompson, S (2003) Test-structuring metadiscourse, intonation and the signalling of organisation in academic lectures, *Journal of English for Academic Purposes* 2, 5–20.

Tonkyn, A (1995) English language proficiency standards for overseas students: Who needs what level?, *Journal of International Education* 6, 37–61.

Vandergrift, L and Goh, C C M (2012) *Teaching and Learning Second Language Listening*, New York/Abingdon: Routledge.

Vandergrift, L, Goh, C C M, Mareschal, C and Tafaghodtari, M H (2006) The Metacognitive-Awareness Listening Questionnaire (MALQ): Development and validation, *Language Learning* 56 (3), 431–462.

Wagner, E (2010) The effects of the use of video tasks on ESL Listening test taker performance, *Language Testing* 27 (4), 493–513.

Wagner, E, Liao, Y F and Wagner, S (2021) Authenticated spoken texts for L2 listening tests, *Language Assessment Quarterly* 18 (3), 205–227.

Wall, D (1997) Impact and washback in language testing, in Clapham, C and Corson, D (Eds) *Encyclopaedia of Language and Education: Vol. 7. Language Testing and Assessment*, Dordrecht: Kluwer Academic, 291–302.

Weir, C J (1983) *Identifying the language needs of overseas students in tertiary education in the United Kingdom*, unpublished PhD thesis, Institute of Education, University of London.

Weir, C J (2005) *Language Testing and Validation: An Evidence-based Approach*, Basingstoke: Palgrave Macmillan.

Weir, C J and Chan, S (2019) *Research and Practice in Assessing Academic Reading: The Case of IELTS*, Studies in Language Testing volume 51, Cambridge: UCLES/Cambridge University Press.

Weir, C J, Hawkey, R, Green, A B and Devi, S (2012) The cognitive processes underlying the academic construct as measured by IELTS, in Taylor, L and Weir, C J (Eds) *IELTS Collected Papers 2: Research in Reading and Listening Assessment*, Studies in Language Testing Volume 34, Cambridge: UCLES/Cambridge University Press, 212–269.

Westbrook, C (2019) *The impact of input task characteristics on performance on an integrated listening-into-writing EAP assessment*, unpublished PhD thesis, University of Bedfordshire.

Winke, P and Lim, H (2014) The effects of testwiseness and test-taking anxiety on L2 listening performance: A visual (eye-tracking) and attentional investigation, *IELTS Research Reports Online Series* 2014/3, available online: www.ielts.org/-/media/research-reports/ielts_online_rr_2014-3.ashx.

References and further reading

Woodrow, L (2006) Academic success of international postgraduate education students and the role of English proficiency, *University of Sydney Papers in TESOL* 1, 51–70.
Wray, A (2002) *Formulaic Language and the Lexicon*, Cambridge: Cambridge University Press.
Wu, Y (1998) What do tests of listening comprehension test? – A retrospection study of EFL test takers performing a multiple-choice task, *Language Testing* 15 (1), 21–44.
Wu, W M and Stansfield, C W (2001) Towards authenticity of task in test development, *Language Testing* 18 (2), 187–206.
Zhang, X (2013) Foreign language listening anxiety and listening performance: Conceptualizations and causal relationships, *System* 41 (1), 164–177.
Zheng, Y and Cheng, L (2018) How does anxiety influence language performance? From the perspectives of foreign language classroom anxiety and cognitive test anxiety, *Language Testing in Asia* 8 (1), 2–20.

Author index

A
Adolphs, S 83
Ahern, S 37
Ahn, H 101
Alderson, J C 6, 16, 30, 33
Allan, H 48
Allen, D 19
Allison, D 97
Allwright, J 26
Anthony, L 79
Arkoudis, S 14, 18
Aryadoust, V 61, 62

B
Baddeley, A 67
Badger, R 70, 71, 102, 122, 133
Baik, C 14
Balasubramanian, C 98, 100
Banerjee, J 26, 42
Barney, H L 95
Batty, A O 94
Bax, S 144
Bayliss, A 15, 19, 26–29, 62, 74, 96, 131
Bayliss, W 145
Bekleyen, N 54
Bellingham, L 23, 26
Bent, T 98
Berne, J E 105
Berry, V 39, 42, 43, 46, 48, 51, 52, 53, 91, 128
Blackhurst, A 107
Blackmore, J 39, 40
Boroughs, R 106
Buolamwini, J 146
Bradlow, A R 98
Braxton, M A 72
Breakspear, T 145
Breeze, R 28, 29

Brindley, G 112, 117
British Academic Spoken English Corpus (BASE) 83–85, 88, 92, 132
Brooks, G 15
Brown, A 78
Brown, G 65
Brunfaut, T 85, 127
Buck, G 62, 68, 106, 113
Buckendahl, C W 50
Bunta, F 98, 100
Burns, A 83
Butler, J 98
Bybee, J 96

C
Calvert, D R 86, 96
Campbell, C 83, 92
Canagarajah, S 97
Capic, T 39, 40
Carter, R 80, 83
Cervantes, R 104, 105
Chalhoub-Deville, M 9, 13, 23, 129, 140, 144, 145
Chamot, U 71
Chan, S 2, 3, 4, 51, 125, 127, 128
Chang, A C-S 104
Cheng, L 54
Chiang, C S 74
Cho, H 125
Chung, J M 71
Clapham, C 6
Clopper, C G 98
Cohen, A D 70
Coleman, D 14
Coleman, G 89, 104, 112
Coniam, D 94
Conrow, F 23, 24, 26, 76
Cotton, F 23, 24, 26, 76

Council of Europe 9, 11
Criper, C 22
Cross, J 39, 40, 51
Cruikshank, K 39
Cumming, A 125

D
Dai, D W 101
Davies, A 8, 14, 22, 73, 99
Denham, P 24
Devi, S xii
Deroey, K 82, 83
Dooey, P 23, 28
Dörnyei, Z 71
Dudley-Evans, T 82
Dunkel, P 74
Dunn, K 79

E
Eberharter, K 72, 122
Elder, C 14, 17, 18, 19, 23, 24, 99, 127
Elliott, M 53, 56
Ellis, L 98
ETS 30, 108

F
Faerch, G 71
Feast, V 23
Ferguson, G 23
Fernández-Cerero, J 145
Field, J 10, 15, 16, 23, 32, 54, 64, 65, 67, 70, 71, 75, 78, 79, 81, 83, 85, 86, 87, 90, 93, 96, 99, 102, 103, 105, 107, 110, 111, 113, 116, 117, 118, 119, 121, 122, 133
Figueras, N 30
Fiocco, M 23
Fitzmaurice, S F 98, 100
Fleming, S 19, 24
Floccia, C 98
Flowerdew, J 82
Foote, J A 146
Fortunati, L 146
Freedle, R 111, 117
French, R 98
Frost, K 127

G
Gainer, G 104, 105
Gardiner, J 133
Garner, M 39, 47, 128
Gathercole, S E 67
Gebru, T 146
Geranpayeh, A 9, 30, 31, 32, 34, 59, 61, 76, 100, 107
Gernsbacher, M A 4
Gilmore, A 81, 82, 83, 90, 92
Gimson, A C 65
Ginther, A 94
Girard, F 98
Goh, C C M 62, 71
Golchi, M M 54
Golder, K 19, 24
Goldinger, S D 96
Goldman-Eisler, F 96
Goodwin, S 89
Goslin, J 98
Graham, S 71, 72
Green, A B xii, 17, 30, 32, 37, 53, 56
Green, K P 93
Gribble, C 39, 40
Griffiths, R 96
Gruba, P 94

H
Hall, D 39
Hall, G 37
Hansen, C 74
Harding, L 100, 132
Hardison, D M 94
Hashim, F 18
Haslett, S 47
Hawkey, R xii
Hawkins, S 96
Hayes, B 16, 17, 136
Heap, S 89, 104, 112
Henning, G 104
Herron, C A 90
Hill, K 14, 23
Hirsh, D 47
Holzknecht, F 72, 122
Hopkins, N 79
Horwitz, E 54

Howlett, S 133
Huckin, T N 82
Hyatt, D 15

I
Ingram, D 15, 19, 26, 27, 29, 62, 74, 96, 131
In'nami, Y 54, 111
Inoue, C 127
Intersegmental Committee of the Academic Senates of the California Community Colleges, the California State University, and the University of California 4
Isaacs, T 146
Itzlinger-Bruneforth, U 105

J
Jafari, K 18
Jenkins, J 100
Jensen, C 74
Johnston, J C 67, 111
Jones, N 30, 107, 145

K
Kachlicka, M 145
Kang, O 101
Kasper, G 71
Kerstjens, M 23
Khalifa, H 9, 30–34, 56, 76
Kiefer, T 105
Knoch, U 39, 127
Koester, A 86
Koizumi, R 111
Konopczynski, G 98
Konrad, E 72, 122
Kormos, J 56
Kostin, I 111, 117
Kremmel, B 72, 79, 122
Kuijper, H 30
Kulmhofer, A 105
Kunihara, T 145
Kwon, S K 144

L
Lai, C 125
Laka, I 69

Lam, D M K 127
Larsen, J A 48
Laufer, B 80
Laver, J 4, 96
Lee, J 55
Lee, S 101
Leitner-Jones, C 105
Li, J 71
Liao, Y F 85
Lidster, R 101
Lim, G 30, 31, 32, 34, 76
Lim, H 18, 54
Littlemore, J 86
Liu, M 54
Low, G 86
Lu, Z 54
Luckin, R 143
Lumley, T 14
Luque-de la Rosa, A 145
Lynch, B 23
Lynch, T 81, 88, 91

M
McCarthy, M 80
McCray, G 72, 122
McDonald, J 93
McDowell, C 15
McGurk, H 93
McNamara, T 14, 37
Macaro, E 71, 72
Mackintosh, M M 48
Macmillan, K 145
Macqueen, S 39
Major, R C 98, 100
Mareschal, C 62
Martinez, R 83
May, L 39
Mecartty, F 81
Merrifield, G 41, 42, 49
Merrylees, B 15
Messick, S 13, 140
Milanovic, M 30, 32
Miller, P 28, 29
Milton, J 79, 80, 81
Minematsu, N 145
Mlakar, H 105

Montenegro-Rueda, M 145
Moore, T 39
Moran, M 101
Morton, J 39
Morrissey, A M 39, 40
Motteram, J 101
Murray, D 14
Murray, J 39, 40, 51
Murray, N 7, 13, 14, 24, 26, 51, 130

N
Nation, I S P 80
Nery, K 23
Nesi, H 83
Nguyen, T N H 18
Nold, G 30
Nygaard, L C 95, 96

O
O'Loughlin, K 15, 17, 18, 19, 20, 23, 51, 130
O'Malley, J M 71
O'Neill, T R 50
O'Sullivan, B 9, 13, 19, 36, 37, 39, 42, 43, 46, 48, 51, 52, 53, 56, 79, 91, 128, 129, 140, 144, 145
Ockey, G J 94, 98, 101
Oliver, R 23
Olsen, L A 82
Oner, J 24
Owen, N 144

P
Papageorgiou, S 89
Park, S 101
Pashler, H 67, 111
Pastorino, C 144
Pearson 30
Patterson, R 82
Peterson, G E 95
Phakiti, A 55, 56
Picard, M 24, 76
Pickering, L 91
Pill, J 39
Pisoni, D B 95, 96, 98
Plake, B S 50

R
Read, J 16, 17, 37, 39, 47, 104, 136
Reeder, K 19, 24
Richards, J 66, 67, 68
Richardson, S 14
Roever, C 37, 101
Rogers, M P H 82, 86
Rossi, O 85
Rugea, S 39, 42, 43, 46, 48, 51, 52, 53, 91, 128
Ruhm, R 105
Rukthong, A 127

S
Saito, K 145
Salisbury, K 92
Sanz, M 69
Sarasola Sánchez-Serrano, J L 145
Saville, N 13, 30, 145
Sawyer, W 39, 40
Schmidt, E 144
Schmidt-Rinehart, B C 74
Schmitt, N 79
Scott, M L 71
Seay, I 90
Sedgwick, C 39, 47, 128
Segalowitz, N 67
Shaw, S D 9, 13, 56
Sherman, J 108, 134
Shin, S Y 101
Singh, M 39, 40
Sitajalabhorn, W 127
Slatyer, H 112, 117
Smith, H 47
Smith, J 83, 92
Smith, P A 48
Snow, C 81, 82
Spötti, C 72, 122
Stankov, L 55
Stansfield, C W 90
Starfield, S 14
Stevens, R 89
Storch, N 23, 39
Study.com 145
Styles, E 67

Sueyoshi, A 94
Suvorov, R 94, 95, 144

T
Tafaghodtari, M H 62
Takala, S 30
Tanenhaus, M K 69
Tannenbaum, R J 30
Tardieu, C 30
Tatsuoka, K 68
Tauroza, S 97
Taylor, L 8, 9, 14, 30, 32, 33, 50, 51, 52, 56, 59, 61, 75, 99, 100, 130
Thighe, D 107
Thompson, P 83
Thompson, S 91
Thomson, R I 101
Tonkyn, A 23
Trofimovich, P 146
Turner, C E 23

U
Uccelli, P 81, 82

V
Vandergrift, L 62, 71
Vanderplank, R 71, 72
Vicente-Macia, I 39, 47, 128

W
Wagner, E 85, 94, 101
Wagner, S 85
Wall, D 16
Wallis, C 39
Webb, S 82, 86
Weideman, A 82
Weir, C J x, xii, 2, 3, 4, 8, 9, 13, 30, 32, 33, 36, 52, 56, 62, 75, 125, 128, 140, 142
Westbrook, C 127
Wette, R 39, 47
White, E 23
Wigglesworth, G 127
Winke, P 18, 54
Woodrow, L 23, 24
Wray, A 67, 69
Wu, W M 90
Wu, Y 111
Wylie, E C 30

Y
Yan, X 70, 71, 102, 122, 133
Yule, G 78

Z
Zehentner, M 72, 122
Zhang, X 54
Zheng, Y 54

Subject index

English language tests
Certificate in Advanced English (CAE, now known as C1 Advanced) 31, 32
Certificate of Proficiency in English (CPE, now known as C2 Proficiency) 85, 86
English Language Testing Service (ELTS) 6
English Proficiency Test Battery (EPTB) 6
IELTS Academic 25, 31, 36, 74
IELTS General Training 25, 36
IELTS Life Skills 52
Internet-based Test of English as a Foreign Language (TOEFL iBT) 10, 14, 18, 19, 74, 76, 77, 94, 97, 108, 125, 127, 135
Occupational English Test (OET) 47, 125
Pearson Test of English (PTE) 7
Pearson Test of English Academic (PTE Academic) 7, 10, 14, 34, 125
Secure English Language Test (SELT) 50
Test of English as a Foreign Language (TOEFL) 7, 16, 18, 34, 61, 98, 104

Key concepts in academic listening assessment

A
Academic discourse 27, 75, 76, 78, 80–86, 89, 90, 92, 97
Anxiety 54, 106, 127, 133
Authenticity
  Delivery 3, 10, 81, 83, 88, 90, 92, 93, 96, 97, 101, 137
  Improvised 90–93
  Recordings of real-life speech events 90, 92
  Scripted material 4, 5, 31, 33, 81, 83, 84, 85, 90–93, 97, 101, 132
  Semi-scripted 5, 90–93, 132
Automaticity 4, 62, 66, 67, 69, 70, 95

B
Background information 5, 29, 74
Bias 13, 25, 74, 76, 81, 99, 100, 112, 132, 137
British Academic Spoken Corpus (BASE) 83, 84, 85, 88, 92, 132

C
Cognitive model of listening 1, 2, 61–70, 117
Common European Framework of Reference for Languages (CEFR) 9, 11, 30–35, 49, 50, 52, 63, 67, 116, 131, 135, 136
  Aligning IELTS to CEFR 30–35
Communicative Language Teaching 6, 48–50, 54
Computer-based testing 95, 107–109, 134–135
Construct-irrelevance 4, 20, 62, 69, 108, 118
Critical thinking 4, 26

D
Dialogue 4, 8, 55, 56, 76, 83, 86, 88, 89, 96, 97, 100, 137
Differential item functioning 62
Discourse construction 4–5, 64, 66, 69, 117, 118, 120

169

Discourse markers 66–68, 78, 82–85, 88, 115, 126
Discourse types
   Analytical/interpretative 78, 79, 132
   Argumentative 78, 79, 132
   Critical 78, 132
   Descriptive 78, 132
   Discursive 32, 77–80, 84, 132
   Expository 32, 77, 78, 131
   Informational 5, 78, 101
   Instructional 16, 54, 68, 78
   Narrative 32, 78, 80
   Persuasive 78, 132
   Process-descriptive 78, 132
Domain specificity 7, 126, 126

E
Emotional state 53
English as a Medium of Instruction (EMI) 100–101
English as a Second Language (ESL) 94
English for Academic Purposes (EAP) 6, 15, 16, 17, 21, 50, 59, 61, 82, 83, 85, 90, 91, 94, 100, 103, 110, 125–127, 130, 133, 136
External validation 9, 26, 30, 31, 32, 34, 37, 43, 135
Eye-tracking 72, 94, 95, 137

F
Formal discourse 48, 55, 56, 68, 80–85, 88, 90, 97

G
Gap filling 105–107, 110, 111, 113, 114, 117, 119, 133, 134
Global listening 106
Grade Point Average (GPA) 22
Grammar 16, 66, 79, 81, 82, 85, 114, 115

H
Higher-level listening skills 4, 45, 62, 69, 120, 131, 134

I
Inferencing 37, 62, 67, 69, 113, 118, 119, 122
   Fact + fact inference 120
Informal discourse 48, 55, 56, 75, 77, 80, 85, 88
Information density 62, 82, 83, 86–88, 90
Input decoding 64, 67, 118
Integrated skills testing 45, 46, 125–128, 135
   Listening-into-speaking 127
   Listening-into-writing 127, 135
   Reading-into-writing 125–128, 135
Intonation 3, 65, 97
   Signals 68, 91
Interaction 3, 53, 65, 73, 88–89, 93, 97, 104, 128, 130, 131
   Seminar 4, 75, 92
   Tutor-student 39, 52, 75, 77
Item design
   Density 62, 82, 83, 86–88, 90, 116–117
   Length and complexity 18, 75, 87, 116–117
   Number of items 8, 34, 79, 116, 118
Item Writer Guidelines 12, 32, 34, 64, 76, 77, 79, 84, 85, 86, 89, 92, 101, 104, 113, 117, 118, 121, 131–137

K
Knowledge
   Speaker 69, 81
   Topic 69, 71, 74, 81
   World 37, 65, 69, 81

L
Length
   Recording 8, 86–88, 137
   Utterance 81
   Word 86–88
Lexis
   Overlap 117
   Paraphrase 88, 95, 103, 113, 117, 120, 134

Subject index

Search 54, 65, 67, 117, 118, 119
Verbatim 113, 119, 120
Literacy
  Academic 7, 14, 20, 130
  Assessment 14, 20, 42, 43, 50, 130
  General 7
Local listening 5, 88, 106, 108, 113, 137
Lower-level listening skills 31, 45, 55, 62, 69, 71, 78, 104–106, 115, 118

M
Meaning construction 64–69, 117–120
Medical practitioners
  Suitability of IELTS Listening test 28, 40–49, 51, 53, 91, 128, 130, 131
Mental model building 94, 108
Metacognitive processes 62, 71, 111
Metadiscourse 91
Mode of listening 3–4, 68
Monologue 4, 8, 55, 56, 86, 88–89, 96, 97, 137
Multiple choice 5, 8, 16, 18, 19, 55, 90, 103, 105, 107, 108, 110, 111, 113, 114, 116, 134
Multiple matching 8, 112, 113, 114, 121, 134

N
Nature of information, abstract/
  Concrete 43, 48, 52, 63, 64, 65, 74, 82, 85–87

O
Overseas trained teachers (OTTs) 37, 39–40, 46, 48

P
Parsing 64–69, 81, 117–119
Performance descriptors 14, 15, 20, 30–35, 38, 43, 51, 52, 53, 67, 126, 127, 131
Pronunciation 69

Q
Questions
  Order 45, 103, 108
  Pre-set 103
  Written 102–103

R
Real-world behaviour/demands 2, 5, 9, 10, 17–20, 24, 34, 38, 45, 47, 53, 59, 61, 62, 71–89, 91, 93, 94, 97, 102, 103, 106, 107, 110, 111, 117, 125–128, 132–139
Recording
  Number of plays 48, 54, 55, 75, 87, 104–107, 108, 112, 133, 135, 136
  Speech 10, 79, 82, 83, 91, 101, 132, 136
  Text 10, 79, 88, 90, 92, 93, 111, 132
Reliability 10, 14, 20, 23, 42, 62, 63, 66, 75–76, 83, 98, 101, 107, 110, 114, 115, 119, 122, 126
Response method 110
Richards' taxonomy (1983) 67–70
Rubric 71, 89, 103–104, 108

S
Scores
  Comparison between countries 41–42, 49–50
  Comparison between skills 14–20, 22, 31, 43, 46
  IELTS band score system 22–26, 31, 33, 34, 39–43, 46, 49, 51, 52, 75, 105, 107, 115, 131
  Minimally qualified candidates 42–43
  Skill-specific 126
Self-assessment
  Of understanding of instruction 26–27, 61–62
Self-monitoring 54–56
  Appraisal calibration 55–56
Short-answer question 8
Sociocognitive approach 9
Socio-cultural factors 26, 29, 77
Speaker characteristics 95–101
Spelling 114–115
Stakeholder perceptions 9, 11, 13–16, 20, 24, 38–40, 42–46, 51, 136

171

Stakeholder requirements 32–35, 38–40, 42–46, 51, 129–131, 138
Standard setting 30–31
Strategy use 70–72
   Compensatory 17, 21, 25, 40, 68, 70–71, 126
   Cognitive 71–72
   Metacognitive 71–72
   Social-affective 71–72
   Test-wise 1, 16, 17, 20, 70, 103, 108, 111–112, 122, 133, 135, 136, 138
Structure Building Framework 4–5
Sub-skills 62, 66–70
Summary completion 8
Syllables 65–66, 96
Syntax 3, 65, 69, 81

T

Test components/purpose
   Exam preparation 9, 11, 16–21, 37, 47, 56, 71, 98, 136
   Goals 3, 11, 14, 16, 17, 20, 32–34, 117, 118, 129, 136
   L2 content 37–41, 100–101
   Practice 16–21, 136
   Study skills 3, 16, 17, 28, 126
   University admission/pre-enrolment 7, 14, 20, 25, 34, 35, 40, 51, 77, 125
Test design/content
   Everyday use 8, 48, 52, 75, 77, 80, 89, 92
Test fairness and justice 13
Test format
   Balance of formats 110–113
   Constructed response 11, 106, 110, 114
   Selected response 11, 110, 113, 114
Test taker characteristics
   Experiential 11, 36–57
   Non-academic 37–50, 73
   Physical/physiological 56–57

Test use
   Immigration 36–38, 49–53, 75, 77, 89, 128, 130
   Use of IELTS for professional purposes 7, 33, 34, 36–53, 77, 126, 128–131, 138
Topic 5, 32, 67, 69, 71, 74, 76–77, 78, 89, 104, 137

V

Validity
   Cognitive 10, 11, 59, 61, 91, 102, 107, 112, 119, 125, 126, 136
   Consequential 9, 11, 13–21
   Context 7, 9, 11, 59, 61, 82
   Criterion-related 9, 11, 22–35, 37, 76
   Ecological 75, 91, 107, 125
   Scoring 10, 11, 52, 61, 62, 76, 110, 114–115
Verbal reports 19, 21, 24, 48, 62, 63, 68, 71, 102–106, 122
Visual support 56, 87, 93–95, 102, 103, 135
   PowerPoint slides 5, 92, 94, 95, 102, 135
Vocabulary 16, 18, 24, 65, 66, 67, 69, 79–81
   Coverage 80
   Frequency bands 79–80
Voice 95–96, 98, 100, 104, 108
   Accent 97–101, 132
   Accent training 98
   Exemplar theory 96
   Function words 65, 80
   Normalisation 95–96
   Speech rate 28, 85, 86, 93, 96–97, 100, 101, 137
   Word forms 65, 79, 80, 96, 132

W

Washback 9, 11, 13, 16–21, 136
Working memory 4, 53, 67, 69, 112